The Tommy Taylor Story

"The Smiling Executioner"

Brian Hughes MBE

Foreword by Sir Walter Winterbottom

EMPIRE
PUBLICATIONS

First published 1996.
Reprinted by kind permission of Collyhurst & Moston Lads Club 2002

EMPIRE PUBLICATIONS
1 Newton Street, Manchester M1 1HW

ISBN 1 901 746 21 6

Photographs courtesy of the author & Manchester United Museum
Front cover photograph courtesy of Manchester United Museum
Jacket design: Ashley Shaw & Paul Windridge

Front Cover: Tommy soars above the Brazilian defence - Wembley, May 1956.

Printed in Great Britain by:
MFP Design & Print
Thomas Street
Stretford
Manchester
M32 0JT

Acknowledgements

I tried to make this book as much as a one-man effort as possible. But nothing can be a total one-man effort, and I would like to thank those people who helped this one man to complete this book.

The first person I would like to thank and without who's help this book would have been impossible to put together is Peter Slingsby. Peter's kindness and patience provided me with the will to carry on with the project when I felt like chucking everything into the waste-paper basket. He proof read and corrected the manuscript.

I owe a deep debt of gratitude to John Donohue, who was a source of enthusiasm and inspiration beside being a mine of information on football matters. My wife Rosemarie and my children, Anthony, Damian, Christopher and Rachael for their support all through the years.

With special thanks to the families of Jimmy Murphy and Sir Matt Busby for their unstinting support for the book.

Wilf Breen, Billy Clynes, Harry England, who was Tommy Taylor's "best pal", and always at the end of the phone ready with his help and advice. Mrs. N. Slate, Mrs. I. Topping, Mike Conroy, and the many United followers of the 1940s and 1950s who sent me material and information. Sean Kelly; John Evans & family for the photos. Mr. Bill Wall; John White.

The staff at the John Rylands Library in Manchester, were tremendously helpful and supportive in all my requests, putting every newspaper and cutting at my disposal.

Mr. Neville Bolton, Editor of the Manchester Evening News; Jeff Hodgson of the Manchester Evening News, for his help and support and the use of the photographs. The News of the World.

Ken Barnes and Roy Clarke of Manchester City who were very supportive and helpful. They were class! Brian Clough.

Arthur Bower, the Barnsley F.C. historian; Dickie Bird, Tommy's school chum. Johnny Steele, Doug Kelly, and Gordon Pallister of Barnsley Football Club. The folk of Barnsley who shared their memories of Tommy with me.

Len Noad for his reminiscing about the transfer saga, and stories about Jimmy Murphy and other important details.

Nat Lofthouse who put his records at my disposal and was a mine of information. He was ever so helpful in every respect, as was Tom Finney. Ronnie Clayton and Brian Douglas.

Sir Walter Winterbottom and Frank Taylor for their kindness, and for writing the foreword and Introduction for the book, as well as their words of wisdom. Paddy McGrath for his cheerfulness and memories of the 1950s.

Fred Eyre for all his encouragement. Likewise, Jimmy Wagg of BBC GMR for his total support all through the years of research.

Last, but by no means least, a special thanks to all the former Manchester United players who helped with countless requests for interviews and information. Allenby Chillton, John Aston Snr, Henry Cockburn, Jack Crompton, Lol Cassidy, Jackie Blanchflower, Sir Bobby Charlton, John Doherty, Wilf McGuinness, Ian Greaves, Ronnie Cope, Colin Webster, Ken Morgans, Albert Scanlon, Freddie Goodwin, Alex Dawson, David Gaskell, Denis Law, Nobby Stiles. Harry Gregg wanted to contribute his thoughts to the book but unfortunately it was too late. With a special thanks to David Sadler for his patience and unstinting help. A special thank you also to Mark S. Wylie, curator, Manchester United museum and Tour Centre

A million thanks to Dennis Viollet who, though busy and living in Florida, took thc trouble to tape his memories for me. It was deeply touching and moving.

We acknowledge with gratitude those who gave permission for the use of material. Every effort has been made to trace all copyright holders and we apologise to anyone who has not been found or properly acknowledged.

Barnsley-born author and television personality Michael Parkinson remembers his Yorkshire friend Tommy Taylor with admiring affection, and has wished this book every success.

If I have forgotten anybody, please forgive me, it was certainly not intentional, I assure you.

Contents

Foreword

Sir Walter Winterbottom

It is a great privilege to write a foreword to this biography of Tommy Taylor of Manchester United and England. To be a great centre-forward a player must have talent for goal scoring and a big heart to take the knocks from determined defenders. Believe me, Tommy had these attributes in abundance along with many more I hasten to add.

Tommy was very hard-working and enthusiastic in all his play and, as the England team manager, I held high expectations of him becoming one of the greatest centre-forwards ever, not only for his club, but also internationally. It was very much a tragedy that he should lose his life so early and before he could fulfil his own aspirations.

Physically, Tommy Taylor was ideally suited for the traditional role of a central striker. Being tall and athletically powerful, he could out jump most opposition defenders to head the ball. He had a rangy stride, deceptive in its speed of acceleration, and a quickness of turns that made him an elusive player to defend against.

Many of the goals he scored were outstandingly courageous flying headers and first time drives from crosses making opponents fearful of his striking abilities.

Even when he did not score, Tommy contributed immensely to England's play, working tirelessly and intelligently in positional movement when not in possession of the ball and being ever alert for openings to pass the ball to other players in a better position to score.

Tommy was well liked and respected by his England team-mates, for he was always cheerful of countenance and brimming with confidence in his attitude before matches.

Tommy scored two fine goals at Wembley when England defeated Brazil soundly by the sore of 4-2, and in the process England missed two penalties. This victory filled the English squad with confidence to do well in the World Cup Qualifying competition. Tommy Taylor played a great part in the four qualifying matches against Denmark and the Republic of Ireland, scoring eight goals, quite a remarkable achievement. With this team, England held hopes for the World Cup finals.

But just four months before the tournament got under way, the terrible Munich air crash changed all that by taking out the spine of the England team with the deaths of Tommy Taylor, Duncan Edwards and Roger Byrne, a trio of enormous talent and assured competence.

Personally, I not only lost three very valuable players to my team, but more importantly, I lost three charming, friendly and loyal friends. Even though it is more than thirty years ago, the loss of these young and brilliant footballers in a tragic disaster still stuns the mind.

Yes, Tommy Taylor was a very exceptional player. A brilliant individual in his own right, and a world-class centre-forward. But a wonderful team player into the bargain.

I shall personally remember fondly his rising skywards to reach the ball floated into the opposition penalty area. The method of his vaulting was exciting for the crowds, and his contact when his forehead met the ball was first-class. The sheer power and ferocity in his headers was truly amazing. Tommy Taylor will always be remembered.

Sir Walter Winterbottom

Introduction

Frank Taylor

Centre-forwards live or die by the number of goals they score. To achieve this Courage has to be paramount in their array of talents. Tommy Taylor had courage a plenty! Like Denis Law, the man who was to succeed to his position many years later, Tommy was prepared to stick his head among the flying boots in the penalty area and take all that defenders threw against him.

But for me the outstanding impression that big Tommy left behind, was that he looked such an elegant player for a big man. His ball control was not in the George Best class, but in the penalty area, he was one of the most feared players who ever played in top professional in this country. You didn't see much of Tommy in midfield, where the "deep-lying centre-forwards" such has Hidgekuti the brilliant Hungarian; Di Stefano of Real Madrid fame and Don Revie of Manchester City; flourished. But when play was in the opposing team's penalty area, that was where Tommy was feared most.

I recall having a discussion with the Arsenal players at that time who asked me; "Who is the best centre-forward in England?"

I said I liked the way that Don Revie and Tom Finney were so elusive in midfield creating moves. The Arsenal players replied; "No it is the big feller at Old Trafford. The dangerous area is the penalty area . . . and when we play Manchester United and the ball is lofted into our penalty area . . . that's when we have a posse of players guarding big Tommy. He is deadly. Especially when the ball is in the air."

The world-famous centre-half Marquitos of Real Madrid said: "Trying to keep an eye on Taylor is like trying to catch the Scarlet Pimpernel. He doesn't stay still. First on the right then on the left . . . a very hard man to mark indeed."

Sir Matt Busby said later: "The lad is a marvel. I don't know how Tommy got his head to that ball . . . It was a fantastic goal."

Tommy Taylor, as a centre-forward, often took a beating from the critics. Even my good friend Henry Rose once wrote of him: "If Tommy Taylor is the best centre-forward in England, I am Santa Claus." But big Tommy, the lad with the ever-ready smile and all-action power-play as an attack leader, is badly missed. On his day, he was the best in the business, a header in the Lawton-Lofthouse class. And they were world-class in every respect. I know that Jimmy Murphy, for instance, rated big Tommy as the greatest centre-forward ever. Praise indeed.

Roger Byrne once remarked: 'Tommy's greatest asset — and sometimes his greatest fault — is that he gets in such wonderful positions. He's always looking for the ball, always taking a pounding in the middle, and taking the weight off the other forwards. If he had Hughie Gallacher's ball control, he would be the greatest ever — but then, Hughie probably wasn't as good in the air as Tom.'

There were a lot of fantastic goals in Tommy's short football life. The young Tommy Taylor went to a Barnsley school where the world-famous cricket umpire Dickie Bird was one of his best friends. Both dreamed of winning fame in sport. Tommy Taylor at soccer and Dickie Bird at cricket.

They both reached for the stars, and their dreams came true. Sadly Tommy Taylor's hours of glory were brief.

For him it ended on the snow-bound airfield at Munich. It is now thirty-five years since the tragic Munich Air Crash, but for those who saw Tommy Taylor play, the memories do not fade. The Big Feller with the Big Heart, the elegance, the sheer joy of his non-stop style of play — a great player taken before we had seen the best of him.

A working-class boy from Barnsley who loved his soccer . . . just like the lads coached and trained by Brian Hughes at Collyhurst and Moston Lads' Club. Good luck, boys. If you take Tommy Taylor as your sporting idol . . . you will be on a winner.

Frank Taylor O.B.E.
Life President of the International Sports Writers

The Smiling Executioner

I had just watched my son, Damian, score a hat-trick while representing Oldham Boys school football team. I was excited and overjoyed as any father would be under the circumstances. Driving home, myself and Damian started to analyse his play and as we did I made comparisons with goalscorers from the past. This brought us on to my favourite subject of goalscorers and goalscoring.

Goalscoring is indeed a very special art. The goalscorer is, simply, the hero or the villain. He is the extremist of football in the view of everybody connected with his team and the fans and press. They either score or they miss.

If he scores, then he gets the applause and headlines. But if he should miss, he will receive the moans and groans and criticism in the sports pages. We also discussed the subject of world goalscoring forwards, players such has Kocis, that great Hungarian header of a ball, Pele, Muller, Cruyff, Seeler, plus many more.

Then we talked about great goalscorers from the United Kingdom whom we were more familiar with players like Clough, Greaves, Law, Best, Lineker and Tommy Taylor. I must confess to being a failed centre-forward for my school and Youth Club, but I idolized goalscorers in any capacity.

Damian and my other two sons, Anthony and Christopher, who also played football for their schools and youth club, had been brought up listening to the feats of the great goalscorers. I had often told them about my own particular all-time "great," Tommy Taylor. My lads knew everything there was to know about Tommy's play from my vivid descriptions.

In his bedroom, Damian had a bookshelf of soccer autobiographies of players such has Ian Rush, Gary Lineker, Denis Law, Jimmy Greaves, Geoff Hurst, Tommy Lawton and Nat Lofthouse, along with many more: "Has there ever been a book published about Tommy Taylor?," asked Damian, knowing my admiration for big Tommy. "No," sadly, there wasn't, I told him. Later, myself and my sons and young daughter Rachael, got around to exploring the possibilities of writing this book. "People don't know the real Tommy Taylor," said Anthony, my oldest child. "All they know is what the various books written about Manchester United expose them to."

He was right of course. Taylor did receive mentions in the many fables of Manchester United, but there was no in-depth book on his career. "Let people understand who Tommy Taylor was, what he stood for, and what he accomplished throughout his short life," said my younger son Christopher. "I'll help with the research," said Rachael.

When football reporters and television commentators discus strikers, they tend to rave over the great goalscorers of the past, players such has Dixie Dean, Tommy Lawton, Nat Lofthouse, Jimmy Greaves, Denis Law, Brian Clough and Geoff Hurst, as "the greatest." They are apt to overlook the brilliant Barnsley product of the early 1950s . . . Tommy Taylor!

Despite his six or seven years in the spotlight, Tommy Taylor remains largely unknown. Stories about him have been written and embellished. New generations of football followers are born and to them Tommy Taylor is more legend than reality, part of Manchester United's distant past.

Tommy is only mentioned when the subject of the famous "Busby Babes" is brought up, or the terrible events of Munich are discussed and that's a shame. This book is an attempt to achieve that goal. (Pardon the pun.)

There will be those who will object to the very principle of this book, claiming that football is a team game and that to glorify the individual is wrong. That may be so, but without wishing to detract from other members of Manchester United's brilliant "Busby Babes" who sadly perished at Munich, I submit it is the brilliance of individuals that thrilled millions of supporters throughout the world.

There have been many books written about the crash and also about other members of that fabulous team. I have written about the 'team' in some detail, but forgive me if I dwell on the best centre-forward I have ever seen. Watching Tommy Taylor in action was rather like drinking a bottle of vintage champagne; it was invigorating, exciting and effervescent. Not only was Taylor one of the most successful goalscorers, he was also one of the most thrilling.

This book is certainly not an attempt to mythologize Tommy Taylor. It is simply an effort to show him as he really was; a wonderful, warm-hearted person who excelled at what he did best i.e. scoring goals, but who also had his flaws.

In his short spell on this planet, he was arguably the greatest centre-forward ever! Nat Lofthouse, the Bolton and England centre-forward, the Lion of Vienna, himself a living legend says: "As a youngster, I idolized Tommy Lawton and as much as I admired him, the greatest centre-forward of all was Tommy Taylor.

"And I don't just say that because he is no longer with us. He pushed me out of that position for England and I can tell you, I was a proud man representing my country. Playing for England meant a great deal to me, but I couldn't have handed that number nine shirt to a better man. And he hadn't reached anywhere near his peak, because he was only twenty-six when he died."

In preparing this book. I had an obligation to the memory of Tommy Taylor and his family and friends not forgetting his former team-mates to be completely honest. This is no glossed over book about a man unfortunately no longer with us, I assure you.

Tommy Taylor's story is a true life "Roy of the Rovers" type of achievement. I've spent hundreds of hours researching and speaking to anyone and everyone who could tell me anything about the subject.

I believe everyone has been completely and totally honest with me. I asked each person to tell me the good, the bad and the ugly. I was prepared to print facts that perhaps were critical of Tommy. This was not a case of telling tales but rather me asking contributors to be candid and open. Though I delved, the only "smut" was that like the majority of young men, Tommy liked the fairer sex and his pint of ale.

Throughout, there are many opinions expressed. I may not agree with every contributor, but I have tried to incorporate as many varied views as possible.

I have sometimes joined separate statements from the same source but I am confident I've done nothing to distort what the speakers said.

In the main, the Tommy Taylor story is told by himself, his friends from Barnsley, some of his England colleagues, members of Manchester United's fabulous 1948 team and his team-mates from the all-star Busby Babes era.

With that doyen of soccer reporters, Frank Taylor, writing a tribute, former England team manager, Sir Walter Winterbottom has also expressed his admiration for this supreme marksman. It is going on for forty years since Tommy died on that snow covered runway at Munich airport, and with the passing of time I don't think there will be another book based on Tommy Taylor's life and playing career. I like to think that this book is a tribute to a wonderful human being and a truly remarkable centre-forward.

For me personally and countless more who look back on the 1950s with a feeling of nostalgia, watching Tommy climb up for those high crosses and heading the ball into the net with the power of a trip-hammer can never be extinguished from our memories. Tommy Taylor, "The Smiling Executioner" will never be forgotten.

Up Like an Eagle

It was a beautiful, sunny July day in 1994. The temperature was up into the high seventies. Unusual for Manchester even in the mid-summer. I was in my deck chair in the back garden reading a newspaper full of the transfer of twenty-one-year-old Chris Sutton from Norwich City to Blackburn Rovers. The radio was playing a touching song by Bette Midler, "The Wind Beneath My Wings."

Five million pounds! I shook my head in astonishment and read the report again to see if I had read it correctly. Good luck to young Sutton I thought, but that huge fee for an untried centre-forward and a wage of £12,000 a week!

It seemed the transfer market had gone barmy in the summer heat wave. The Bette Midler song was in full flow now and putting my paper down I closed my eyes and my mind drifted back to March, 1953, when, with schoolboy friends from Collyhurst, the tough inner-city neighbourhood which was football crazy, we were getting prepared to cheer on our hero's, Manchester United, that afternoon.

We were making our way down Rochdale Road, into the city centre where we would join the queues boarding the "Football Special" buses bound for Old Trafford, the home ground of our favourites, Manchester United. Wearing our red and white scarves and with rattles at the ready nobody could be in any doubt which team we supported. On this particular day, there seemed more people than ever making their way to the shrine of my favourites.

A younger lad from our school, Saint Patrick's, was also catching one of the specials, with his older brother Charlie, and his dad and uncle. This lad would one day become a world-class star footballer for United and England . . . Nobby Stiles.

Everybody was excited and talking about the twenty-one-year-old centre-forward manager Matt Busby had signed that week from Barnsley.

The supporters were full of hope and expectation the young player would strengthen the team. There was a buzz in the air. The buses were packed solid, looking out of the bus window, thousands were also walking to the ground.

It was a cracking atmosphere. Everyone seemed to be asking the same question: "Is he any good? After all, he has only played in the Second Division," everyone seemed to be saying.

Matt Busby's wonderful free-scoring championship-winning team of 1952 were getting a little past it. The team was growing old, results were not encouraging, but Busby was not worried, because he had young players in the reserves who were just waiting for their chance in the first team. Players like Dennis Viollet, Don Gibson, Ian Greaves, Geoff Bent, Bill Foulkes, Mark Jones, Jackie Blachflower, Eddie Colman and Duncan Edwards. These youngsters were among the most brilliant footballers ever produced by one club.

They had come from all parts of the British Isles, and had been coached to near perfection as possible by Busby's right-hand man, Jimmy Murphy, assisted by Tom Curry and Bert Whalley and the others on a dedicated training staff. These kids had great pride in the club and a passion to make Manchester United the best club in world football.

"When you put on this jersey, you will feel ten-feet tall," Jimmy Murphy used to tell the United players, holding up the club's famous red jersey.

Murphy, the Welshman with an Irish name was from the valleys. and often added: "It will make you run through brick walls. Wear it with pride lads." United's galaxy of glittering young stars in their reserve and youth teams were world beaters.

They all respected Murphy. He was like a bulldog, and when explaining his point of view he reminded you of an old-time preacher full of fire, brimstone and passion. His total enthusiasm rubbed off on young players.

But back to the championship winning side. Busby was loyal and understanding to the players who had won the First Division title, but he knew that he would have to promote the youngsters sooner rather than later. He maintained Tommy Taylor would complete his new team-building plans. The Barnsley lad was the final piece of his jigsaw.

My particular idol in those days was the "Gunner" himself, Jack Rowley. I worshipped all goalscorers and Rowley was phenomenal. He was nearing the end of his brilliant playing career with United, but still doing a great job helping to nurture these kids. It was obvious to us all the new centre-forward had been bought to replace Rowley, though Jack could also play on the left wing, or at inside-forward.

How ironic then that it was my idol, Jack Rowley who would help Tommy Taylor score his first goal for his new club and settle into the United first team perfectly. But I am running ahead of my story.

On this Saturday, United were playing Lancashire neighbours, Preston North End. And in those days Preston were a very good First Division team, with Tom Finney their biggest star, but backed up by the terrier tackling of Tommy Docherty who, many years later, would become manager of United.

And with class players such as Jimmy Baxter, who had been at Barnsley with Taylor. Wayman, Cunningham and the rest, North End were unchanged for a seventh successive game an indication they had been playing good football and getting winning results.

The "Reds" on the other hand had lost to Stoke the previous week, and Busby made seven changes for the Preston match. Old Trafford was heaving with supporters with many of the gates locked half an hour before kick-off.

The United team was: Crompton; Aston, Byrne; Carey, Chilton, Cockburn; Berry, Rowley, Taylor, Pearson, Pegg; with no substitutes allowed in those days. The ground was a cauldron of deafening noise from a crowd of 52,590, which was by far United's biggest gate of the season.

Old Trafford is now known as the "Theatre of Dreams" but in those days it was our theatre too. We were all hoping for a better quality of life and going to watch United took away a lot of the greyness of life in the 1950s.

There was plenty of good natured singing, chanting and banter, but not a single obscene shout or threatening gesture. In short, no aggravation between fans. It was a wonderful, warm atmosphere with everyone looking forward to an exciting and entertaining match.

As United ran out, all eyes were on Taylor, a big strapping fellow. He certainly looked the part — big and strong with a thatch of black curly hair. If you could have programmed the perfect centre-forward, then big Tommy would have been thc ideal. He moved like a gazelle . . . And this was just in the warm-up before the game started!

"Is he worth £30,000?", we heard old-timers asking. "We'll soon find out," said another. The shrill of the referees whistle brought the captains to the centre circle. Once more the cheering and rattles were at full throttle.

The first time Taylor touched the ball, you could tell he was class. He breasted a high ball down to his feet and stroked it out to Johnny Berry on the right wing. A murmur of approval, like the sound of a rising wind, passed around the ground. "He'll do," exclaimed an old man removing his cap.

"He's got it up here," he added, pointing to his own head. Up to this point the big Barnsley lad had been quiet. Then, in the seventeenth minute, Rowley, tearing after a cunning pass by Carey, looked up, saw Taylor making his run on the far post, and then sent over an inch-perfect centre.

The whole stadium was almost silent. Taylor soared like a trout to a fly and a glorious header whizzed into the Preston net. Within a split second, a thunderclap of noise hit the afternoon air as the United faithful celebrated the Yorkshire lads first goal for his new club. As he scored, Taylor looked magnificent. His hands stretched in a salute above his mop of black curly hair, a big melon-sized smile across his handsome face. The fans took to him instantly. He quickly became my new hero, though I could never forget "Gunner" Rowley.

It was a vintage performance from the whole team. Taylor's arrival had given the whole club a boost. They went on to a 5-2 victory over Tom Finney's side.

Young David Pegg, a "Tyke" like Taylor, scoring two cracking goals, followed by one from Jack Rowley.

Charlie Wayman got the Preston goals, one in each half. But this was a splendid team effort from United. Roger Byrne played Finney, the Preston genius, out of the game, while little Johnny Berry looked world class on United's right wing.

"Old International," of the *Manchester Guardian* said: "Certainly from the point of view of tactical common sense as well as physical proportions Taylor seems ideally equipped. He stands just over six feet in height, has a clean trim appearance and a powerful set of shoulders, and can ride easily any but the heaviest charges. Moreover he has springs in his heels and can use his head to telling effect."

Tommy Taylor's storybook debut was a credit to the lad. He overcame the psychological handicap of having to look, think, and react like a player worthy of that £30,000 transfer label; a bullet-speed header brought thunderous applause and he certainly deserved the handshakes of his colleagues who mobbed him all the way from the goalmouth to the centre circle.

A few years later, talking about his debut, Tommy said: "Manchester United became my choice because they were not too far from my home and they had a good side. They could obviously help my future. Was it a wise move? Well, I got my answer a few days later in a First Division match against Preston. All my colleagues wished a very dazed and bewildered young player good luck.

"On the field they set out to assist me, especially inside-left Stan Pearson. It was Stan who passed on tips throughout the game, pointing out that I was playing on the wrong side of the opposing centre-half, Joe Marston, and encouraging me to get a couple of goals.

"Matt Busby, too, has a fine manner with players. He goes out of his way to help and does not 'tear a strip off you' in front of others. Instead, he joins us in training, falls in beside the player he wants to talk to, and quietly gives his advice or criticism while lapping the pitch."

Taylor's arrival in top-class soccer was a Roy of the Rovers story in every respect. No disrespect intended against Chris Sutton, but if he is worth £5,000,000 what would a Tommy Taylor be worth today?

In 1954, the Hungarian's had the finest header of the ball ever seen, in Kocis. One Hungarian said they only used the centre from the wing because they had a player like Kocis, otherwise they would have cut it right out of their play.

That is what forwards such as Taylor and Kocis meant to their respective teams. These players were also good on the floor. But it was for aerial power Taylor, like Kocis, became world famous. Over the coming years, opposing defenders were aghast at Taylor's workrate, pace and headwork.

Somewhere between seventeen and twenty years of age, most players reach their best form. After that they mature, but don't often improve. Those who did, like Taylor, Dennis Viollet, Jimmy Greaves and Denis Law are exceptions. These great players went on improving beyond the age at which most others come to a full-stop . . . Taylor kept on improving until his tragic and sudden death!

His fantastic scoring record — twenty-six goals in only forty-four first-team games for Barnsley — was astonishing, as was 112 goals in 166 league games for United's first team. With eleven in fourteen European Cup matches. Fantastic! In nine F.A. Cup games he scored five times and he claimed sixteen goals in nineteen appearances for the full England team. A truly amazing record.

Yet there was much more to his game than just scoring goals. He was described by team-mates of the three teams he played for as the most "unselfish" forward they had ever played alongside. His bravery knew no bounds. He made chances for others and didn't care who scored as long as it was for his team.

Modern-day football experts, supporters, managers and coaches, would smile and shake their heads in disbelief at the manner in which Tommy Taylor became a football legend. The greatest centre-forward the British Isles has ever produced!

Taylor left school at fourteen to work down the pit, and one wonders what incredible heights this young man would have achieved had he not been killed at Munich just days past his twenty-sixth birthday, with his best years still to come. Tommy was the current England centre-forward. But, not anywhere near his peak when his life was snuffed out on that snow-covered airfield in Germany in February, 1958.

My Name Is Tommy Taylor

Tommy Taylor was born at number four Quarry Street, in an area of Barnsley called Smithies, which was built on a hillside overlooking Barnsley, on 29 January, 1932. The Smithies neighbourhood was a small, friendly community where the residents were real down-to-earth Yorkshire folk, mostly from the mining industry — coal being the only major source of energy in Britain in those times.

The second-youngest child of Charles and Violet Taylor's six children (their first child died when only three years old, suffering from spinal meningitis.) Thomas was a mischievous lad with a lovely friendly smile. He was soon "Tucker" to his friends. It came from the nursery rhyme: "Little Tommy Tucker Who Sang For His Supper."

Tommy attended Burton Road Junior School and he was certainly not the "brains of Britain" by any means. He was not a dunce either, just average in the "B" section and moved on to Raley Secondary Modern School. This was well equipped in sporting terms, with its own rugby and soccer pitches, in addition to a gymnasium and indoor swimming pool. This was a rare in those days. Nobby Stiles, Brian Kidd and Wilf McGuinness, for example, played their schoolboy football on red-shale pitches. The champion shot-putter Arthur Rowe and test cricket umpire Dickie Bird were both former Raley pupils. Tommy was like most of the youngsters of those times, he appreciated the simplest of things in life, playing football with his friends and going down to the canal for picnics and a swim.

Taylor, in an interview on his early life, was quoted as saying: "I have been asked to tell the story of my early years in the game, so here goes. Well, I suppose I was born to play football. My grandfather was a footballer, and a pretty good one. He played for Barnsley St. Peter which, I understand, was the parent club of the present league team. He was a centre-forward, like myself, so maybe when I'm playing football I am a chip off the old block. I was only a lad when he died, so I never had the chance to talk football with him. Maybe if I had, he would have given me a few tips and advice, and made a better footballer of me.

"My father was also pretty good, but was a centre half. He played in the Yorkshire league, having a spell with Wakefield City, among other teams. When I tell people about my football ancestry, they always ask if there were any others in the family, so I had better jump ahead and tell you that I have a brother Bill, now aged eighteen, who is a centre-half. He has just signed amateur forms for Barnsley. I have other brothers, all keen but not first-class. I rather think Bill has it in him to become a pretty good player and, who knows, one day he may figure in league football and have the job of trying to stop me scoring goals!"

Surprisingly, for one who was to make such an impact on the professional game, as a schoolboy footballer, Tommy was somewhat lacking in total enthusiasm. In his last school year he played for his school team and also Barnsley Boys, but was reluctant to participate outside of school hours. His first season for Barnsley Boys was at centre-forward, while in the second season he was moved to left full-back.

For his school and the town teams, young Tommy played no more than a dozen competitive games. While at school he harboured no dreams of becoming a professional — as soon as lessons ended he was off home with his pals from Smithies, After twice arriving without his football boots on days when he had been selected for inter-school matches, he was never again selected for either school or the town team! It was said he was dropped from his school team because he did not own a pair of football boots, just a pair of clogs!

Says Taylor: "I started playing at the age of twelve as a left-back. In due course I moved to centre-forward and was picked for Barnsley schoolboys. This, however, was during the war when there was little competitive football, so I never played in the England Schools Shield, that grand tournament which has given so many boys their first taste of serious competitive football."

In December, 1944, after scoring a goal playing for Barnsley Boys against South Elmsall Boys, Tommy got his first mention in the newspapers. Usually these games were played on local grammar school grounds and, on occasions, at Frickley Colliery Football Club's ground. Then to his joy, Taylor was selected to play at centre-forward for Barnsley Boys against Leicester Boys at Oakwell, the home ground of Barnsley F.C. on New Year's Day, 1946. He was ecstatic and scored a "scorcher" in a 2-2 draw. Tommy was later moved to left full-back. Nobody knows why these positional changes came about, but the least concerned person was young Taylor himself. He would have played anywhere. His Headmaster at Raley, Edward Parkinson, says Tommy was one of the smallest boys in the team, but full of energy and boundless enthusiasm. "The ideal type to represent the town team."

Taylor obviously possessed great natural footballing ability and he was strong and extremely robust, but had a couldn't-care-less attitude which, in the long run, was to benefit him. Think how many brilliant players you have seen or played along side in school days who did not make it as seniors. Some were burned out or didn't have that vital something which made them different.

Tommy never owned his own football boots while at school. He borrowed a friend's, and it seems that a certain teacher gave him an ultimatum: "If you have no boots, you can play in your clogs." Young Taylor refused, and was sent home. He never played for his school again. The same teacher never selected Tom's brother, Bill, although he had real ability. A few years later, when Tommy was making a big name for himself, he was walking through Barnsley centre when his former teacher was walking towards him, the teacher obviously delighted that his former pupil was headline news wanted to stop and speak. Tommy completely ignored him, which as everyone knew was totally out of character for this lad with the ever-smiling face and the bubbling personality. Deep down Tommy had never forgiven this teacher. Not for dropping him from the team, but for holding a grudge and denying his younger brother the chance to play for the school team.

What about coaching? Taylor's views were as follows: "Coaching, of course, was not possible on peace-time lines. So many of the masters were away in the services and, generally, we had to work out our own tricks, lay our own plans and cure our own faults. However, I was lucky in one respect Mum and Dad were dead keen. "They travelled with the team to see me play and they were so anxious for me to do well that I was never without a proper kit."

Tommy's disinterest in making football his chosen career continued after leaving school. He got work on the pit top at Wharncliff Woodmoor Colliery. It was physically hard graft for the youngster but he was always ready for some fun with his workmates. Football never entered his head at that time. He was palling around with a group of lads who would remain amongst his closest friends. Bob Nicholls, Joe Harvey, Keith Hibberd, Jimmy Cooper, Bob McCormick and Harry England; Harry remaining very close to Tommy throughout his life. In fact, Tommy spent a great deal of time in the England household. As they got older these lads liked a drink and having a kick-about on the "bog" and a game of snooker in the Regent, or listening to gramophone records. Tommy also loved riding horses. Harry Kay, the local "Arthur Daley" who's son Peter was a professional show-jumper, had some horses and Tommy and his mates would often clean out his stables. In return they could ride the horses. Tommy would build jumps and fences and enjoyed getting on the horses and going over the self-made jumps. Taylor later explained: "We were a working-class family and when I was fourteen, the time came for me to leave school and go to work. Barnsley is a mining centre, that I should think of another occupation never entered my head. So I became a surface worker, and whether it was the complete change from school life, or whether I was not strong enough, I lost interest in soccer. I stopped playing and missed the better part of two seasons.

"This is supposed to be a period of a players most important development and I think I must have been very lucky to be able to pick up the game again. I was on the small side in those days. Had I been quick-growing and lazy, getting back into the game would have been impossible.

"How I restarted was a pure fluke. A team called Smithies United were a man short, and they asked me to play. I was centre-forward and I had a good game. I also scored, but what I remembered most was that I played well all round despite my long lay off."

Two years elapsed before Tommy again had any football involvement. Then fate took a hand in his destiny. Smithies United, a team based at the Woodman Pub, where Tommy's aunt, Esther Raynor, was the licensee, were short of a player — young Tommy was asked to play. It was a tough match against rivals Cudworth North End in the Becket Hospital Cup. It was quickly pointed out by some members of the team that he was not a signed player.

Tucker Taylor, Tommy's uncle, was a registered player for Smithies, but was not playing because he was injured. He suggested that his nephew should "use" his name when signing the referee's team sheet. "We are both called Tommy Taylor," said his uncle. "Our Tommy only has to sign his own name."

The problem was solved and the sixteen-year-old played. The teams in the Nelson League were rough, tough opposition for mature players, let alone a sixteen-year-old like Tommy, but he was not frightened and acquitted himself well.

Tommy Taylor said a year later: "They kept me in for three games-and then wonderful things began to happen for the small boy who worked at the pit head. Fancy! Only three games and there were scouts from Hull City and Barnsley watching me play.

"It just shows how well organised is the scouting system of many first-class clubs. It makes you realise what a vast organisation is league football, and also that no boy can ever complain he never had a chance."

While playing for Smithies United, young Taylor very quickly came to the notice of two Barnsley scouts: Tommy Hunt was suitably impressed and recommended that Barnsley should sign him immediately; and Horace Plant, a local youth team manager who did some part-time scouting for Barnsley. A third Barnsley scout, Harry Wass, was also very impressed with Taylor's ability. Hull City were also at these games and a representative made an approach for Tommy.

Tommy Hunt recalled: "He was a keen lad, with immense bravery and good skills on the ground, but in the air he was unbelievable. I couldn't believe what I was seeing. He rose up as if he had wings quite fantastic. He also had a long-striding run. And he was very strong indeed for one so young.".

Tommy Taylor is reported as saying: "My case proves that every young player of any promise at all comes under the microscope. Barnsley were first in with a definite offer for me to join their ground staff and when Hull City sent a representative, I had to tell them I was fixed up. With so much football in the family there was no objection at home and I was able to say goodbye to the mines and enter upon an entirely new life.

"The man who signed me was Mr. Angus Seed, one of two famous football brothers. It was he who managed Barnsley then, and it was under his eye that I made whatever progress I did. When he died last winter (7 February, 1953) many footballers lost a good friend. What a change for a boy! Suddenly I was transported to a new world. For though I had to do odd jobs at the ground, I had footballers all around me, and some of them were very good ones too.

"Talk was now of soccer and, young as I was I had a sudden ambition to do well. I could see way ahead, and it became even more mysterious how I ever lost interest. The old enthusiasm I had when at school returned with a rush I had no need to be persuaded perhaps that was my granddad coming out in me. I suppose what's in the veins stays there through many, many generations."

After a successful trial Tommy was offered a job on the groundstaff with Barnsley. Smithies United were paid the massive sum of ten pounds, not a bad fee for the future England centre-forward was it? On 7 February, 1948, the raw sixteen-year-old from Smithies signed amateur forms with Barnsley.

It's hard to imagine that he had nearly two years away from the game. On 25 July, 1949, Tommy signed professional with Barnsley.

Taylor came under the watchful eye and supervision of Johnny Steele, a former professional player who was a brilliant inside forward renowned for his remarkable dribbling skill and technique. Steele served Barnsley over many years, first as a player, and coach, then as manager, secretary, general manager and a director. Johnny was the Barnsley youth coach when Tommy arrived at Oakwell to start his life as a footballer. He recognised his potential straight away.

Steele had this to say about the teenager: "Tommy carried a little too much 'puppy fat' but we advised him about his eating habits. He listened and acted accordingly. And he wasn't very tall either at that time.

"But he possessed a terrific shot in both feet and he also had that uncanny knack of being able to virtually "hang" in the air and get tremendous power and direction behind his headers. He could head the ball much harder and a lot further than many players could by kicking it. He was a natural, but he still had to be taught the right and wrong way of doing things on the field, but we brought him along slowly, through the junior team, the "A" team and so on."

Getting a job on the Barnsley ground staff was a far cry from his humble beginnings. In those early days Tommy was very popular with everybody at Oakwell, he had become friendly with Doug Kelly, another newcomer to the ground staff. Wherever he went and whatever the company he was well liked and respected. He was the clubs practical joker, always laughing and playing little tricks on the training staff, squirting the hosepipe on them, dropping fireworks outside the staff's quarters on bonfire night much to the delight of the rest of the ground staff.

His grin was infectious. But, he was a lad who never forgot what he was there for. He proved a willing listener and an eager learner. Most days he had to be chased home from the ground he loved so much hours after training had finished as Steele confirmed: "He would have slept at the ground if we'd let him. He loved the club, the staff and the supporters. In those days Tommy was no Charles Atlas in physique and despite non-stop activity on the Oakwell training ground he was still slightly plumpish."

Taylor's view of his early days at Oakwell reveal his affection for Barnsley. "They were not enjoying the most prosperous spell in there history but still had some splendid players and great tradition for cup fighting and turning out a succession of fine footballers who had passed on to other clubs and to the highest honours.

"I found myself in the period immediately after the war with such men as George and Ted Robledo, Johnny Kelly, Jimmy Baxter, Danny Blanchflower, Beaumont Asquith, Gordon Pallister, Gavin Smith and others who made up the professional staff. The Robledo brothers afterwards moved to Newcastle United for a big fee and George of course, made a big name. It was he who scored the winning goal against Arsenal when Newcastle won the cup in 1951–52. Now he, and his half-back brother Ted have gone back to Chile where they were born. Johnny Kelly was a wonderful winger on his day. He seemed to have a perfect flair for doing the right thing without bothering to think about it and often he would move off at an unexpected angle or make a surprise pass without having to think about the why's and the wherefores of it.

"Jimmy Baxter moved to Preston and he made a great reputation at Deepdale as a thoughtful, constructive inside-forward. He seems to have fitted perfectly into their style of play. Danny Blanchflower went to Aston Villa, and is considered by many to be one of the finest wing-halves in the four home countries.

"As George Robledo played for Chile in the world cup. John Kelly was capped for Scotland and Danny Blanchflower has already won eight full caps for Ireland, you can see I was among players of great skill. As a ground staff lad I did a good many odd jobs, trained on a schedule laid down for the younger element and turned out on Saturday mornings.

"Although, only occasionally, in the Northern Intermediate League. This was a medium for young footballers in which Barnsley were very interested. Soon I found myself promoted to the "A" team. I was satisfied with my progress and I suppose the club were because having once been promoted to a higher grade, I was never put back."

Gordon Pallister, served Barnsley for sixteen years after joining them from Bradford City in 1938. For six years he was club captain. He retired from active playing in 1952, at the age of thirty-five due to a back injury. A year later, he became a director, holding this position for over thirty years until he retired. He

Tommy as a young Barnsley player.

is now Barnsley's vice-president. Gordon has fond recollections of Tommy Taylor. He has recalled: "I can remember quite clearly when Tommy first came to the club as a boy and training with us, then we signed him on professional forms.

"I was of course the captain when he made his first team debut. I can remember him scoring a goal at Coventry; it sticks out in my memory very clearly. It was a heavy ground, the ball was like a lump of bloody lead, soaking wet, the old caseball type with a lace in it. He met this ball with his head he must have been twenty yards out, and he met it perfectly, the ball left his forehead like a rocket. I can picture the ball flying into the net. I couldn't have shot it harder.

"Even then at his age and he was only about seventeen or eighteen at the time, I said to the coaching staff. 'This lad is nearly as good as Dixie Dean and Tommy Lawton now!' That's how good he was at heading the ball, brilliant, really brilliant at heading.

"Even as a kid he was so powerful and strong, no matter what the conditions were like, he took some knocking off the ball. And when he played for Manchester United he was better still. You have to remember that Barnsley in those days had good forwards. Players who could dribble and beat defenders with ease, but we assumed that if a player was classed as a forward then that meant scoring goals. And Tommy was better than most at doing this as his record shows. A great centre-forward! I had the pleasure, or I should say the displeasure of playing against Tommy Lawton, when he was player-manager with Notts County. Believe me, I always classed Lawton the best header of a ball without a shadow of a doubt. But I have to say with all honesty that had he have lived, Tommy Taylor would have become even better than Lawton. And I don't say that flippantly."

Football coaching in those days was almost non-existent. Training usually consisted of a few laps around the pitch, a few sprints and perhaps a few weights, maybe a five-a-side game, ending up with a little shooting and heading practice. The players saw very little of the ball. This train of thought came about, it was said, that if the players didn't see much of the ball during the week, come Saturday, they would be hungry for it, thus making them play better.

Many people have argued since that those methods produced better individual and more skilful players than what are coming through today with the benefit of modern coaching. Certainly players such as Tom Finney, Jimmy McIlroy and that superb coach, Malcolm Allison, were not happy about all the emphasis on coaching or the lack of sensible coaching, and in the late 1950s expressed their concerns.

Tommy Taylor was determined to improve himself as a player and he took measures in this direction as we will see later. He spoke his mind about things which he thought were wrong or unjust. He was never what could be termed a trouble maker, not in the least, but however he was forceful with his opinions.

Tommy was desperate to improve his all-around play, and trained hard and diligently in this respect.

The Barnsley trainer, Bob Shotton, used to chalk a line on the wall at the back of the stand. This would be a certain height, Tommy would practice jumping for hour after hour, then Bob would chalk the marking higher, Tommy never once complained. He would practice harder and more diligently until he got well above the chalked height. This was one of the reasons why he could leap so high for the crosses which were sent over from the wingers.

Tommy's first game of importance was in the Paisley Charity Football Cup on 2 May, 1950: St. Mirren 0, Barnsley 1. This was the headline in one of the Scottish newspapers with a brief report of what was Taylor's first ever first team appearance. Mind you, Tommy was hardly mentioned at all. The Barnsley team was: P. Kelly; Lindsay, Pallister, Blanchflower, White, Glover, Smith, Taylor, Wright, Baxter and J. Kelly.

Thoughts of professional football were soon checked by National Service in the Royal Artillery. "I became Gunner Taylor 22366853. I was posted to Oswestry and I ought to say here that I was now much bigger than when I went into the Smithies team for those three fill-up games that had such a big effect on my life. The training, the fresh air, and care about my way of life all had their effect."

Barnsley knew they had a future star on their books in young Taylor. His development was astonishing even to hardened professionals like Steele and the rest of the Barnsley training staff. But it was his fierce determination and his attitude which struck these men most forcibly. Tommy wanted to make up for the lost two years when he lost his inclination for football. Though he loved laughing and joking, the lad was as keen as can be to learn everything about the game. He watched the older players and more important, he learned from them.

Taking two years out to do his National Service would hamper his progress it was feared by the club officials. Joe Richards, later to become Sir Joe Richards, the Barnsley chairman was also a well respected and influential business man in the Yorkshire town. Richards sat on many committee's in Barnsley. One of them was the Coal Board Committee.

It was suggested Taylor should be given a token job in the coal mining industry. This would mean Taylor, to all intents and purpose was a miner. Under the regulations he would not have to serve his two years and could continue playing for the Barnsley club. Working down the pit was a reserved occupation!

It was a dodge to avoid National Service which was compulsory in those days. It was a legal dodge. Many clubs did this for players they didn't wish to lose for two years National Service. Here Taylor's true character shone through. In truth, nobody wanted to give up two years of their life in military service. When it was suggested to the lad steps were in motion for him to avoid going for his National Service by becoming a miner again. Taylor declined and immediately put a stop to this course of action. He served his time like every other young man in the British Isles.

Harry England confirmed the above, saying: "Tommy could have had it cushy. He had no need to have gone into the forces. Officially he would be employed by the Colliery, but instead of being stuck working down the pit, he would have been carrying on his life as a Barnsley footballer. And remember, he had already lost two vital years between fourteen and sixteen, when he hadn't played any football whatsoever.

"Barnsley wanted him to take the pit offer, but he was a single minded lad, with principles. He served his time like the rest of us. No easy options for him. That wasn't his style."

And military service helped the youngster as coach Steele pointed out. "It wasn't the training Tommy received at Oakwell that improved him. It certainly helped, but that fell to the British Army. The discipline and rigorous training brought the best out of him physically and mentally. After two years in the Royal Artillery his appearance changed drastically. He went to do his National Service as a boy and after two years emerged as a man. The transformation was remarkable.

"In that two years, Tommy had lost that puppy fat but had put on a couple of stone, which was solid muscle, and he had grown two inches in height and he had gained immense strength. He could run all day his stamina was envied by a number of other players. Yes, army life seem to suit Tommy and it certainly developed him physically and in ability."

Tommy enjoyed it too and is on record as saying: "Fortunately, I was able to get in some good-class football while in the army, and I was very lucky to be able to play along with such men as John Charles, Geoff Twentymen, Johnny Anderson (Leicester City) and Jack Parry (Derby County). There were others too, all good players and good sports and we had some happy times together.

"I was chosen to play for The Army, and went to Austria and France. It was great. I picked up a lot of hints playing with these good players.

"This was the standard of football which suited me down to the ground. I found that I was on a completely different level as far as skill and thinking goes. It was terrific."

Clarry Oldfield, a Barnsley lad, was a fair footballer himself. He was good enough to be on Huddersfield Town's books and had the "great" Bill Shankly personally chasing after him. Shankly, of course, was working with Huddersfield at that time.

Clarry recalls how he met his Barnsley chum while doing his National Service: "I had completed my basic training and was awaiting being posted to some army unit. I was walking across the parade ground and bumped into Tommy."

The two Yorkshire lads, of course, knew each other from the Barnsley area. After exchanging pleasantries, Tommy asked Clarry what duties he was doing and where he was going to be posted.

Says Oldfield: "I was a bit depressed, and to be truthful I didn't like the army discipline one bit. But like every other young fellow my age, I received my call-up so I had no option but to serve two years. I was wishing my life away and couldn't wait to get discharged."

On telling Tommy that he had not a clue what posting was in store for him, Tommy quickly detected that Clarry was homesick and down in the dumps and needed cheering up. Tommy, smiling, told his Yorkshire pal: "Don't worry, I'll speak to Captain Gibson who is in charge of my unit. He is also in charge of the football team at the camp."

Tommy went to great pains to help his fellow Yorkshireman. After a great deal of talking, Taylor managed to get Oldfield transferred to his unit. This achieved army life became much easier and bearable for Private Oldfield.

Oldfield explained: "I was forever grateful for Tommy's help. He had no need to go to any trouble to help me, because though we knew each other from living in Barnsley, we were not close mates.

"He got me on the football team which was terrific because we got certain privileges if playing football, and we were treated much better. I remember Tommy used to score hat-tricks as regular as clockwork. What a wonderfully brave player. He was an automatic choice for our unit side. The rest of the team had a saying about him that he would dive in front of a moving bus to score a goal. What a courageous lad. Nothing nor anybody ever frightened him.

"Some of our team would express their reluctance about facing certain opponents but not Tommy. It never bothered him. Even if the defender marking him was a giant with an awesome reputation for handing out unmerciful stick. Yes, he had bags of grit and courage. And believe me, he could handle himself could Tommy. It was astonishing really, the way he could get up so high for those headers. Whenever a ball was crossed into our opponents penalty area, we would turn and run back to the centre circle, fully expecting that he had headed a goal. Yes, that's how confident we were in his ability to put the ball into the back of the net.

"Captain Gibson thought very highly of Tommy. This officer would do anything for him, he liked Tommy's pleasant and easy going nature. And he thought Tommy was a sensational player with the correct attitude. Yet Tommy wasn't even an established or regular first-team player for Barnsley.

"I'll say without contradiction, that playing regular for the army team helped develop the lad into what he became much later. You could tell though, that Tommy had that little something which separates ordinary players from the potentially great ones!

"I remember that there were always plenty of first division club scouts at our games. Mind you, later on we also had Ronnie Clayton, the Blackburn Rovers wing-half in our team along with some other players from league clubs. It was smashing playing with these fellows they could pass the ball about. But honestly, Tommy was outstanding in our forward line.

"Money was a big handicap for me, the lack of it. Like most other soldiers, I hardly had any spare money or clothes. Tommy came to my rescue again, he was so unselfish, taking me and other soldiers out for a few pints. He really was a wonderful chum and very loyal."

Throughout most of his Army life Taylor was stationed mainly in Oswestry, though he was later posted to Tonfirnan, in North Wales. He played first-team football for the Northern Command and also his Regimental side in Division One of the Welsh League. His team became League Champion's for two consecutive seasons — 1950–51 and 1951–52, Tommy's goals playing a major part in this success.

The commanding officer in charge of the team was a very kind and understanding man, Captain Gibson, who it appears was football daft. Regimental Sergeant Major McLean, was in overall charge of the training. The strict training and discipline were beginning to take effect on Tommy's physique.

It was while Taylor was serving in the Army that he was introduced into the Barnsley first team. He had of course played in the Charity Cup match against St. Mirren in May, 1950. But this was the real thing, the big test, a highly competitive game. His first league game was against Grimsby Town, in October, 1950.

He was selected to play inside-right alongside the quicksilver Cecil McCormack who scored a rivetting hat trick. Tommy didn't score but his robust all-action play enabled McCormack to score all his goals. The Oakwell crowd loved Taylor's enthusiasm and never-say-die spirit. And he quickly became a folk hero. He loved the Oakwell supporters and they loved him.

Tommy talking about making his break through into Barnsley's first team said: "I really felt things were going my way. I felt that I was improving my knowledge of the game, picking up useful tips here and there. I made my league debut in 1950, against Grimsby Town and two weeks later I was fortunate enough to score my first ever hat-trick, in competitive football."

Barnsley considered Taylor an inside-forward in those early days. A centre-forward was usually a big robust type of dreadnought, a battering ram who would terrorise opposing goalkeepers. Though by now standing over six feet tall and with the build of a top class cruiserweight, Tommy was developing into a cultured and gifted forward. With the added ingredients of being both brave and courageous as a lion.

After watching McCormack score his hat-trick and as if to show he had noted exactly how it should be done, Taylor's next game saw him score a sizzling hat-trick in a 7-0 victory over Queen's Park Rangers. This was only his second league game. Tommy was only eighteen years old, the match was played at Oakwell. Barnsley, in October, 1950. His club got a special forty-eight-hour leave from the Army for Tommy to play, because Jimmy Baxter was missing due to a knee injury. Johnny Steele or Fred Semley, the club masseur or both, would make the four-hour drive to Wales to bring Tommy back to Barnsley.

What a superb performance from the teenager as he scored in the twenty-ninth, eightieth, and eighty-fifth minutes. The crowd went wild; they had found a new, swashbuckling hero. And what pleased them even more, was that he was one of their own, a Yorkshire lad through and through. Taylor's service for Army requirements limited him to just sixteen first-team appearances in two years.

The Army played in two Cup competitions. There was the Inter-Command Challenge Cup, and also the Triangular tournament held between the British, Belgian and French Army teams for the Kentish Cup. Tommy was selected for a short three match tour with the Army team. This would be his first ever trip outside the British Isles.

"This trip opened Tommy's eyes, says Oldfield. "He realised the more successful he was playing football, the more he could travel and see the world. Some of us Barnsley lads had never been further than Blackpool or Scarborough. He loved visiting these other countries."

In Austria he played in a match which contained seven current Austrian Internationals. This had no effect on the Barnsley lad because he scored a riveting twenty-minute hat-trick. He was dynamic, with bags of energy and the never-say-die spirit.

There was no question that he was the star of this tour. There were many hectic schedules during his Army playing career. While representing the Army he played against various League clubs including Aston Villa, Everton and Sheffield United. Tommy also played against the might of the Irish Football League in Belfast.

Though he was on the losing side by the score of 4-2, he was the outstanding player on the field. He scored when his thumping header from thirty yards rebounded back into play off a post. Tearing after the loose ball he moved like greased lightning to bang it into the net. On Wednesday, 26 April, 1951, The British Army played Corinthians on the KAC ground, in Austria. More than 4,000 spectators, a number not often seen at these games attended the high-class match, won by the guests in a sure manner. Taylor (3) Nutt and John Charles, a penalty; were the marksmen.

Yes, it was the same John Charles of Wales, Leeds and Juventus fame. And it is interesting to observe that though the big Welshman could play in a number of positions, he was mainly used as a free-running centre-forward around this period.

But Tommy showed so much potential that it was he who was selected to lead the British Army's attack. Tommy talking about the early part of his National Service said: "I must say that everything went splendidly during the first part of my National Service.

"True, I was missing the intense training which is generally considered so essential for the young footballer, but I was getting a share of good games, and to watch such a variety of players in action and to learn from them, was adequate compensation for any disadvantages. All clubs tend to run to certain styles, and I think it must have been a great benefit to me to watch so many different team mates most of them more experienced than I was and I was brought into a wider world of football than I would have been had I been a youngster on the staff of a Second Division club in pre-war years."

Disaster struck while playing in a match for the fifty-fifth Training Regiment at Litchfield, against a team which selected from the North Staffordshire Regiment. Jumping for a high cross with the opposing goalkeeper, Tommy went down in a heap, the goalkeeper landing on top of him, with his full weight on Tommy's knee. He lay motionless.

A cracked bone, torn ligaments and severe cartilage damage was diagnosed. He was taken back to Barnsley, and admitted to the Becketts Hospital where he had two operations. He was out of action for nearly a year.

Here's how the player reacted: "Then out of the blue came disaster, or what seemed like a disaster at the time. I was playing in an army game and unfortunately it turned out very rough. I don't think some of the fellows realised how rough it was.

"Some of them were not high class footballers and they just sailed in regardless of the consequences.

"There were a number of minor casualties and one very bad one that was me. The goalkeeper landed on my leg and a good many things went 'crack.' I went home to Barnsley and the club doctor's did everything they could for me. There was a cracked bone and also some cartilage trouble. It was decided to avoid an operation if at all possible and I spent weeks in bed with weights on my legs. I was in bed for six weeks and there was a period of eight weeks when I did not put my foot on the floor. Can you wonder that I thought my football career was over? Eventually it was decided that an operation would be necessary and the cartilage came out and about the same time my Army career (such as it was) finished. I was discharged in May, 1952, and I need hardly say the outlook looked very bleak for a tall perhaps slightly out grown youngster."

Oldfield remembered Taylor's mishap like this: "I remember Tommy getting a very serious injury; we were all sickened at what happened to him. Medical knowledge in those days regarding football injuries was very limited. It was nothing like it is today. The damage he suffered would have finished the majority of players careers, make no mistake. In fact I remember the talk going the rounds was that Tommy was finished for good, "he would never be able to play again. But this lad was so determined to get himself better and become a top forward that you wouldn't have bet against him achieving it.

BARNSLEY F.C. 1950–51
Back: D. Blanchflower, A. Glover, E. Bannister, P. Kelly, G. Pallister, J. Baxter;
Front: G. Smith, E. McMorran, C. McCormack, T. Taylor, J. Kelly.

"It always amazed me how he went on to play for Manchester United and England after the damage to his knee, but like I said he had a fierce determination to succeed. I always followed his career. We lost contact with each other after his injury and I got demobbed.

"But I cherished wonderful memories of Tommy, and I will never forget his kindness and infectious personality. He was always ready for bit of fun and he was very popular with everyone. A great, great person and a world class centre-forward!"

The damage suffered in that extremely rough army game was, in fact, very serious and was indeed career threatening. Barnsley had signed the youngster as a full-time professional on completion of his National Service. This was a grand gesture on their part.

Several medics, after diagnosing the injury expressed their fears of the knee ever getting back to normal again. Two major operations followed in the Becketts Hospital, in Barnsley. Fred Semley, the Barnsley masseur, also expressed his fears about whether Tommy would ever play League football again. But Tommy was one of those special breed of human beings that perhaps come along, if one is lucky, once in a lifetime. With the injury not seeming to be improving, Tommy felt a little disheartened. As a last resort, He travelled up to Newcastle, to visit a specialist.

"Of course you will be able to play again," the specialist told a very relieved young footballer and his family. He assured them that he would be able to sort out the injury problem. This medical genius certainly did as he promised.

"I was not hopeful but I knew that I would have to give my heart and soul to getting fit if I wanted to play again, said Taylor. "I had eleven months of inactivity, and looking back, I have to think soccer was in my blood. I have no doubt that the natural strength that came from being the third generation of "miner-footballers" came to my rescue."

Though at times, Tommy clearly despaired of ever playing again. He was down in the dumps, but with encouragement from his family, mainly his mother, Tommy went through a rigorous routine of four hour stints to strengthen the knee. As he lay on the floor in front of the fire, he would lift weights on his damaged leg, carrying out these exercises day in and day out until the injury was behind him.

With the damage cleared up it was back to normal. Tommy once again became his happy-go-lucky self, always with a smile on his face. He was having a whale of a time especially with Harry England and his other mates from Smithies. He couldn't really believe that he was getting paid to play football.

Though many of his friends who were working down the pit were earning nearly as much, if not more, he reasoned that life in the fresh air compensated for that. These were of course, the days before Jimmy Hill won his wage battle and brought in the new wage structure.

Tommy loved the life of a footballer and the freedom to go wherever he chose after the morning's training was over. It is doubtful if any player before or since loved a club as much as Taylor loved Barnsley Football Club. But Steele and other members of the training staff and everyone else who worked for the club occasionally had to warn him about his liking for a few pints of beer.

"When August, 1952, came, I was ready for the fray. Regular exercise, the summer months and the feeling of a new football season, Taylor remembered. "I felt as right as could be, and I was in the Barnsley team," Taylor remembered.

"They were playing me at inside left with the Irish International, Eddie McMorran, at centre-forward. Nothing went right for us. I know that every club that does badly, pleads bad luck and I plead that now for Barnsley. The run of the ball, injuries, mistakes that normally would be got away with, cost us goals. It went on week after week and it wasn't for lack of trying. There were some fine fellows in the team, full of fight, but nothing we could do seemed to come off. I got a goal or two, but we were soon facing the virtual certainty of relegation.

"At Christmas I was moved to centre-forward and soon I realised I had found my best position. Perhaps it was because there was more scope for movement than in the inside position where one has a set task to perform. Anyway, I quickly settled there and was very happy at the job. I was living at home in a happy home nothing seemed nicer than the prospect of playing centre-forward for Barnsley. Although we were facing relegation we still kept our cup fighting traditions going in the cup."

On 10 January, 1953, in a momentous F.A. Cup third round tie against Brighton, after thirty minutes Brighton looked a safe bet for the fourth round after taking a 3-0 lead. The crowd of over 17,000 were stunned.

With relegation a distinct possibility, it looked as if Barnsley were now to be unceremoniously dumped out of the F.A. Cup competition. Many supporters had left the ground before half-time, but as Gordon Pallister said, when you have forwards with the spirit and fighting qualities of Tommy Taylor, no cause is lost.

In a rip roaring comeback in the second half, Barnsley scored four goals in sixteen minutes to wipe out Brighton's lead. Kaye, who had moved to inside forward, scored the first. Brighton were rattled by a magnificent goal from Taylor in the sixty-eighth minute and McMorran scored to make it level. With a quarter of an hour to go, the home crowd, silent for so long, roared for more. Quick Brighton raids were stifled. Strained nerves led to frayed tempers and several players were called to the referee.

Taylor, unrecognisable by first half standards, scored the winning goal eleven minutes from time. This was Taylor's debut in the F.A. Cup, and what a brilliant debut he had, marking the occasion with a brace of goals. This was one of Barnsley's greatest cup fight-backs in their long history. The whole town celebrated, none more so than the community of Smithies where the ale flowed freely.

Tommy Taylor wrote later: "Poor results had been followed by poor gates and a deaf man could not have missed hearing the rumours that the club would have to part with me. Transfer talk began to get into the papers. I paused for some time, before agreeing to move and I took some time to decide which club I should move to. But at the time I had no real desire to leave Barnsley. I had not long finished a spell of almost two years National Service and the hospital.

"I was among friends in short I was content despite the rumours. I felt I still had a job to do for Barnsley and I carried on playing and trying to help them avoid relegation."

Tommy celebrated his twenty-first birthday on 29 January, 1953, but there was no party or festivities. Barnsley were playing Plymouth in an F.A. Cup tie. They lost, but his team-mates decided to take him to a night-club named the *"The Seven of Clubs."* This happy band of footballers drank a few pints and everyone had a good time, but unknown to the players tragedy was awaiting them.

On the train journey back to Yorkshire, poor Angus Seed became quite ill. The guard was informed and arrangements made for an ambulance to be waiting at Gloucester where the train stopped. Angus was rushed straight to hospital. Tommy and all the Barnsley squad were upset, but Tommy took it very badly.

Angus Seed passed away on 7 February, the day after his sixtieth birthday. This was also the day that Barnsley played Rotherham United. It was a vital game for the Oakwell outfit, who were struggling against relegation. The players were obviously upset about Seed, but the game had to go on.

"Only a great revival can save Barnsley from relegation following their defeat by Rotherham their seventh in succession and they fully deserved a draw. Taylor headed Barnsley's first goal and ten minutes from the end he got another after Norman Smith's shot had been partially cleared. Then with only six minutes to go, and Barnsley fighting desperately for an equaliser, Taylor missed a penalty."

This is a brief report of the game played against Rotherham United, on 7 February, 1953. The final result was Barnsley 2, Rotherham 3. Tommy scoring his club's two goals.

By missing a penalty in this game Taylor was denied the opportunity of registering his second hat-trick for Barnsley and earning his team a draw.

This was one of the last games Tommy played for the club. In fact, he only played three more times, scoring two further goals before being transferred. There had been speculation and transfer talk for several months before he eventually did move from his home town club.

The Barnsley Chronicle reported him saying: "I don't really want to leave Barnsley Football Club. Despite all the rumours going the rounds.

"I love the club, the staff, everything about the place. My girl friend is a Barnsley lass and all my family live in Smithies. And I certainly don't like the idea of leaving a sinking ship. I know the club need the money which they will receive if I move to another club."

I digress here to let one of Tommy's close friends from his days as a Barnsley ground-staff boy relate his fond memories when both were starry-eyed teenagers playing for their favourite club.

My Pal Tommy

Doug Kelly joined the Barnsley groundstaff exactly a year after Tommy. They became close friends. Doug was a school friend of Mark Jones, who had joined Manchester United. Doug and Mark played for Darsfield Secondary Modern School and both represented the Don and Dearn district team. Kelly was a player at Barnsley for seven years before moving on to Bradford City. He was a pall-bearer at the funeral of Mark Jones.

"Tommy Taylor and I became great friends when we were both on the groundstaff at Barnsley. Tommy seemed to make friends easily. He was exactly a year older than me. We were two of a kind really, very laid back, we liked a laugh and a bit of fun but we preferred others to lead the way. In the junior teams Tommy wasn't really outstanding. His greatest assets were his strength and his unselfishness. He was a typical inside or centre-forward and hard working. Mind you he had two good feet, being able to shoot with either foot, but remember, Barnsley had some good forwards in those days.

"His life from when he turned professional at seventeen, to when he was eighteen centred around the games he played in the Hatchard League and also the Yorkshire League, with the occasional match in the Northern Intermediate. Looking back I suppose his first full season as a professional was very ordinary and Tommy's good fortune started by the misfortune of other people getting injured, while he was in the forces.

Barnsley then had a spate of injuries and when Tommy was eventually selected to play in the first team he hadn't even played in the Central League with the reserves, but once he played in the first team he was an instant success.

"During the first two years he played wherever he could, even though he picked up a nasty knee injury while he was serving in the army. This injury put him out of action for nearly a year. But at the beginning of the 1952–53 season, Tommy really began to make his mark.

At that time at Barnsley, we never really had a settled forward line. There was me, Tommy Lumley, Eddie McMorran and Tommy as well as Cecil McCormack and we all played in the centre-forward position at one time or another. We had a wonderful team spirit and though Barnsley were struggling there was a good atmosphere at the club.

"I've said this many times before, but I can only recall Tommy playing for the reserves at Oakwell just the once and that was against Manchester United, and he scored a brilliant hat-trick. I believe it was during this game Manchester United realised they had found what they had been looking for . . . a future star centre-forward.

The Barnsley manager, Angus Seed, was like a second father to Tommy and me and the day he died, we lost at home to Rotherham United, and we were sickened. Angus was a gentleman. Managers in those days usually came to the ground in suit and tie. They left the training to the trainer while they went about other business. Angus was a very kind and considerate person.

"As young lads we were the dogsbodies at Oakwell. We didn't mind the jobs we were given although I must say the one we hated most was sweeping the stands after the matches. We came in and trained on Mondays, Tuesdays and Wednesday mornings and it was always with the first team.

Sometimes on Wednesday morning instead of training we would go playing golf at the Barnsley golf club. Tommy and myself didn't play a great deal at that age. We used to go looking for golf balls.

On this particular Wednesday, Danny Blachflower took it upon himself to book a restaurant in the town centre for a meal for all of us after we had played golf. He had also ordered taxis to and from the golf club. Very few players owned a car in those days.

The next morning Angus Seed played merry Hell with him, because the club picked up the whole bill. He really belittled Danny in front of everybody. But Danny was a brilliant talker, oh, he was fascinating when he got that Irish blarney going, but he had to keep quiet this day. Me and Tommy sat fascinated.

"Tommy's greatest strength was always in the air, but there is always a difference between heading a ball and jumping for the ball. Tommy was an expert at both and there are not many players today who can do that. And remember, he could really get some power into his headers. The ball then was a proper caseball, with laces in and very heavy indeed. Yes, if you didn't head the ball correctly you would have a nasty headache for a few days. Tommy was marvellous when it came to jumping and heading; he was something special.

"There was no special method of training like there is today. Tommy would practice jumping and heading the ball. Behind the stand at Oakwell we used to have half a dozen posts, like a "T" post, with balls hanging down. They were quite a distance apart and starting from a low height upwards. That was the only special training I remember him doing, for he was just a natural header of the ball. No matter what anybody says now, no one at Oakwell ever said that Tommy was ever good enough to play for England. Some of the old timers say now, that they knew from the beginning that he would eventually play for England. But, that's easy to say forty-odd years later, but back then nobody ever forecast it.

"It's ironical really Barnsley Reserves had played Everton and Sheffield United and both Tommy and myself were in the first team. The reserves had a mid-week game against Manchester United. The boss (Angus Seed) dropped Tommy from the first team, who the following Saturday were due to play Rotherham. United brought all their stars, Chilton etc., and my mate, Mark Jones, marked Tommy. If memory serves me right, Tommy got three or four goals and their assistant manager, Murphy was in raptures over Tommy's display.

"I was at the game, right near Murphy, and I heard everything he was saying. He was furious with his defenders, but drooling over Tommy's display. Mind you, Tommy never feared any opposition, be it United or anybody else. He used to get stuck into defenders and goalkeepers, and that night he gave United's defenders a torrid time. From that day Murphy hounded him until they signed him. The point I'm making is that it was Murphy who spotted Tommy's potential. Murphy who saw how good Tommy could become with the right players around him. At Barnsley he was just another inside or centre-forward.

"On the strength of his display against United reserves, Angus Seed dropped me and promoted Tommy back into the first team the following Saturday.

"I gave Tommy some stick over that I can assure you, all in good fun though. If Tommy did have any faults at all as a player, they soon knocked it out of him when he moved to Manchester United.

"Matt Busby was an artist at buying the best players for certain positions and letting them go out and play. The full back had a certain area to cover, as did the wing half, then the centre half knew which area he had to cover and so on.

"Now the forwards were different. Your centre-forward stayed up front in the middle, the inside forwards had to bring and fetch the ball and also get goals. Wingers, well, they just stayed out on the flanks, sometimes not in the game for long spells and the workrate of a winger was virtually zero. That's why Stanley Matthews could play until he was fifty. Today, he would be expected to drop back and work hard behind the ball. Stanley would have been finished in his thirties if he were playing in modern football.

"Me and Tommy socialised quite a bit in our spare time, along with Norman Smith, Maurice Jackson and Maurice Hudson. We'd meet up at the ground before the game and afterwards we went out together in the evenings. Although I must say that at that time, we never drank too much because the club officials kept a very strict eye on us.

"I always remember a little story which makes me laugh even now. We played a cup-tie down in Plymouth and we heard that the game was being filmed by "Pathe News". A couple of cinema's in Barnsley use to feature the "Pathe News" and we spent most of this particular day going between the two cinema's watching the clip, even though the clip lasted less than five minutes.

"I'm convinced that if Barnsley had had a good run in the F.A. Cup in that 1952–53 season, Tommy would not have been sold. A good cup run would have brought in the money which the club badly needed, and the cup was all about money. But it wasn't to be, and Tommy was sold to United.

"Tommy never came back to Oakwell after he left. Once he left the club, he became a Manchester man. I don't mean to say that he snubbed his friends in Barnsley. This was because Tommy was so busy settling into his new environment.

"In those days players began their pre-season training in July and there were also pre-season tours as well, so you could be at it virtually eleven months of the year. So Tommy was kept busy.

"That's why we never saw a lot of him, but I can honestly say that in all the time I knew him, I never saw any wrong in Tommy Taylor. He never had any edge to him, certainly no big-headedness which might affect other players who might have achieved what he did with United. The last time I ever saw Tommy in person was in fact at Maurice Hudson's wedding.

"He gave me a badge which he had brought back from South America, where he had been playing for England. I got married in 1957, and we went on honeymoon to the St. Nicholas hotel in Scarborough and I insisted that at the night time we all go into the basement to watch United play Real Madrid, in the European Cup. There I was on my wedding night, cheering a flickering television screen.

"I was proud and pleased as I watched my pal Tommy, and also big Mark Jones, whom I knew very well because we went to the same school and played in the same team.

"Two grand Yorkshire lads, and tremendous players indeed! In that era, the length of a footballer's career depended a lot on what position he happened to play in. If he played at the back as a defender, or even on the wing he would last longer, perhaps four or even five years than say an inside or centre-forward. A goal scoring forward took the blame when his team lost (for not scoring enough goals to win the game).

"But if the team won and he was the scorer then he obviously took all the credit. A centre-forward could play for ninety minutes and hardly kick the ball, but if a couple of kicks brought two goals, then he'd had an absolute "blinder" of a game. In those days a centre-forward's job was to score goals. Nothing else. No dropping back in defence. Score the goals that was his job.

"Then a forward could charge the goalkeeper into his net during a game as long as it was fair and square. This was something Tommy Taylor was an artist at doing. Believe me, Tommy was a great, great centre-forward. Yes, one of the best in the world of football without any doubt at all.

"He started his career at Barnsley as a promising talent, but it was at Manchester

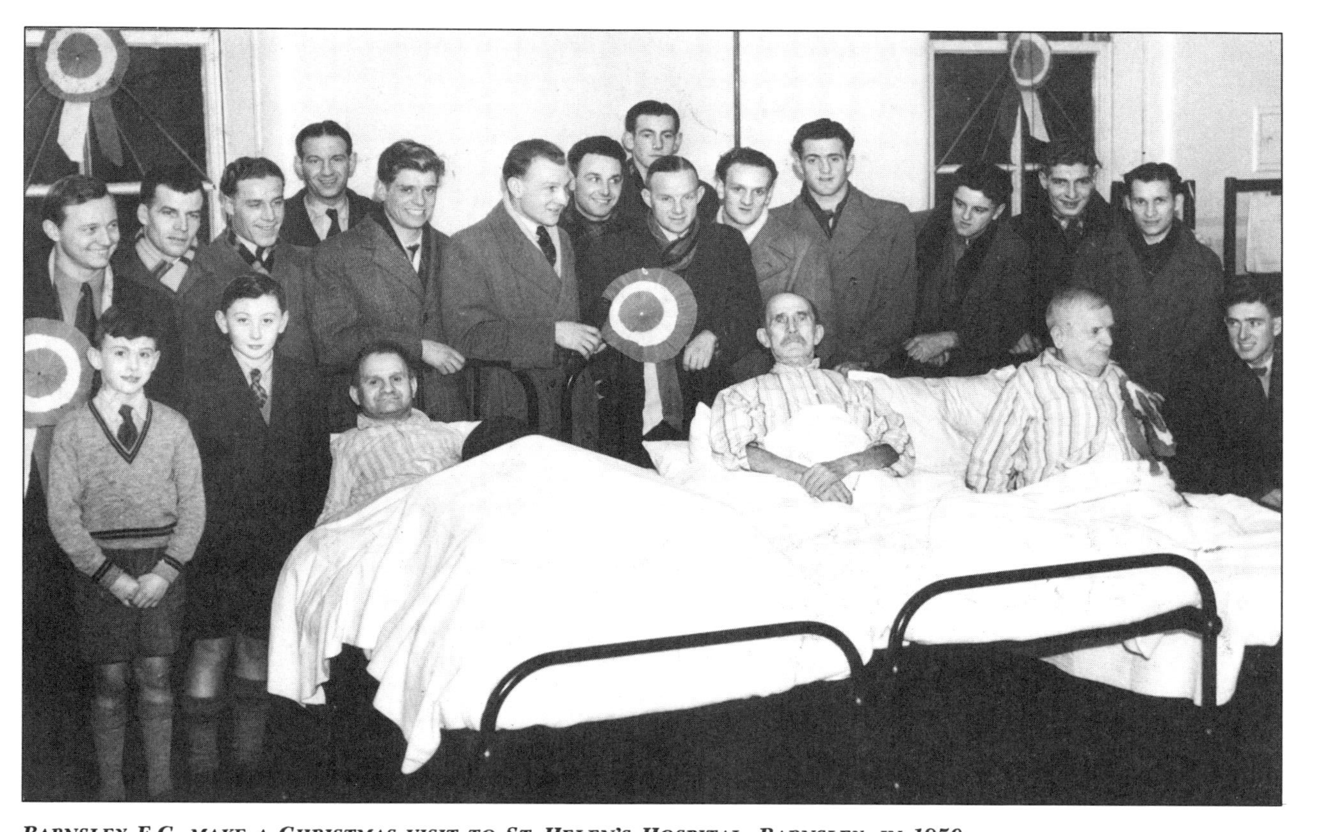

BARNSLEY F.C. MAKE A CHRISTMAS VISIT TO ST. HELEN'S HOSPITAL, BARNSLEY, IN 1950

The players: J.C. McCormack, G.Smith, S. Normanton, G. Pallister, K. Lambert, H. Hough, G. Innocent, D. Lindsey, J. Allen (behind), A. Callaghan, E.J. McMorran, T. Taylor, R.B. Robinson, W.E. Deakin, R.D. Blanchflower (seated).

that he blossomed and became England's greatest ever centre-forward. I should know because I grew up with him as a teenager at Oakwell and I saw first hand his improvement from a puny kid into a truly magnificently built centre-forward.

"The goals he scored were superb and the like of this kind of player will never be seen again in our game, for the simple reason is when they made Tommy they threw away the mould. It was my privilege and pleasure to have known him as a close friend, a marvellous player and a first rate human being!"

The Transfer Trail

The transfer of Tommy Taylor to Manchester United was neither as smooth nor as clear-cut as we are led to believe when reading about this event in the many publications on the subject of Manchester United. In fact, it was a long drawn-out affair before Matt Busby was able to sign this shy youngster. In their respective books, both Matt Busby and Jimmy Murphy glossed over the transfer events rather quickly.

The Taylor transfer saga was an irksome four or five day transaction, according to both Busby and Murphy. But in reality, this was certainly not the case. The truth of the matter was that Matt Busby and Jimmy Murphy chased Tommy over a seven month period. They had many problems to overcome before they landed their man. Once United had decided that Taylor was the centre-forward they wanted more than any other player in Great Britain, it was all systems go in an effort to land the biggest catch of raw talent seen on the football field for many years. Jimmy Murphy was delegated to make sure United got their man.

Players who score goals regularly, season in and season out, are worth their weight in gold. And if he happens to be a physically big and brave fellow into the bargain, so much the better. These kind of players make the turnstiles click faster because football supporters are excited by forwards who can put the ball in the back of the net. They are similar to knockout punchers in boxing. Crowds flock to watch them, because they provide excitement!

A new generation of goalscorers was suddenly emerging in the early 1950s. The "regulars" among the list of goalgetters was rapidly disappearing and in their place were youngsters of exceptional promise who were proving themselves by being able to take advantage of the half-chance in the toughest area of the game.

Nat Lofthouse says : "In those days you could name half a dozen or more centre-forwards who were good enough to play for England. There were some brilliant goal scorers. Competition was fierce, because there were so many good ones around. I am not talking about inside-forwards. They were providers and goal takers, but a centre-forward was the main man in the forward line, a completely different player to an inside forward. You would be hard pushed today, to name six centre-forwards who could play for England! The centre-forward was the main player for scoring. Everything came from him. If he didn't score, the whole team was in trouble."

Busby and Murphy believed that Tommy Taylor was the finest of this new generation. Big, strong, fearless and the possessor of a hard shot in both feet. Above all else, however, he was the tenacious type, and among the hardest men in the game to shake off the ball once in full flight. He got many a goal because of his courageous approach to the game. Many good judges saw him as a leader of potential greatness. They all shared that view. To Busby and Murphy, Taylor was a raw diamond who, they reasoned, with their polishing and coaching, would in time become a world beater alongside the Dixie Deans, Nat Lofthouses and Tommy Lawtons of the soccer world.

Brian Clough, who has become a household name, a folk hero and a legend in soccer, was just starting his career with his hometown club, Middlesborough at about this time. His prolific goal scoring exploits as a centre-forward for Middlesbrough and later, Sunderland brought him 204 goals in only 222 games, an amazing feat of marksmanship. Clough knows a thing or two about goalscorers, front men, strikers or whatever they are called in modern football.

Brian Clough: "I'm often asked what makes a striker and the answer is simple the ability to put the ball in the back of the net. Of course, that's not the be all and end all of the subject. We can talk about pace, heading ability, bravery, ball-playing skills and so on. But, at the end of the day, a striker is judged by the number of goals he scores over a period of time not just in one season.

"On every player's passport is stamped the words 'professional footballer' but if any of them had put down the word 'striker' they wouldn't get out of the country for three or four years!

"Strikers are very much like goalkeepers. They have to learn their trade and when they score or save goals consistently over a long period then they can be recognised as what they profess to be. And in my book when you judge a goalscorer you have to go by the number of times he scores in League football.

I will always argue that League goals are the yardstick for judging a striker's record. And although you might have felt I was over simplifying the matter when I referred to strikers needing the ability to put the ball in the net, there are some players over the years who have specialised in doing just that.

"In my era Jimmy Greaves was a class apart from the rest when it came to scoring goals at the highest level. He could score them from anywhere, anyhow at any time. I had a record at one time that matched his, but I'll be the first to admit that mine were in the Second Division while Jimmy's were in the First, for England and against mean Italian defences in his brief spell on the Continent. We did have something in common in that we were both labelled 'lazy' players. And that never ceased to stagger me.

"Lazy or not I used to come off the field feeling absolutely shattered. The people who used to criticise invariably didn't know what it was like to be a centre-forward or front player (call them what you will) who was knocked from pillar to post every Saturday afternoon.

"Peter Taylor used to always tell me that Hughie Gallagher was the best striker the game has known but the first ones I really admired were Tom Finney, Tommy Taylor and Ferenc Puskas.

"One thing is certain . . . the Greaves, Laws, McDonalds of this world will always capture the attention of the football public. Goals are the commodity that people pay to see . . . and will go on paying to see for a long time to come. Greaves had a marvellous record, but there were others who come to mind like Denis Law, who really excited crowds with his striking qualities. His pace and reactions were nothing short of electric."

This was what a modern day manager thought about goal scorers or more important, a centre-forward. They were like gold, hard to find, and players of the calibre of Tommy Taylor were found once in a life time. Most centre-forwards in the 1950s stood about 5ft-9ins; this was the normal size for forwards. There were, of course, odd exceptions.

Tommy Taylor was an exception. Defenders, though, were burly six-footers or bigger. In the main, this was what managers looked for in their defenders. United's own Mark Jones, Roy Hartle, John Higgins and Tommy Banks, all of Bolton readily spring to mind; Dave Ewing of Manchester City was another big defender.

Before commencing their search for a centre-forward, United had already experimented with various players in the centre-forward position, but all to no avail. They wanted a big, powerful leader for their attack. This was another reason why Busby and Murphy were desperate to land Taylor.

Busby told his board of directors that the player he was seeking would cost around £30,000. This huge amount stunned and shocked some of the old-fashioned United directors, but they trusted Matt's judgement. If he thought this player was worth this vast amount then so be it. "Go out and sign him," they told the manager.

The truth about how and when United first became interested in Tommy has become a little distorted with the passing of time. Lol Cassidy, was with United from 1946 until 1956 and is a former Headmaster of Saint Patrick's school in Collyhurst. Manchester. This was the inner-city school which produced later "Busby Babes" in Terry Beckett, Nobby Stiles and Brian Kidd. Lol had heard talk about Taylor's potential long before United eventually signed him.

Lol Cassidy: "I played mainly in United's reserves and "A" teams. Around the early 1950s, Matt Busby and Jimmy Murphy were revamping the whole structure of the playing staff. There were lads coming from all over the British Isles, brilliant youngsters and it was an exciting period.

"Mark Jones was one of them, a huge lad with a magnificent physique for one so young. I played many games with Mark.

"I was only a part-time professional because I was teaching, but I will always remember Mark saying to me one day: 'There's a good player in Barnsley. His name is Tommy Taylor, he can't half leap for those headers. He'll be a hell of a player, I think some big club will sign him before long.'

"Now, I could get up high to crosses from our wing men. And I thought to myself: 'This fellow Taylor must be some header of the ball for Mark to keep harping on about him.'

"It was of course no secret that Matt was looking for a big powerful centre-forward. They were grooming a young lad named Eddie Lewis, but though Eddie was good, he lacked pace. The club were experimenting with various players at centre-forward. They had marvellous youngsters in almost every other position, but there was no natural front man to use the modern day terminology.

"Matt was still searching for a leader for the first team. I knew that, because he would to say to me 'Lol, you need to go full time, then you would improve a lot more.' I don't know if this was Matt's way of suggesting I might be the answer, or whether it was wishful thinking on my part, but I had no intention of going full-time.

"Johnny Carey was only on £6 a week; I was getting my teacher's salary plus part-time money with United. It did not make sense to go full time. Every time I had a conversation with big Mark, he would be singing the praises of his friend, Tommy Taylor. So I knew quite a bit about Tommy's reputation long before he ever joined United.

"What I am saying is simply this: If I knew all about him, you can be absolutely certain that Matt and Jimmy also knew all about his pedigree. I was not the answer being over thirty and I just enjoyed a game of football."

Taylor's old Barnsley friend, Doug Kelly, related his version of when he felt United first became interested in Tommy. It was late in 1952 or early 1953.

United's reserves were playing Barnsley at Oakwell. Albert Scanlon, a sixteen-year-old left winger of immense promise was selected as twelfth man to travel. Those were the days of course before substitutes were allowed.

Tommy Taylor was the opposing centre-forward. Albert sat in the dug out next to Jimmy Murphy, Bert Whalley and Bill Inglis. As the game wore on, United were being torn apart. Tommy Taylor was causing havoc to United's tattered defence.

He gave the young Gordon Clayton and Mark Jones a torrid time, with these two on the receiving end of a real buffeting. Tommy was like lightning, and United's reputation had not phased him in the least. To him they were just another team to be beaten. He was winning everything in the air, and this was one of Mark

Jones's best attributes. But he could not match Taylor's aerial ability and Murphy was agitated and angry at his players, puffing away on his cigarette. Jimmy was barking out instructions to the players, but on this night his coaxing was of no avail. United lost 3-0.

As the final whistle blew, Murphy dashed out of the dug out and headed straight for Gordon Clayton, United's goalkeeper. "What do you make of their centre-forward?," asked an angry and irate Jimmy. A nervous Clayton did not really know what to say. If he said Taylor was a world beater this might well have brought more scorn from Murphy. If he said Taylor was no good, then another scathing comment might ring in his ears. So big Gordon quickly replied: "He's alright, not much skill."

Before poor Gordon could utter another word Murphy screamed at him in no uncertain terms: "Not much skill? He scored a hat-trick against you." Jimmy's choice of words was colourful to say the least. Albert Scanlon had been suitably impressed with the rival team's centre-forward's display and goal plundering. He vividly recalls this incident.

Albert Scanlon: "We were all frightened of Jimmy Murphy. Don't get me wrong, he was a lovely man and well respected, but we all knew that 'he' was the one person who would say whether you got into United's first team or not. Obviously, the boss, Matt Busby, relied on Jimmy to inform him who to promote into the first eleven.

"The competition was fierce for places not only in the first team, but also in every other team for United. Jimmy was a perfectionist. If we won 10-1, he would scream about the one goal we conceded and have us all back in for training the next day, "where he would analyse why we gave away that one goal.

"So you can imagine what kind of temper he was in that night. United reserves were used to winning by double figures, not getting beaten by the likes of Barnsley."

The next day at Old Trafford, an excited Jimmy Murphy could not wait to tell Matt Busby that Tommy Taylor could be their man. "He's the player we are looking for Matt. We must get him. He's as brave as a lion."

Busby was secretly excited about what his trusted right-hand man had told him. He designated scouts to watch Taylor at every opportunity.

The hunt to capture Taylor was well and truly in full flow. Every United official must have crossed the Pennies dozens of times to watch Taylor in action.

They did not just watch him playing for Barnsley's first team. They scrutinised him playing in any other games and the more they watched him, the more certain they were that he was the player to help bring glory and honour to Manchester United.

Yes, here indeed was the centre-forward United's backroom staff had searched the length and breath of the British Isles to secure. He had the United stamp all over his play.

One day, Busby asked his club captain and his trusted friend, Johnny Carey, to drive to Leicester, to watch Barnsley play. "Watch a boy named Taylor, who plays in the forward line," said Matt.

The normally cool Irishman was visibly excited on his return to Old Trafford. Carey couldn't wait to see his boss. "Taylor is the genuine article. He looks class on and off the ball, and he's so unselfish. We must get him," Carey told his manager.

Busby was at his desk. Looking up at his captain he thanked him profusely for his opinion and smiled: "That's another good report I've received on this young man. I will have to go and see him play myself."

After watching Tommy play for thirty minutes in a Barnsley game, Busby knew his staff were spot-on with their assessments of Taylor's ability. He had a warm glow inside him at the prospect of Taylor playing for his club. Here was an unpolished diamond who would, with patience and United's coaching, shine even brighter than any other new forward.

In quieter moments, Busby would sit in his office at Old Trafford, lean back in his chair, light his pipe and, as the smoke swirled through the still air, he could picture Taylor linking up with another youngster he was developing and ready to blood in United's first team, the slight but quick-silver Dennis Viollet who needed a big fellow to play off.

Busby envisaged what Taylor would be like running on to those beautifully flighted through balls from Roger Byrne and sixteen-year-old Duncan Edwards another diamond he was getting ready to promote to the first team or soaring up for those wonderful crosses from his winger's, Johnny Berry and seventeen-year-old David Pegg, who had already seen action in the first eleven.

Len Noad is a former newspaper reporter. A close and trusted friend of Jimmy Murphy, he also acted as a scout for Manchester United in the 1950s. Len was instrumental in the negotiations to sign Taylor.

Len Noad: "Tommy Taylor was a young, promising player quickly developing into an all-round forward. A great goal scorer, terrific at taking up positions across the front line, he had a marvellous physique, wonderful running power and was totally unselfish."

It was Len who, many years later, brought Lee Sharpe to United's attention when Sharpe was a Y.T.S. on Torquay's books. Now retired and living in Newton Abbot, Devon, he recalled the saga behind the transfer of Tommy to United. It was a real cloak and dagger affair.

Len Noad: "I can recall the Tommy Taylor transfer quite clearly, and the little part I played therein. My great friend, Jimmy Murphy and myself had frequent get-togethers at the Seymour, a public house near Jimmy's home in Whalley Range, in Manchester. The reason we met in the Seymour was quite simple really. We could chat and discus business without interruption from anybody.

"On this particular occasion Jimmy opened by saying: 'Len, Tommy Taylor at Barnsley is the best young centre-forward in the game. We want him here. Do you know him?' Now that was all that was necessary between us. Jimmy knew that I would act accordingly. I then made several trips to South Yorkshire to contact my various friends and I also popped into Woolworths in Barnsley frequently. I knew I would find Tommy at the record counter. He loved his records and had a good collection.

"Time moved on apace in the chase for Tommy's signature. I learned from sources in Barnsley, that their chairman, Joe Richards, who was top man in the Yorkshire coalfield, had privately arranged with his opposite number in South Wales for Tommy to join Cardiff, a First Division club in those days. I, of course, passed all this information back to Murphy.

Jimmy instructed me to keep a close watch on the situation 'If you lose him, Len, we'll cease to be friends!,' he told me. On receiving news that things were hotting up, Matt Busby and Jimmy decided to move quickly. The three of us motored to Barnsley in Matt's Hillman Minx and we went out to Taylor's home to meet his parents. Matt was brilliant with Tommy's mother and father, speaking in a quiet tone of voice he won them over with his charming manner. Tommy was as good as signed."

John Aston: "At the time of the Taylor transfer, I was still playing in the first team, so details of Tommy's move to United, didn't concern me. We needed a centre-forward that was obvious. You have to remember though, that many players had served in the forces and this took its toll on them. Later I was coaching in a full-time capacity, working closely with Jimmy Murphy. Many years later Jimmy would tell me the problems he and Matt had during the Taylor transfer and why it took such a long time to sign Tommy. 'But He was well worth it,' he often told me smiling. Both Busby and Murphy thought very highly of Tommy as a person and a player."

Len Noad: "Busby and Murphy in those days were revolutionaries as far as football thinking was concerned.

"They had seen most of the other League clubs bury their heads in the sand, and proclaim that English soccer was still the best in the world despite the superb Hungarian team and other brilliant continental sides of those times.

"There was very little 'thinking' taking place in boardrooms and out on the training grounds. After all, these foreigners were merely "fancy Dan" footballers who would wilt under a stiff challenge. That seemed the general consensus of opinion in England, but not at Old Trafford!

"Busby and his staff knew that soccer was now a world game, and that the Europeans and South Americans were improving rapidly. We might have taught them how to play the game, but now we could learn from them. Yes, a wind of change was blowing through our game."

With this in mind the United duo were planning their team building. They knew the soccer world was changing rapidly and drastically.

The back room set-up was geared to producing world beaters. Plans were near fruition but they needed a big, brave centre-forward and Taylor fitted the bill. The United manager had spoken to Joe Richards about the possibility of Taylor becoming available.

Busby knew Barnsley were not a rich club. Nor were they attracting big crowds. It was a shame, but a fact of life that clubs like Barnsley had to sell their biggest assets to survive. Richards indicated that he would have to put Tommy up for sale in the near future. He gave United first option when the Oakwell club decided to sell him and off the record, the chairman told Busby that it would be difficult to get Taylor to move from his home town club.

Joe Richards: "The lad loved Barnsley Football Club. The coaching staff thought very highly of his ability. They didn't want to see him leave. Tommy himself did not want to leave. We would not sell players such as Tommy under normal circumstances, but to balance our books we were forced to sell our best players."

Secretly, Jimmy Murphy was sent to speak with Tommy about moving to Old Trafford before Barnsley officially put him up for sale. It can be assumed that all parties knew about this transaction taking place. But in the football world nothing is certain until it is signed and sealed.

Jimmy made the trek across the Pennies several times in an effort to convince the youngster that Manchester United were the only club for him. For his part, Busby considered Taylor was the greatest prospect in the game at that time, even though £30,000 for a Second Division player was outrageous. But Tommy was steadfast in his resolve that he wanted to go nowhere.

Cecil McCormack, a teammate, who was also a prolific goalscorer, advised the young Taylor a year before his eventual departure that if Barnsley sold him, then his best move would be to try and join United.

"They play football smoothly and always have two good wingers. A first class footballing side," Cecil told Tommy. He still suffers pangs of remorse from giving the lad this advice.

Others at Barnsley were also whispering in Tommy's ear, urging him to stay put. Among them were the coaches, who were more concerned with performance and results than the football politics and finance.

Richards got to hear what they were doing and sent for them. He was hopping mad. "I know what you are doing, and what you are saying to Tommy. I'm telling you now that you had all better stop this nonsense and alter your attitude, because there is a dire need for the fee which Taylor's transfer will bring to this club," he told all concerned.

Matt Busby was dignified, a known charmer. He put everyone at ease and made them feel that here was a person who could be trusted. His very presence brought instant respect and he spoke in clear, quiet tones. On the other hand, Jimmy Murphy had Celtic pride. Murphy always spoke with the pride and passion of the valleys.

He was like one of those old-time preachers, full of fire and brimstone. Anyone he was talking to could hardly be bored by Jimmy's conversation or untouched by his sincerity. Murphy told the Barnsley lad about the brilliant youngsters who were being groomed at Old Trafford.

"They will be world beaters and so will you, when you join us. Look, you can't be responsible for the plight which Barnsley are in. It's not your fault. Besides, you're much too good a player to play in the Third Division," Murphy added.

Len Noad: "When the speculation was at its highest. Bob Shotton, Barnsley's first-team trainer, deserved a creditable mention. He took Tommy into the treatment room one morning and asked him if I was helping him. Tommy blushed and Bob said: 'It's all right, Tommy. Len won't let you down. You can trust him.' This was a lovely tribute and I thanked him."

After Taylor's last game for the Oakwell team, which was a 1-1 draw at home to Lincoln on 14 February, 1953, a match played in five-inches of snow. There had been constant speculation that before the week was out, Tommy would be transferred. Annoyed, he sought out the chairman. Together they walked slowly along the corridor beneath the main stand, stopping outside the office where the afternoon's gate receipts were being counted.

Tommy, head down and obviously upset by the rumours said: "I don't want to go, Mr. Richards." The chairman was agitated, annoyed, very brusque and directly to the point he replied: "You've got to go Tommy. That is the end of it. I don't want to hear any more." Can you imagine this scenario taking place in the 1990s?

Tommy Taylor: "I soon realised that it would be for everyone's benefit if I moved and so I chose Manchester United. Firstly, Manchester was not far from Barnsley; secondly they had a great reputation in post-war football, and I knew that I would get absolutely first class coaching and advice from Matt Busby."

Finally the day of the transfer came. It was the 4 March. It was a hectic day for Joe Richards and his directors. The club was managerless due to the sudden death of Angus Seed a few weeks before.

On the day Tommy was transferred, the Barnsley outfit let Eddie McMorran, another prolific scorer move to nearby Doncaster for £10,000.

Twenty First Division clubs were reputed to have wanted Tommy's signature for their clubs! This was whittled down to seventeen and when Joe Richards announced the fee (£30,000), there was only a handful of clubs left. United were firm favourites and Busby had agreed to pay the "huge" amount. Tommy still stalled. He just did not want to leave Barnsley.

Both United officials had gone to great pains to explain their hopes and plans for the future, and the glittering young stars about to be unleashed into the First Division when official talks began Tommy asked if he could still live at home with his family and train at Oakwell Busby readily consented, and when the United manager thought he had sealed the deal, Tommy wavered and came up with another request. He wanted six weeks to think things over!

Matt Busby told him: "Look son, you are hedging. You will have the same decision to make in six weeks time. Why not sign now and we can all go home and get some sleep."

Tommy asked Busby to hand him the pen. Then, sheepishly, asked: "Would it be possible for my mother and father to get a couple of tickets to watch me play?"

Behind the scenes, it was known that Cardiff, in an all-out effort to clinch the deal, had upped their offer to £35,000. Barnsley were quite ready to do the deal with the Welsh club and disregard United's offer but Taylor put a quick halt to that.

"I'm joining only one club, and that is Manchester United and beside, Cardiff is much too far from home for my liking," he told club officials.

Doug Kelly: "Tommy used to show me glossed up brochures and post cards from the Cardiff people showing what a lovely place it was. They sent him all sorts of stuff. I don't know if this was from the Cardiff directors or the fans. But the bottom line was he honestly didn't want to leave Oakwell.

"The day he finally signed for United four of us, myself, Tommy, Maurice Jackson and Maurice Hudson were sat in the Empire Cinema in Barnsley. A notice flashed on the screen saying: 'Would Tommy Taylor please report to the football club immediately.' Yes, that's how he signed. He had told us that there had been a great deal of talking and it was making him fed-up, but I think at the end he had resigned himself to moving"

Though Barnsley wanted £30,000, Busby did not want to burden young Tommy with a price-tag of that magnitude so it was agreed to make the official price, £29,999. The odd pound was given to Lily Wilby, a Barnsley employee, who had made constant cups of tea in the boardroom during the hectic transfer negotiations. When everything was done and dusted, Busby and Murphy were overjoyed, but didn't show any emotion until everything was finally signed and sealed.

There was no back-handed payments to anyone which was rumoured at the time.

Len Noad: "It was said that I received a gold watch from United for my part in the transfer; that is rubbish. What I did was because of my friendship and admiration for Jimmy Murphy."

Wilf McGuinness: "I was only a kid when Tommy joined United. With the benefit of hindsight, well intended though Matt Busby's action's were in paying only £29,999, it attracted more publicity than if the fee had been a straight £30,000."

Len Noad: "The fee was the largest Manchester United had ever handed over for any player at that time. But the transaction proved to be one of the best they ever made. Tommy Taylor was a first-class clubman. He was only interested in playing football, he had no vices and was the sort of boy anybody would be proud to have as a son. After training he usually trotted off to a record shop in Manchester city centre.

"I could always find him there for a chat. He proved a steal as his goal tally showed. And he became one of the most popular players to grace the Old Trafford turf. He soon settled down at United made new friends and indeed loved life in Manchester."

Dennis Viollet: "I didn't know much about Tommy until after United signed him. And like everybody else, I read about it in the newspapers. I was doing my two-years National Service and I missed out on a lot of things which were going on at the club. I wasn't classed as a first-teamer in those days, I had played in the odd game here and there.

"What I do know was that the great Manchester United team of 1948 was starting to get the wrong side of thirty Busby and Murphy were looking for new blood. Jack Rowley was coming to the end of a fabulous career with United. They tried several players as the spearhead, including Lawrence Cassidy. They bought Johnny Downie, but nothing worked out.

"The first time I actually met Tommy was while I was home on a short leave from army duties and popped in to do a spot of training at Old Trafford. I remember asking the lads what sort of a person he was. I heard very positive things about him. What a nice feller they thought he was, but more important, what a terrific player they believed he would become. I knew he had scored quite a lot of goals for Barnsley.

"I really got to know him better when I made my first-team debut at Newcastle in April, 1953. I played on the right wing against a fellow named Alf McMichael, the Irish international full-back. I can't remember who Tom was facing. I have never known ninety-minutes pass so quickly, but what I do remember was Tom scoring with a beautiful header I remember thinking, God, how this fellow can get up so high of the ground. It was startling really. He just soared high above everyone else.

"That was the first of many, many great goals I saw Tom score with his head. Those headers were absolutely superb. He was only slightly older than myself, but he kept an eye on me all through the match. I think this was to make sure those tough defenders didn't get to physical with me."

When Taylor joined United, the game was changing rapidly. The old-time battering ram type of centre-forward charging at defences like a bull in a china shop was fast disappearing. Tommy was the forerunner of a new breed of centre-forward. He had a touch of velvet about his play, moving out to the wings, taking up different positions, centre-halves were puzzled and didn't know what to make of this style of play Busby encouraged him in every possible way.

Defenders were used to having physical battles with the opposing number nines. United encouraged Tommy to use this ploy of movement and thinking. This was the big difference between United and the method of other clubs.

Critics said that because he was so big, Tommy, at times appeared crude when the ball was played to feet. If this was so, it soon disappeared once Murphy got him on the training ground.

Jimmy was a hard task-master, but he loved working with the big raw-boned forward who, in turn, enjoyed the sharp-tonged Welshman's wit and the training chores.

Tommy knew Murphy was making him a better player. In time, his ball control improved drastically. Matt Busby and his staff were working flat out to blend their dream team together. They had the best young talent in English football in reserve and junior teams, but like all great clubs they needed time to develop and "gel" together as a unit.

Dennis Viollet: "There was a certain kind of magic atmosphere about Old Trafford in those days. Tommy's signing seemed to trigger it all into action. He was surrounded by very talented players."

John Aston: "There were brilliant youngsters such as Viollet, Pegg, Jones, Blanchflower, Edwards and many more, with the likes of Charlton, Scanlon, McGuinness, Colman and Bent coming later. Many others fell by the wayside, but the job of making United a top club was being achieved. Busby used a softly, softly approach. Murphy did the screaming and rollicking, driving home the simple things which help make a world class footballer.

"They were all the better for the grounding Jimmy instilled into them. 'Keep it simple. Pass the ball to a red shirt,' was what he preached; simple instructions really, but very true. This was what Tommy Taylor learned and why the boss went to a great deal of trouble to secure his transfer Tommy was a bargain buy."

The Big Money Burden

To conclude this chapter on the transfer saga of the Tommy Taylor story, in 1953, the record transfer fee was the £35,000 which Sheffield Wednesday paid Notts County for inside-forward Jackie Sewell, in March, 1951.

When United paid Barnsley the £29,999 fee for Taylor's services everyone thought it was a ridiculous sum to pay for any player. Jackie Sewell talking about the burden of such a huge fee said: "After long deliberations I agreed to sign for Sheffield Wednesday. After I completed the transfer forms. I had the most restless and sleepless night of my life. The next morning, spread across the newspapers, was the figure £35,000 and my worries were increased. I wondered if I had done the right thing; my head was in a whirl for weeks after.

"I went to Meadow Lane to collect my boots and the first person I met was Tommy Lawton. He could tell I was worried. He took me for a walk around the cinder track, put his arm around my shoulders and said: 'You don't want to worry, Jack. The money has nothing to do with you. Forget it, you'll repay them every penny,' His words certainly steadied me.

"When Tommy Taylor was transferred to United for £30,000 I had every sympathy for him. His story was so similar to my own, a jump from the comparative peace and tranquillity of a mining village, to the glamour of a big city and big-time football with one of the most famous clubs.

"Though Wednesday and United paid those huge amounts of money for our services, do you know what Taylor and myself received? Ten pounds!

"Yes, that was all that we received, and under the rules, all we were entitled to get from the transfer fee. I wanted to see a scheme which would benefit the player, where he would be entitled to a cut of the fee. But at that time no such scheme could be operated because of the way a players contract existed. It was unfair.

"Taylor was a wonderful centre-forward. I played with Lawton, and he was the best. Brilliant at going up for high balls. This was one of Taylor's strong points, he was great at heading and led the forward line brilliantly. He was with a good club, United had Busby and Murphy, and they would polish any raw edges Taylor might have had.

"I have mentioned the encouragement I received from Tommy Lawton. Believe me, no young player could have had a better counsellor, friend and coach. I shall never forget the day he said to me: 'Jack, one day you'll be a real star. Do you know why?' I confessed I didn't and he replied: 'Because you are a good listener. And when you can listen you can learn.'

"I mention this little story because it is perfectly true, and the perfect maxim for young players. Tommy Taylor was a good listener. Within weeks of his transfer, he was selected for the South America tour, on international duty.

"Tommy would listen and act, on what Walter Winterbottom advised him to do. He always wanted to improve his game. Players such as Billy Wright, Alf Ramsey, Tom Finney and others would suggest certain techniques to help improve his play. He always listened intently and would act upon their suggestions and advice.

Taylor was a wonderful centre-forward and he became a big star. England had quite a few quality leaders in those days. Some were world class. Stan Mortensen, Roy Bentley, Nat Lofthouse and a few others were goalscorers of the highest merit, and Tommy was in there with them.

The king of them all though was Tommy Lawton. He and Taylor were absolutely fabulous when the ball was in the air. Both had the knack of hovering in the air. Their heading ability was feared throughout football. Lawton of course, was coming to the end of his illustrious career as Taylor was just commencing his, with the magnificent Busby Babes team which brought pride and prestige back to English football. Great players, wonderful characters, and perfect gentlemen.

Moving to Manchester

After signing for United on the Tuesday, Tommy, accompanied by his girlfriend Norma Curtis, a Barnsley lass, arrived at London Road station (Piccadilly Station, as it's now named) to have a look at Old Trafford. As the couple got off the train they were met by a smiling and excited Jimmy Murphy. After exchanging pleasantries, they were whisked from the station directly to United's ground, where Murphy took them on a tour of the facilities. Albert Scanlon was busy cleaning the dressing rooms as Murphy, Taylor and Norma, walked through the area under the main stand.

Albert Scanlon: "I recognised Tommy straight away. He had a big smile as Jimmy showed him round. 'I know who you are,' I thought. 'You're the feller that scored that cracking hat-trick against us at Oakwell.'

"I busied myself sweeping up, not wanting to attract attention when, suddenly, Jimmy stopped and looking at me, said: 'Albert, son, what are you doing tonight?'

"I told Jimmy I was going to watch Manchester City play Glasgow Rangers at Maine Road. City were one of the few clubs at that time who had floodlights."

Jimmy Murphy responded: "Oh good. Would you mind taking Tommy and Norma with you to Maine Road? I'll arrange the tickets."

Scanlon recalled: "I got washed and changed while Murphy and some other members of staff were talking with Tommy. Later, I took Tommy and his girl friend to our house in Hulme. My mother made a lovely tea and off we went to City's ground. The tickets were waiting for us and after the game we walked from Maine Road back towards Hulme. Tommy had to visit his 'digs' situated somewhere near Lancashire County cricket ground. Tommy and Norma thanked me and jumped on a bus heading towards Old Trafford.

"What impressed me was his down to earth attitude. He could so easily have ordered a taxi, but no, the bus was good enough for him. There were no airs or graces about him. He was a big, big star at that time. He never forgot my mother's kindness. Every Christmas he sent her a present."

Having located his digs, and met his landlady, Tommy and his girl friend returned to Barnsley that night. The next day, he received a telegram from United telling him a BBC television crew would arrive at the Taylor household in Smithies, on the Friday morning to film the new star. After the filming, the twenty-one-year-old returned to Manchester alone.

He was met at the station by Matt Busby and Johnny Carey and a posse of reporters and photographers. Tucked under his arm was a brown paper parcel his football boots. How down to earth could you get?

Tommy was a little nervous, but thrilled at the prospect of pitting his wits against First Division defences. He was determined to make his move a success. He vowed he would watch, listen and learn.

Johnny Aston started his footballing career as an inside forward, but became a classy full-back and gained seventeen England caps. Aston was an excellent tackler and proved to be one of the most loyal servants the club produced. He turned out at centre-forward and other positions for the club.

He joined United in 1937 turning professional in 1946. Illness ended his career in June 1955. He played in 253 post-war League games, won an F.A. Cup winners medal in 1948 and in 1952 a League Championship prize, joining the backroom staff in 1956. A lovely soft spoken and well-mannered man he remembers Tommy Taylor's arrival clearly.

John Aston: "In the 1950s the area near to the ground was a hive of industrial activity with thousands of people employed in Trafford Park. A corner house on a street right near to the ground was owned by a lady called Mrs Rimmer. In the morning she sold sandwiches etc.

"There were home made lunches at mid-day, snacks and soft drinks. She did a roaring trade. I'll never forget a little incident just a day or so after Tommy signed for United.

"The papers were full of the story that Tommy, a mere twenty-one-year-old Second Division player could be worth a £30,000 fee. Though I was still in United's first team I was nearing the end of my career and I fancied staying in the game, I liked coaching. I used to help Bert Whalley with the youngsters.

"Myself and Bert Whalley would often take a couple of young apprentices to Mrs Rimmer's for lunch. One day, we were asked to take Tommy for something to eat. He said he fancied some home-made cooking. About six of us sat down at the table and it was busier than usual for some reason or other.

"Mrs. Rimmer had the pans on the stove and there was steam everywhere. It was hectic. She was serving, clearing plates and cups from another table. People were shouting out their orders. The talk from everyone was obviously about football, and in particular the Taylor signing.

"Mrs. Rimmer wasn't a football fan. In fact she wouldn't have known a tennis ball from a caseball. 'I'm fed up with all this talk about silly old football, have you lot got nothing better to talk about other than a load of men kicking a silly little ball about?' she said, as she hurried from one table to another. Then, looking in our direction she blurted out: 'And who in their right senses would pay £30,000 for somebody to kick a ball for them. What's the world coming to? It's ridiculous, it really is!'

"Tommy was sat at the table unconcerned and couldn't have cared less. He was tucking into his meal, Mrs Rimmer was spouting that no footballer was worth sixpence, let alone £30,000. At this remark Tommy looked up, laughed, and in his thick Yorkshire accent replied: 'Your right love. I couldn't agree with you more.' After finishing his meal Tommy excused himself and he and the lads walked back over the bridge to the ground. Mrs Rimmer had no idea who she had just served was. When somebody said jokingly to her: 'Do you know who that fellow is that's just walked out?'

Unconcerned but slightly puzzled Mrs Rimmer was told that the chap who had just thanked her for an excellent meal, was the man who had cost United £30,000. She blushed bright red and was speechless. Back at the ground, we all had a good laugh about the incident. None more so than Tommy. Honestly, he was a great person.

"In the dressing-room before Tommy's first game against Preston, everyone wished him well. There was not the slightest bit of resentment.

"We had young David Pegg playing as well, then only seventeen years old. Tommy seemed remarkably calm and collected with no outward sign of nerves. When he stripped, his physique was quite impressive. He was head and shoulders above me.

'Come on lads, let's show what we can do,' said Allenby Chilton, our centre-half. Preston were a very talented side then, and there was a huge crowd. Tommy scored his first goal with a header, from outside the penalty area.

"I had played with Tommy Lawton and I always thought he was the best header of a ball I had ever seen I soon put young Taylor in the same bracket. The amazing thing was the power he got into those headers. It really was tremendous.

"We had not been playing well and were all in agreement that for a newcomer in his first game in the top flight Tom had done wonderfully well. He scored a couple of goals against Preston."

Allenby Chilton arrived at Old Trafford in 1938 and served United until leaving in March, 1955. He captained the club and was one of United's most regular first-team players from 1946 to 1954.

Allenby Chilton: "Being an ex-boxer, I thought young Tommy had done a bit when he stripped before the Preston match. You have to remember at that time we were all under a bit of pressure. Our results were not consistent and perhaps a few of us were getting on a bit!

"Basically we were still a good team. Tommy's arrival was a shot in the arm in many ways. All the attention was focused on him. I must say, he was remarkably, calm and collected about all the publicity. During the game he busied himself, took up good positions and scored two cracking goals. It was after his second goal, which I had a hand in making for him, that I realised he was a fine player. I remember saying to the lads: 'Matt's signed a good 'un in this lad.' He was so laid back and casual. He had a great debut and went on to prove a world-class centre-forward".

Tommy received a favourable press on his debut and one paper suggested he was another Trevor Ford. *The Manchester Evening News* reported: 'Tommy Taylor's storybook debut . . . He deserves a large slice of credit for the way he overcame the psychological handicap of having to look, think, and react like a player worthy of that £30,000 transfer label. After his bullet-speed header brought him his first goal. He deserves great praise.

"George Follows's article was headlined: 'Tommy Taylor Has The Lawton Look.' Then went on: 'Enter the shy and smiling executioner, Tommy Taylor. The home-sweet-home boy from Barnsley kisses all round from the family afterwards is deadly in the penalty box. And Manchester United have bought a full £30,000 worth of goal-filled footballer perhaps more. He looks a little like Trevor Ford, a little like Jack Rowley. And in his ruthless execution near goal hc is a lot like Tommy Lawton.'

"Another report said: 'Take his goals. There was the one he headed in from Rowley's fine centre. Not a difficult goal, but it flashed in with a finality that is a goalkeeper's despair. There was the one he shot in from Pearson's equally fine through pass.

"He breasted it down, ran two, three, four strides . . . and flogged it in from fifteen yards.

"And this above all there was the easy way he bore the price of fame, and the sudden transplanting from Oakwell to Old Trafford. Yes, Tommy was impressive on his debut. He had begun brightly. Then for a time the game went away from him. There was no panic or rush to justify all those headlines. He waited for the game to come back to him . . . and it did!

"But he was just one of eleven men who had a wonderful afternoon. United put on a super-show. Tommy could dispel any last lingering doubts in his mind that Old Trafford was the right place for him to come to."

Tommy Taylor: "When I first played for United, I was given a wonderful reception by the crowd. I knew I was on trial as far as they were concerned and I was longing for a goal. My first chance came following a corner.

"I timed the dash alright, but my header sailed wide. I was sorry I did not score, but though it was a miss, I knew I had done the right thing and the "feel" of it put me right for the rest of the match. I scored later on, but it was the 'miss' that I appreciated the most."

Tommy scored a further six goals before the season ended, making it seven goals in eleven appearances a good return. He was settling down splendidly to life in Manchester. Busby and Murphy were delighted with their capture from Yorkshire.

Tom Jackson of the *Manchester Evening News* and Alf Clarke *Manchester Evening Chronicle* were very impressed with Tommy's potential but both thought that he needed a scheming type of forward alongside him like Stan Pearson.

They each wrote they had great faith in his ability and felt sure that once things started going his way Tommy would be well to the front as a marksman. Towards the end of his first season with the Reds, playing at Newcastle in April, 1953, United fielded twenty-four-year-old Les Olive in goal and nineteen-year-old Dennis Viollet their debuts in the first team.

Tommy scored twice and helped both lads to settle into the team though only a novice himself as far as experience was concerned. The spluttering stop-start performances of the team saw Tommy tried at inside right with Jack Rowley at centre-forward in the hope of galvanising the forward line. It was not the success it had been hoped.

Tommy had all the essentials in his soccer make-up, and people were convinced he was a vital cog in United's future attacking machine. Around this time, Tommy had to serve his army training was hardly ideal preparation for matches. In fact he had to miss one or two first-team matches because of army duty. It was clear though that centre-forward was his best position.

Wilf McGuinness, Collyhurst born, and christened at St. Patrick's, the church school which produced other United players such as Lol Cassidy, Nobby Stiles and Brian Kidd, captained Manchester, Lancashire and England schoolboys before joining United in 1953.

His future looked bright indeed, but he was desperately unlucky to break a leg in December 1959 at the age of twenty-two. The injury ended his playing career. He had played in eighty-one League games.

McGuinness became United's youth team manager and was a member of the club's training staff. In 1966, he was part of Sir Alf Ramsey's coaching team when England won the World Cup. Wilf was popular and highly thought of at Old Trafford. He was Matt Busby's choice as Chief Coach and then manager when Matt retired in 1970. There could be no one more loyal to United's cause than the big-hearted north Manchester lad.

Wilf McGuinness: "Though I joined United just after Tommy signed, I had to work for two years, training only on Tuesday and Thursday's. I saw a great many of United's first-team games and also, of course, some training sessions. The first time I watched Tommy train was pre-season in 1953. He ran out of the tunnel at

UNITED BREAK OFF FROM TRAINING
Dennis Villoet, Tommy Taylor, David Pegg, Bert Whalley (behind), Wilf McGuiness, Roger Byrne, Matt Busby, Ray Wood, Billy Whelan, Duncan Edwards, Mark Jones, Billy Foulkes, Johnny Berry,

A BIT OF A KNEES-UP DURING TRAINING
The fully visible players are Wilf McGuiness, Dennis Viollet, David Pegg, Tommy Taylor and Duncan Edwards.

Old Trafford wearing a big, thick, polo-necked sweater. God, he was imposing! He ran like a true thoroughbred with a beautifully controlled long striding gait.

"I was thinking to myself: 'Why couldn't I be as tall and graceful as him. And have his kind of acceleration from a standing position.' He was magnificent, and what's more he looked the part in everything he did. We younger kids had to watch our Ps and Qs with the first-team players, but Tommy was different. He seemed to have a perpetual grin and was always ready for a laugh and a joke."

Colin Webster was known as the "fiery" Welshman. He joined United from Cardiff in May, 1952, after winning an Army Cup Final medal. It was Dennis Viollet and a United director who recommended him to Matt Busby. A utility forward, good with both feet, Colin gave United over six years of loyal and grand service. Playing mostly in the reserves but getting sixty-five first-team games under his belt, scoring twenty-seven goals. He was the understudy for Tommy Taylor.

Colin Webster: "I joined United on the day they played Arsenal and beat them 6-2 to win the First Division Championship. I got a £10 signing-on fee and a complimentary ticket to watch the game. I was taken to old Ma Watson's daughter's house in Hornby Road, which was just around the corner from Ma Watson's. This was my digs. Blanchie (Jackie Blanchflower) Gordon Clayton, Big Dunk, and a few more United lads were in both houses. All the lads used both Ma Watson's main house, and her daughter's house. In 1953, we heard the whisper that the club were going to pay big money for a centre-forward. But we didn't know who it was until this huge curly-haired lad walked into Ma Watson's front room with a big smile on his face.

"That's how I shall always remember Tommy. We had some laughs. I bought a really good thick, warm overcoat, and we called it the communal overcoat because everybody wore it. One bitterly cold night I was going out and went to the coat rack, put my coat on and as I stuck my hands in the pockets, there was £80 there. It wasn't mine so I asked Blanchie and Tom if it was their money. 'No' they both said. So we had £20 apiece and gave old Ma Watson £20. She was delirious with joy.

"Big Duncan had red sauce with every meal. I bet he went through a bottle of it every other day. It was comical. We would all be sat eating and 'Dunk' would put a big dollop of the stuff all over his food.

"Tom said to him one day: 'I bet you wouldn't put that stuff on your porridge in the morning.' Duncan said he would. The next morning Duncan was sat at the table with his big bowl of thick porridge, he was just about to put some treacle on his food, when Tom said: 'Hey, wait a second, you said you would eat your breakfast with red sauce on it.'

"Without blinking an eye, 'Dunk' picked up the ketchup, poured it over his porridge and ate it.

"Tom loved winding Dunk up but in good-natured fun, though. I loved going for a pint with Tom; he was great company."

When Tommy came to live in Manchester it was Coronation year (1953) and things were changing rapidly and not just in Manchester, but practically throughout the whole of the British Isles. Jobs were still plentiful and authority in our schools had to be obeyed. It was the year Everest was finally surmounted, (by Sir John Hunt and his team). A year later, Roger Bannister, ran the first four-minute mile. The age of the crooner and ballad singers were making way for vibrations of a new sound of music rock and roll. Bill Haley and his Comets, and Elvis the "pelvis" were livening things up considerably.

There was an air of optimism everywhere; teenagers were no longer satisfied to be seen and not heard as their parents had been. Younger people wanted a big say in their futures.

This was rebel without a cause time. Marlon Brando and James Dean were wearing blue jeans instead of suits a symbol of the changing times. It was the Teddy boy era, with their drainpipe trousers and velvet collars. Tony Curtis hair styles, slicked and well-greased.

It was a funny and exciting period and a complete reversal of the drabness of the post-war, ration book austerity. There was a demand for better housing and standards of living conditions. The backstreet, little terrace houses were still there with cold water, gas-mantled lighting and outside toilets; but this was about to change.

The South American Tour

Ten weeks after joining Manchester United Tommy was shocked and very surprised at the news that he had been selected to go on tour to South America, with the full England team at the end of the season. He could not believe it. He never imagined for one moment that he would be in with a chance of being selected.

He had to pinch himself to make sure that he was not dreaming. Tom Finney, Billy Wright, Alf Ramsey and Nat Lofthouse were among other players selected. Johnny Berry, his United team mate, was also in the squad. This honour was more than Tommy could have hoped for or expected.

Being selected for England was the furthest thing from his mind. To his way of thinking, England only selected established players, and he had played only eleven First Division games ruling him out of contention, he reasoned.

He talks about that period: "First Division football proved very exciting though the play was often widespread. Players kept their positions well, the tackling was close, and there was less time for thinking. I felt I was learning all over again, but the team was very helpful.

"What followed next was beyond my wildest dreams. I was home at Barnsley, I went to a cinema, and on coming out bought an evening paper. There I read I had been selected to go to South America with the England team. I can honestly say that you could have knocked me down with a feather.

"Almost every newspaper had tried choosing the party on behalf of the selectors, and centre-forwards like Bill Holden and Bedford Jezzard had been named as possible second choices to Nat Lofthouse. No one picked me.

"So there it was. The boy who had given up football for lack of interest, the youth who had been almost crippled in that Army game. A centre-forward with less than a third of a season's experience of First Division football was the surprise choice for the tour. Can you wonder if I went home (happily) dazed? Although I had played in representative Army teams, meeting a full touring side of internationals was quite a different thing, and I was very nervous when I reported to the meeting place in London.

"There were football greats in the party, men like Billy Wright and Tom Finney who had been automatic choices for England pretty well ever since the war and other experienced battlers like Bill Eckersley, Alf Ramsey, Jimmy Dickinson, Harry Johnston, Jack Froggart and, of course, Nat Lofthouse, England's number one centre-forward.

Harry England: "This was a wonderful honour for Tommy, he was overjoyed and he really couldn't believe it, that he, a kid from Smithies, had been selected to play for his country, and going to South America.

"Yes, a lot of good things happened for Tommy in 1953. We celebrated his selection with a few drinks in the pub. If Tommy had not joined United, he would have been getting ready to play in the Third Division with Barnsley.

"Instead, he was going to South America with all those great players, representing England. He promised that he would send us post cards from the various countries he visited. And he was true to his words as always".

Walter Winterbottom, a world-wide soccer personality, was Director of Coaching to the Football Association beside being the England manager. Walter was a very shrewd judge of a player. He had noted Tommy's progress since going to United.

He also knew that Matt Busby, for whom he had the greatest respect as a soccer visionary, only had thoroughbreds in his teams. Matt had indicated to the England boss that young Taylor was good, and getting better. That was the endorsement Winterbottom needed to hear. Everyone at Old Trafford was delighted at Tommy's selection for the national side. Jimmy Murphy inspired Tommy, gave him belief and confidence in himself. Jimmy was a very, very persuasive talker. The young centre-forward couldn't believe what Murphy was telling him, i.e. that he was good enough for England!

Henry Cockburn recalls: "We were all pleased for Tommy and little Johnny Berry when England selected them. Believe me it is a marvellous thrill when you get that letter telling you your country wants your services. I played thirteen times for my country, and I was proud every time I pulled on that jersey with the three lions.

"To be honest, I felt like a lion when I ran out onto the field with the England team. I told Tommy to enjoy every minute of it, because you have no idea when it will all end. I explained to him how disappointed and devastated I felt when I was never selected again.

"I blame this on getting sent off against Manchester City. I told Tommy to just play his normal game. After all, that is why he was selected, He had done remarkably well to get picked after only a handful of First Division games".

Now listen to Allenby Chilton. "I was delighted when Tommy got the call-up from England. He deserved it for the way he had settled down at Old Trafford. Johnny Berry, had been with us for nearly two years before Taylor came. He was a direct little winger. Tommy was a bit raw on some aspects of his game, but you could see that he was going to improve rapidly and become a better player.

"I only played for England twice, but those two occasions were among my proudest moments in football. I told Tommy that he would come back a much better player, after playing and mixing with the likes of Finney, Wright, Ramsey and Lofthouse.

"You had to improve by playing and mixing in great players company. And don't forget, he was only twenty-one. I'm glad to say I was proved correct. When the new season came you could almost see the confidence bursting out of him".

Jimmy Murphy said at the time: "I smiled to myself when he was selected. Some people believed I had over-exaggerated Tommy's potential, but I knew he was a great leader of the forward line. I must be honest and say that I never felt Tommy was at his best for England.

"I could never put my finger on why this was. Whether he never got the right kind of service from his England team mates I wouldn't like to say, but there is no doubt that he wasn't as relaxed nor as fluent playing for England as when he was playing for us."

On Thursday, 3 May, 1953, the England team left London. The flight took them to Madrid, Daker, Reciffe, Rio, Montevideo, and then on to Buenos Aires. These eighteen footballers were to prove among England's finest ambassadors ever sent abroad.

The full squad was goalkeepers Merrick (Birmingham), Ditchburn (Tottenham); Alf Ramsey (Spurs — the same Ramsey who a few years later would manage England when we won the world cup), Eckersley (Blackburn), Garrett (Blackpool), Wright (Wolverhampton), Johnston (Blackpool), Barrass (Bolton), Dickinson (Portsmouth), Barlow (West Bromwich), Finney (Preston), Broadis (Manchester City), Taylor and Berry (Manchester United) Redfern Froggatt (Sheffield Wednesday), Bentley (Chelsea) and Jack Froggatt (Portsmouth).

It was a happy party with plenty of laughing and joking with Bill Eckersley and Ivor Broadis the two comedians, who had everyone in stitches with their antics. These two made the hours pass like minutes. Being a new boy in the England set-up, Tommy was quiet and reserved. Enjoying the frolics and the banter but keeping himself to himself. After all, he was there to do a job for his country!

Tommy, of course, had his team-mate Johnny Berry for company. Tom Finney also went out of his way to make him feel like one of the lads. He became close to his main rival for the number nine shirt, Nat Lofthouse, known affectionately as "Lofty," or "The Lion of Vienna" by the fans. Lofthouse went on to serve Bolton Wanderers and football for over fifty years. And as this book is being written, he is still serving Bolton as their President and founder of their famous Lifeline fundraising scheme. He was honoured with an O.B.E.

Nat was among the top centre-forwards of all time. Playing for his only club,

Wanderers he notched up 452 appearances and scoring 255 goals. In thirty-three Internationals for England he scored thirty goals. What a record. He is a living legend. But more than anything else, Nat is a first class human being, a gentleman and one of the most respected sporting figures ever. And that kind of praise has to be earned, you can't buy it. Nat Lofthouse has it in abundance.

When the plane carrying the England party touched down on the tarmac of the Ministro Pistarini Airport in Argentina everyone was shattered after the long journey, but due mainly to Eckersley and Broadis they were in good spirits. And raring to get into action.

Nat Lofthouse recalls: "Until meeting up with Tommy on this England tour, I had never set eyes on him or even heard of him. Of course I had read about his transfer from Barnsley to United. I found him a big, friendly fellow, easy to get on with. He was a smashing guy but quiet and unassuming. We soon became good friends.

"Billy Wright, Alf Ramsey and Tom Finney were good blokes for helping new lads to feel part of the set-up. And with Ivor Broadis and Bill Eckersley around, you soon felt part of the team.

"Tommy was always game for a laugh, even at his own expense. And I must stress that Walter Winterbottom went out of his way to get a family atmosphere going with his squads. It was one for all, and all for each other. He was a gentleman and everyone liked and respected him."

When it came to booking accommodation and planning a tour, you had to hand it to the Football Association. Few players were studied with greater care than the men who were to wear the white shirt of England. The England teams headquarters were at the Hindu Country Club, Don Torcuato, a few miles outside Buenos Aires. It was a beautiful place a millionaires paradise, with a magnificent golf course, tennis courts, swimming pool. This club was the playground of the Buenos Aires elite! The pitches were bone hard, and before facing Argentina the F.A. insisted that they should have a "representative" game, as distinct from an International, before being exposed to these crack footballers. This game the F.A. aid would be nothing more than a "warm" up to get our lads used to the conditions.

On Thursday, 14 May, a team which bore the label "F.A. XI" played an Argentinian team named for this occasion "Buenos Aires". But to every Argentinian it was a full scale International. To say the Argentinians took this game seriously is putting it mildly. It was their World Cup final.

Any game against England brought out a hostile response from them. Only Tommy, Billy Wright and Bill Eckersley, who were to prove England regulars on this tour took part in this representative game. It was played in the magnificent River Plate Stadium, with nearly 100,000 spectators present. There was a blistering sun and the pitch was like a bed of concrete. The Argentinians produced a brand of football which was "out of this world."

The English team worked hard and Tommy scored our only goal with a nifty header, showing no nerves and causing the Argentinian defenders great concern. These Argentinians seemed to be on a different planet. We lost 3-1.

Nat Lofthouse was among the spectators. "This was the first time I had actually seen Tommy in match action. What impressed me about him more than anything else was his lack of nerves in the hostile atmosphere. Many players would have been quivering in their boots. But here was this young chap, calm, cool, and raring to get at them. I don't need to tell people how tough those Argentinian defenders were. They looked fearsome, too.

"Tommy gave as good as he got, never shirking a full-blooded challenge. He was a strong runner and got through a lot of work. When he went up for the crosses from our wingers, I couldn't believe how high he was leaping it was phenomenal. I treasured my England place, but after this display, I knew I had my work cut out to keep it." The following day every Argentinian newspaper headlined their front pages: "Argentina 3, England 1." So much for this so called representative match!

This was wonderful experience for the youngest member of the squad, Watching these brilliant players in action was a revelation for Tommy. He learned and picked up valuable experience and knowledge which would stand him in good stead in the next few years when United played the crack European teams.

Winterbottom was pleased with Tommy's first game under his management and he retained the Manchester United lad for the official match against Argentina a few days later. The England party met President Perron, who proved both courteous and charming and seemed to know a great deal about soccer.

But unknown to the England lads the president wanted his country to beat England badly. Very badly indeed. So much so, he donated a brand new car to be raffled with the proceeds to be shared among the team. "I want you to beat England. All Argentinians are behind you," he told them.

The game was again played in the River Plate Stadium. It was hot, sultry and humid. Billy Wright looking at the bone hard surface, closed his eyes and said: "How I wish for a bit of rain." As if his wish had been granted, the heavens opened and it started to pour down in sheets. This pleased the English players enormously.

"For the game, against the full Argentine side, I moved from to inside left with Johnny Berry as my wing partner. On my right was Nat Lofthouse and I must say I appreciated this opportunity of playing along side a man whose goal scoring feats for England had made his name a household word," Tommy said later.

"I found Nat all that I expected: easy to play with, most helpful in bringing others into the game, fearless in going for half chances, brilliant in the air. He was a truly great player".

The rain came down heavily. Spectators, who were all out in the open air, were drenched. Alf Ramsey and Billy Wright had stressed the tactics to be used and the rest of the team gave it everything they had. Lofthouse who only knew one style of play, came in for a little rough treatment from the Argentinian defenders.

He said later: "After one clash there were three or four tough defenders around me. They looked rather menacing and jabbering away. Obviously, I couldn't understand a word they were saying, but from the scowling faces they were looking directly toward me. Then, all of a sudden, I heard a broad Yorkshire accent: 'Don't worry Nat, I'm right with you,' It was Tommy rushing into the skirmish.

"Boy, was I glad to see him. These Latins were fiery tempered. All through the twenty-odd minutes the game lasted Tommy was on hand when the flack was flying. It was lovely to know that he was battling away with me. And he was only twenty-one. What a brave lad. Make no mistake, these Argentinian defenders were feared of us. What really frightened them though was when our guys sent over those high crosses, I was reputed to be good "upstairs" (going up for headers) but Tommy was superb too in leaping for the high balls. They couldn't get anywhere near him. The amazing thing was the way he seemed to hang in the air. He was a natural at climbing in the air. I'm convinced of that."

Tommy Taylor: "This game was given up when the ground became flooded and referee, Arthur Ellis, had no option but to call it off, so bad were the conditions. I have never seen it rain so hard. Within minutes of going on the field, we were wet through.

"The next game I was selected for was against Chile and we fielded an unchanged side. The game was fairly level but early in the second half England really got going. Our brand of football was very good for fifteen minutes or so and Nat and I each got a goal.

"They attacked vigorously in reply and scored once, but we held on and ran out winners. I think we just about earned our victory. Next came the big test against Uruguay, the World Cup holders, and this was the match that had really been on our minds since we left London. Our rivals scored first, but at half-time we thought we could wipe out the deficit. However, they piled on the pressure in the second half and scored again and confident with their lead, played some really magnificent soccer. I got a goal back for us, but that was it we were beaten 2-1. Uruguay deserved their win.

"They had not been overrated. If they came here to play internationals against England, Scotland, Ireland and Wales, their brand of football would be highly appreciated and they would have a good chance of winning. They are absolutely first class and I must emphasise that the pitch on which they beat us was in good condition and did not give them any advantage. The tour finished with a game against the United States. I missed this match, which we won 6-3."

The England manager, Walter Winterbottom, worked very hard with Taylor. The Barnsley lad enjoyed this individual coaching. He was eager to learn as much as he could and Winterbottom was one of the most respected coaches in football. He was not a boring type of coach; in fact he was one of the most interesting talkers about tactics ever known.

Walter was a perfectionist and always preached that any job was worth doing well. Beside being a highly thought of coach, he was one of the kindest and charming men you could wish to meet, and above all, very knowledgable about world soccer. His qualities as an organizer, especially in training, was first class. He appreciated that each player was an individual, but coached them to play as a team. He took a great deal of unfair criticism, but the selectors picked the squad, not Winterbottom.

John Aston says: "It was a known fact, that Tommy was most fortunate to come into contact with Matt Busby and Walter Winterbottom so early in his career. Yes he was lucky indeed to have two such understanding people of their nature caring for him, and guiding him in the right direction. This improved his play and also helped mature him as a person."

Once he was back in England, Tommy shook hands with his England colleagues and headed straight to Barnsley for a reunion with his family. "It was a marvellous experience and I enjoyed minute of it," said Tommy. He told the family of his trip to the top of the Empire State Building in New York. Later, he talked about his first season at Old Trafford and his England experiences.

"For me it really ended a chapter in my football career. In the course of a few months I had made something of a name as a centre-forward. I had been transferred for the second highest fee on record, had experienced a brief spell of First Division football, had been right across the world, and managed to score my first goals in international football.

"Very few footballers had been so fortunate to see so much in such a brief space and believe me I knew it. I hope I can say I was not swollen headed. Rather I felt I ought to work at my football in an attempt to live up to the luck that had come my way.

"There was only a brief close-season for me we were still in America in the second week in June and we had to report for training in a few weeks I had mixed with great players for the first time. I had seen them off and on the field. Can you wonder if I resolved to make them my example? I decided during the summer of 1953, that men like Billy Wright, Alf Ramsey and Tom Finney must at some period of their careers, have given their whole life to the game and they must have lived, breathed and eaten football. Here was I, a young man at twenty-one, given chances which I barely deserved, and I resolved that if I could, I too would dedicate my next few years to the game, oblivious of all counter-attractions. I would try to deserve the good things that have come my way in 1953."

TOMMY'S FIRST THREE INTERNATIONAL CAPS
Tommy displays his first three caps with the help of Mrs. Swinchat (his landlady) and Colin Webster.

Early Days At Old Trafford

Tommy soon settled down to living in Manchester He quickly made new friends among his new team-mates, becoming particular close to one of the original "Busby Babes", Jackie Blanchflower, who was the younger brother to the great Tottenham player, Danny. The older Blanchflower was a former colleague of Taylor's at Barnsley.

The younger Blanchflower was a superb player in his own right having represented United in all competitions and in every team, from April, 1948, until he was critically injured in the Munich disaster in February, 1958.

Jackie began his football career as an inside-forward before moving to the pivotal position during the 1955–56 season. He won twelve caps for Northern Ireland, besides gaining two League Championship medals and a F.A. Cup Final medal. In fact, Jackie took over the goalkeepers jersey from Ray Wood early in the 1957 Final after the United keeper was injured in a clash with Aston Villa winger, Peter McParland, and acquitted himself admirably. Tommy was a year older than the mild-mannered Belfast lad, but they became inseparable. These two became know as a pair of "rum buggers" by the United players because of their liking for a pint of Guinness.

Jackie Blanchflower remembers: "Manchester United were having trouble with the centre-forward position before Tommy Taylor arrived. Matt tried everyone at the club. However, what we needed was a big, strong centre-forward, and Tommy was ideal.

"There was absolutely no resentment by the other players about buying him. In fact, they were all of the same opinion. 'If this lad can help us win games, that will be good enough for us'. When Tommy was signed, he went straight into the first team. Jack Rowley moved out to the left wing where he had, of course, played before. Though Tommy took his place as centre-forward, Jack never showed any animosity or resentment. From the day he joined the club, Tommy was a first-team regular and never lost his place other than through injury or being on duty for England. He was the best thing that happened as far as United's fortunes were concerned.

"Tommy used to tell me that he did nothing until he went into the army. 'That made me into a man', he told me. Because he was just messing about with his pals. 'Laking' is a Yorkshire saying for playing around. He had a really broad, Yorkshire accent. We used to say: 'This fellow doesn't speak any English.' We couldn't understand him at times. He took the mickey taking in good part though and never lost his temper at the ribbing about his accent.

"When he first arrived in Manchester, Tommy stayed with myself and ten other United players at Mrs. Watson's house. We were all young, fit men and we were all close and the best of pals. After a while, Mrs. Watson became ill. I don't know if it was because there were ten of us! However, we split up and had to move into separate digs.

"We got on really well and we liked the same things . . . going to the pictures, greyhound racing and Chinese meals. We were close friends and we socialized together regularly. Tommy was a real charmer. We used to go to the Ritz on Saturday nights.

"Eric Morley was the under-manager; Jack Binks was the manager. Little Eddie Colman, David Pegg and the other lads used to go to the Plaza."

It is the soccer coach's job to create a beautifully flowing team, while at the same time he has to encourage the player to improve his skill and technique. What kind of coaching was Tommy Taylor receiving at Old Trafford? Well it was simple common sense.

No player would walk off the training pitch with a worried frown on his face, not understanding what had been drilled into his head. Let us see what the players had to say about the type of polishing Tommy received from United's staff.

Henry Cockburn has a simple theory for the club's post-war success: "Busby and Murphy were brilliant. They didn't have fancy coaching ideas. What they had was common sense! 'Pass it to a red shirt play it simple,' they would tell us during practice matches. Both of them would put on track suits. The old baggy kind obviously, there were no fancy designer track suits in those days!

"They would go on different sides, encouraging or rollicking us whatever the case might be, pointing out our good points while explaining what we were doing wrong. Most of the 1948 team had never had this kind of coaching before. We were all used to seeing the manager wearing his outdoor suit and spending his time in the office. Busby and Murphy were different.

"It was years later I realised just how good their advice was to us players. I was coaching myself, at Huddersfield, and I went on an F.A. coaching course. It suddenly struck me. Busby had produced great teams with wonderful individual players who had flair and were exciting to watch. He did this without using the jargon I was hearing on this course. United played it simple, but look at the success they achieved. And don't forget, that the 1948 team played breathtaking football. I remember a Wolves player saying to me after we had thumped them good and proper 'You lot must be the fittest team in the First Division. What do you do in training?'

"We mainly played five-a-sides etc. We did lapping exercises and perhaps a few weights, but that was it. The reason we looked so much fitter than others was simple. We passed the ball around accurately. This was what Busby and Murphy preached".

No coach worthy of his reputation would be foolish enough to stifle flair or stunt potential, but his job is to get the whole team to "gel" thus enabling ability to be utilised for the good of the whole team. This is what Manchester United's coaches did brilliantly. Each player in United's teams dovetailed easily into their positions. They had world-class individuals, of course, but even these flair players became part of the team.

Wilf McGuinness says: "We were encouraged to play 'off the cuff,' but with the emphasis on teamwork. Busby and his staff loved players who produced something on the field which was different; they would lavish praise upon you for attempting such feats. This was the reason they produced such great teams.

"Matt wanted silky smooth skill and perfection in his players, while Jimmy was the hard man. He wanted players to fight for the ball, give the opposition no rest. They were psychologists as well as teachers, because every player has a different temperament and has to be treated differently.

"I watched Tommy in training," says Wilf. "He used to do a lot of hard stints on his own. He liked a drink, but he trained as hard and with as much dedication as any world boxing champion. It was this aspect of his stature which stood up clearly."

In Tommy Taylor's case, coaching was often a matter of correction, teaching him to overcome his faults. Faults such as holding on to the ball too long, or not long enough, trying to dribble or run with the ball when it should have been dispatched to a teammate. Basic things but important and Tommy was a willing pupil and improved rapidly.

Jackie Blanchflower concludes: "Tommy had a few rough edges when he arrived. Most of us had been brought to the club as schoolboys. The training staff worked on our skills and technique, honing the rough edges and making us into United players. Tommy hadn't had the benefit or 'the foundations' as Matt called it, but he soon learned, he became a great player through the clubs coaching system.

"On the staff was a former boxing trainer — 'Tosher' Powell. He would hang a ball from one of the rafters under the main stand. We had to run, jump and head the ball but not just head it straight. We had to direct our headers. We had no proper gym in those days and so we used to run under the stands and as the season wore on, 'Tosher' would raise the ball and making it harder he would prod a ball with a sweeping-brush. It was a moving, hanging target harder to reach and head. This was done to improve our timing and jumping.

"Tommy used to practice for hours. You had to time it perfectly. Tommy was really magnificent at this. I can still picture him now rising up so majestically.

"Tommy was a wonderful trainer. He and 'Tosher' and Tom Curry, got on well together. "Tosher" was an ex-Newcastle player. A typical Geordie and a lovely, sincere man. Old Tom loved down to earth genuine people. He knew if you were trying to pull the wool over his eyes. They loved big Tommy.

The search to bring the best schoolboys from the four home countries to Old Trafford was well and truly underway. A network of talent spotters were recruited under Joe Armstrong, a former Post Office official. They scouted everywhere that a schoolboy, boy scouts or youth club game was being played. This was how the greatest array of young fledging footballers came to one particular club . . . Manchester United!

Back in Manchester, living in the hostel with the other bachelor youngsters proved to be tremendous fun. Mark Jones, Tommy's friend from Yorkshire was also staying there, as was the shy fifteen-year-old Bobby Charlton. Duncan Edwards, Gordon Clayton and Colin Webster were also residents. Big Mark's idea of looking after the hostel lads was to escort them all to a horror film in the city centre. They all had free passes to get into most of the big cinema's in Manchester. After the film was over, Mark would then march them back all the five miles home!

Tommy laughed at their moans and groans as Jones had them marching on the long trek home. "Swing those arms", he would shout. Coming from Yorkshire he and Tommy were used to walking for miles and miles. Jones, was a couple of years older than the rest apart from Tommy of course, and he smoked a pipe, which meant you were "a real old man" in those times.

Albert Scanlon remembers: "We heard all about the lads being marched all the way from town back to Old Trafford. They seemed to have loads of fun. They were all very close. I put this down to the fact that they were young lads all away from home and possibly for the first time ever.

"They befriended each other and formed a bond, whereas the lads born and bred in Manchester could go back to their own homes after matches or training had finished. Mind you, every kid at United was made to feel important and part of a special club. The spirit was unbelievable. You had to be a part of it to understand exactly what I mean. I couldn't begin to explain how it came about, other than to say it was down to Matt and Jimmy."

Dennis Viollet was homebred. "Tommy trained hard, very hard. I would say he was one of the best trainers at the club in those days. He would lap and lap, then sprint up and down the stands. Even in training he looked magnificent, he had loads of energy. What impressed me about him though, was that he was willing to listen and improve his overall standard of play. The relationship between the management and the players, Matt Busby and Jimmy Murphy was something special. I have never experienced it before or since. We were all very close indeed. Probably Jimmy had more contact with the kids and the reserves in those days, but he was a very, very important part of the Manchester United success story.

"Jimmy and Bert Whalley and the other members of staff at the club, will never know how much they meant to us United players when we were just kids. They were like fathers to us all, as was Matt when we got older and moved on into the first team. In thirteen years with United I cannot remember more than twice having any harsh words with my team mates or staff. Twice in thirteen years can't be bad. It was all down to club spirit."

Wilf McGuinness another Mancunian recalls: "I joined United the same day as Bobby Charlton — 6 June, 1953. We knew each other from playing together for England schoolboys. It is hard to describe the club spirit at Old Trafford in those days; it was like belonging to something really special. It was fun and we had our fights, but bad feeling was never allowed to fester. Tommy Taylor was like an Adonis to us younger kids, he was big, well made, good-looking and confident. Yet he was more a kid at heart than any of us, always laughing and messing around. Mark Jones was about the same age as Tommy. He might have been about a year younger, but he was much more serious in his outlook than Tommy."

Two weeks after joining United, Tommy received first hand evidence of the talented youngsters Jimmy Murphy had been telling him so much about. Jimmy had said many of the kids would be world beaters. Taylor thought this was a bit far-fetched; just Jimmy being his enthusiastic and passionate self.

But he began to change his opinion as he sat in the stands and watched Barnsley's Youth team, play United's kids at Old Trafford in a Youth Cup game which attracted 12,400 spectators. (On the same day, Barnsley's first team played Birmingham City at Oakwell in a Division Two match. In front of a . . . 7,406 crowd.)

United's brilliant youngsters beat Barnsley 3-1. Duncan Edwards, Noel McFarlane and Albert Scanlon scored United's goals to take them through to a semi-final with Brentford. Tommy watched the game, took a deep breath and realised for himself the wealth of football talent which he had joined.

The kids were magnificent. Murphy was right when he told the centre-forward: "Tommy, son, you are the final piece to our jigsaw."

The F.A. Youth Cup a new competition for under-eighteens, had its baptism in 1953. This was to prove a wonderful platform for players like Edwards, Eddie Colman, Scanlon, Pegg, Ronnie Cope and Billy Whelan. And in later years, Charlton, McGuinness, and many more of United's great players, who would play in the competition. Busby and Murphy eagerly welcomed the competition and United's youngsters would go on the attract attendances which made many First

Division clubs envious.

The first game in this knock-out cup was staged at The Cliff Training Ground in Salford when Leeds United provided the opposition. Duncan Edwards made Captain in this first ever match in the competition. United won 4-0, one of the goals being an own goal by a certain Jackie Charlton, brother of United's Bobby.

Victory was rewarded by another home game against non-League Nantwich. This game saw United's youngsters record a score of 23-0, still the highest in the history of this competition. Edwards and David Pegg scored five goals each. The crowds were so vast that The Cliff games were switched from The Cliff to Old Trafford. This gave the youngsters an extra incentive to play well.

One morning, talking after training to a few of United's young players, Tommy was asked how he got started in top-class football. "Luck and sheer good fortune. I didn't play soccer after leaving school for two years. I was working in the pit. I played for Smithies United. They didn't want me to play because it was a man's team," he replied.

"And in those days I was a slim, short youngster. But I turned out and scored. I nearly fell over when a Barnsley scout and one from Hull City asked me after the game if I would like a trial. As a Barnsley boy I picked Barnsley. It was the wisest decision of my life. So the morale of the story is . . . Keep trying and be lucky," Tommy told the kids.

Season 1953–54

August, 1953, was the start of Tommy's first full season with United. He had settled down nicely in his digs, and because of his bubbly character he was popular with both young and old alike at Old Trafford. The first team was not a settled combination. Matt Busby was still biding his time before unleashing his youngsters. Some of the older team members were struggling to hold their form.

There was no gloom at Old Trafford Busby and his staff knew that they had youngsters like Blanchflower, Gibson, Viollet, Whitefoot, Wood, Foulkes, Pegg and Jones and others who needed just a little extra time to develop. This was one of the reasons he persevered with his loyal older players. There were plenty of 'snipers' around who were having a dig about United's poor start to the season. Busby and Murphy were calm.

Tommy Taylor had a view: "The finest thing that happened last week from an Old Trafford point of view was our 4-1 win at Middlesborough. Believe me, we didn't relish that opening sequence of eight games without a win. Old-timers in Manchester tell me that in early Thirties, United actually opened one season by going thirteen games and losing them all.

"Well, though it wasn't as bad as that we began to think we must have killed a cat, or whatever it is that is supposed to bring bad luck. Yet during those eight games our spirits didn't really get down. For one thing, we drew five times, which not only meant five points but gave us hope for that with a little extra fortune we might have made it ten points. We didn't feel we had been playing really badly or that we lacked skill in some departments.

"True, we had failed to 'click' now and then, but we did feel that the step from drawing to winning was a matter of very little difference to our form. A third factor is keeping up our spirits. We have the greatest manager in the game in Matt Busby and although he can be a stern critic, he knew that the store of talent at Old Trafford hadn't run dry all of a sudden. His faith in our recovery was second to none.

"However, Manchester people were talking about Arsenal and United facing the drop into the Second Division. We didn't appreciate that one bit. Finally we registered our first win (at Middlesborough) and you can bet your life we were a happy party on the way home.

"We were soon working out how many home games we had to win to bring our points and matches level. That is the first aim of every team to make forty-two points from forty-two games. We don't boast, but I believe you will see a very different Manchester United in the next few weeks with all the old solid team work coming back.

"Another thing that pleased us about the win was that it took us one point above our Maine Road neighbours. Don't think we wish to see City pushed down to the bottom of the table. We would rather see them high up, say in the second place in the chart if we could be in the first place. The rivalry between the two sets of supporters is very real perhaps keener than in other city's in Britain except Glasgow and Liverpool."

Tommy had scored his first goal of the season in his second game against Liverpool at Anfield which ended in a 4-4 draw. By late October, Busby had decided that the time was ripe to blood the new generation of Manchester United starlets.

Matt Busby: "We beat Aston Villa at home but it was a terrible game, I decided something had to be done and drastic. I intended to make the move which would either make or break Manchester United. The time could not have been more opportune, a friendly match had been arranged against Kilmarnock, in Scotland. I took sixteen players. I played all the young players and they did not let me down as we won 3-0."

Henry Cockburn, joined Manchester United from Gosling's, a well known amateur team, in 1944. He played nearly 300 competitive games for the club, winning thirteen England caps-his first after only six League games. He won an F.A. Cup winners medal and a League Championship medal. He left Old Trafford for Bury in October, 1954. Henry is still a trim, dapper little fellow, sprightly and radiating with life and enthusiasm, he is in his seventies now but as sharp as a tack. Recalling the night Busby made his historic decision to use his young players.

Henry Cockburn: "We played up in Scotland. I think it was to celebrate the first game Kilmarnock switched on their floodlights. I was playing wing half, I went up for a high ball and someone's elbow caught me in the face and broke my jaw. This was a friendly game so substitutes were allowed. Who took my place at left-half? Duncan Edwards! I think I only managed one more first-team game after that.

"The team Busby took over after he first became manager proved to be a great one. People seem to forget that. The team which preceded the 1952 Championship winning side was great, but don't forget, we were the first team Busby managed."

On the following Saturday, United played against Huddersfield Town, who were near the top of Division One. Busby fielded seven players who were twenty-one or under. This is regarded as the first game the "Busby Babes" ever played.

The date was 31 October, 1953. By then, Tommy had netted five goals, but the Reds had won only four games. Once Busby had decided to give his youngsters their heads, results picked up and they were undefeated in their next five matches. There was a freshness about the whole team which the wind of change had obviously blown in.

It was during these changing times that Taylor's lethal partnership with the whipcord Dennis Viollet took formation. Though Viollet had made his debut at the end of the previous season. Tommy benefited by scoring another five goals including a brilliant hat-trick against Blackpool.

Matt Busby recalled: "Dennis Viollet was only small and frail. So I asked Tommy to look after him on the field, because there were plenty of tough defenders in those days. It was marvellous to watch Tommy, only twenty-one himself, looking after Dennis like a veteran. Playing off a big centre-forward such has Tommy Taylor was the ideal ploy for Dennis.

"He would watch Tommy going up for the high balls and Tommy could twist his body in flight flicking the ball down to where he wanted it to go. It was uncanny really. "Dennis would move like radar into position; he got plenty of goals with this play."

"Brilliant Hat-Trick"

On a bitterly cold day in November, 1953, while playing in front of 49,853 spectators huddled together in Old Trafford, Tommy, United's goal machine scored his first hat-trick as a United player. A week earlier at Ninian Park, the home of Cardiff City, United had run riot scoring their biggest victory of that season, (6-1) with Tommy getting a solitary goal, but helping Dennis Viollet get to a couple, with Berry, Blanchflower and Jack Rowley also getting on the score sheet.

The match against Blackpool was a much awaited confrontation and, according to the previews in the newspapers, a "cracker" of a game was in store for the both sets of fans. The Seasiders were very strongly fancied to beat United. They had a settled team with some outstanding individuals such as Stanley Matthews that wizard of dribble, the genius of little Ernie Taylor, centre-half Harry Johnston, and a crashing, dashing centre-forward, Stan Mortensen. These four players had been selected to play for England and would be appearing in Wembley Stadium, opposing "Major" Puskas and his "Magical Magyars" a few days after the United match.

Both sets of fans were comparing the two centre-forwards, Tommy and Stan Mortensen. It was United who handed out the shocks to the star-studded Blackpool team and their featured internationals. The game had started brightly with the Seasiders playing flowing, intelligent football, Ernie Taylor, who in 1958 would join United after Munich, was using delicate little "chips" to left-winger Bill Perry, and Blackpool were dictating the game. It came as no surprise when United's Lancashire rivals took the lead after twenty-two minutes with a stunning goal from the ever-dangerous Perry.

Six minutes later, United were on level terms, and deservedly so, with Tommy Taylor proving the man of the moment with a smart header which fairly whizzed into the Blackpool net beating 'keeper George Farm's outstretched palms. It was a powerful header, thumped home like a Rocky Marciano piledriver!

The move leading up to the goal started with young Duncan Edwards passing a beautiful ball to Jack Rowley out on the United left flank. The "Gunner" moved forward, saw Tommy racing towards the far side of the Blackpool goal and Jack centred the ball in typical Rowley fashion, high and directly to the leaping centre-forward's forehead. A great goal, wonderfully executed and planned to perfection.

John Aston said later: "Tommy's header went in the net like a bullet. The 'keeper had no chance from the moment Rowley centred the ball. I hasten to add that Tommy's header was as powerful as most players could kick the ball.

"Harry Johnston was no slouch. He was a hard, solid centre-half and an international. Harry was usually the master when the ball was in the air, but he came second best to Tommy for this goal."

United were flowing now Edwards was inspiring them like a veteran and within the space of two minutes Viollet crowned a magnificent effort with a goal. Then, Johnny Berry who was in fantastic form and was waltzing past the Blackpool defence as if they did not exist, threaded a ball through to Rowley, who was also having a "stormer" Tommy was well positioned and as the ball came to him his fierce shot surprised Farm as it flashed past him into his net.

The "big fellow" had scored two cracking goals. The United fans were willing him to get his hat-trick. When Berry once again did the business. Aston wanted a crack at goal. He let fly with a ferocious shot. Farm could only parry it and as the ball broke loose, Tommy spurted forward and whipped the ball into the goal. The ground erupted and Tommy, hands aloft like a matador, was overjoyed.

Tommy was cashing in on the intelligent, skilful and articulate ball play of his inside partners, Viollet and his close pal, Jackie Blanchflower. Many knowledgable observers were starting to make comparisons between Mortensen, who was due to lead the England attack against the Hungarian's a few days later, and the young United leader.

This of course was unfair. They were two completely different types of leaders. Both excellent in their own fashion and style. What was more interesting, though, was the great duel fought between Johnston, the Blackpool pivot, and Tommy, whose qualities (and his three goals) had proved the highlight of this fascinating game. It had to be said that Tommy Taylor won convincingly.

A few days later, Tommy, along with other United colleagues were sat glued to a black and white twelve-inch television in their lodgings at Mrs. Watson's. They were absolutely mesmerized as the Hungarians gave England a lesson we have never forgotten.

"I bet your bloody glad you didn't get picked to play for England this time Tom," said the smirking Welshman, Colin Webster. "Thank your lucky stars the selectors overlooked you for this one," remarked Gordon Clayton, United's young goalkeeper, after the Hungarians 6-3 thrashing of England. Tommy smiled, but refused to criticise any England players. Tommy's time would come!

Busby, after worrying how his young players would cope with the pressures of First Division football week in and week out soon realised he had no need for concern. His team was settling down and coping quite well indeed. The end of the season saw his team finish in fourth place.

"Within two years this young team will be much too good for anything else in the First Division," he told close friends. Not long after returning from the tour of South America, Tommy was asked to give his observations about forward players.

"Inside-forwards can usually be divided into goal-getters and goal makers. The ideal forward-line has an inside-forward who plays back, picking up all the loose balls and then opening out the game for his own side; the other should be forceful, always on the look-out for goals. I try to play as a goal-getter. Barnsley, and now Manchester United, have been playing me at centre-forward and I find it helps when I play inside-forward.

"I went to Barnsley as an inside-left and it was while I was there that I was introduced to the double centre-forward game the game I was asked to play alongside Nat Lofthouse on the South American tour," he pointed out.

"To play this sort of game you must have a perfect understanding with the centre-forward. You have to know all his little tricks, you have to be lying handy ready to nip into the middle if he takes the centre-half out on the wing, and above all, you must be watching the run of the game.

"It is no good having a second centre-forward playing well up if your own team is on the defensive for long periods. So I would say to the young player who wants to be a fast forceful direct type of inside man, don't forget that you also have a duty to the wing-half behind you.

"If he is being hard pressed, forget the goal-getting for the time being and get back in defence to help him. Now then, how does this second centre-forward game work out in practice ? Well, I always like to play on the "blind" side of the man marking me.

"Let me give you an example. In one game in South America, Nat Lofthouse wondered away to the left wing. I was left behind the right-back. There seemed no danger, but when the ball came back into the middle, I was able to nip smartly in past the back and score.

"Nat has another knack of snapping the ball back to the inside man, then darting away as if expecting a through pass. He takes the defence with him and for a brief second, the way down the middle is open. It's then that the direct type of inside man has to strike, and strike fast.

"These may appear elementary tactics, but it is the speed of execution that makes them so dangerous. You must have speed in passing, speed in taking up position and, above all, speed in shooting. Get the trainer or clubmate to keep rolling the ball in front of you, run in at top speed and drive them in. Try it with the left foot and the right foot, high balls, low balls and at all sorts of angles.

"So much for shooting. Now what about heading. The first essential is to be able to get up to a ball. Any skill I have in that direction is due to the fact that in the Army I took up long jumping and high jumping. Any sort of jumping is bound to improve a man's spring. But of course, the big thing in heading, as in shooting, is timing.

"That only comes with practice. Personally I always like to be moving in fast to head a ball. For corners I stand back on the eighteen-yard line then run in as the winger is kicking. Some other tips: Keep moving around use that long cross-field pass to the opposite wing whenever possible and above all, be direct".

"The end of mid-week fixtures often means you can look forward to better football. I expect you have enjoyed the early games and admired (at any rate, I hope so) the speed and dash and vigour of players fresh after concentrated training sessions following a summers rest. But the football will be better than at any other time in the season. Two matches a week means several fixtures complicate the always difficult lives of club managers.

"To battle for precious league points means good players are wanted in action all the time and, in turn that almost every team is carrying one man at least not 100 per cent fit. He is "in" because he just cannot be spared. Secondly, practice games are out. A practice game in which the ball can be stopped and a little chat undertaken, are fine for developing harmony and slick movement, but the unfit man cannot be risked! The third reason the football will get better is that many of the early fixtures, being home-and-away return games, produce rather hectic results. The beaten side are all out for quick revenge. Years ago, clubs used to play each other on consecutive Saturdays. That was stopped because it made football too keen. Why then, do the authorities allow these early-season and Christmas and Easter holiday return games? It doesn't seem very logical to me.

"So, one way and another, these August and September games produce helter-skelter football, exciting to watch maybe, but certainly not of the best quality. Soccer played at a little slower pace and with more thought and planning should be the rule until the Christmas holidays, which in turn will be followed by cup ties.

Ankle Injury Threatens His Career

27 March, 1954, was to prove a black day as far as Tommy Taylor was concerned. United were thrashed 3-1 by Arsenal at Highbury and though Tommy was "the outstanding player on the field," (said critic, Henry Rose) he picked up a nasty, troublesome ankle injury. It was to plague him for a long period. In fact, this injury forced him to miss the remaining six games of the season, and was so serious that for a time it threatened to end his playing career. In thirty-five appearances for United's first team, Tommy had scored twenty-two goals and was United's top scorer for that season. United finished fourth in the League, but Taylor was an extremely worried young man. The damage showed no signs of healing.

There were many knowledgable pundits shaking their heads and advocating that Tommy's career was now seriously in doubt. United had their physio Ted Dalton, working overtime on the treatment table with Tommy, but the cheerful Yorkshire lad was in sheer agony with this ankle.

Dalton tried everything he knew to help clear it up, but it all to no avail. It was rumoured around Manchester that Matt Busby was at his wits end not knowing what to make of his ace centre-forward's mystery injury. Ted Dalton and other medical experts could not diagnose anything wrong with the ankle.

Dennis Viollet explains: "Tom suffered from this nasty injury for quite some time. He was getting treatment daily, of course, sometimes twice a day but it wouldn't seem to clear up. He took a lot of unfair criticism after the ankle injury, and could justifiably have used this as an excuse, but he never said a word. I knew deep down Tom was very concerned about the damage."

In late March, Taylor had an operation on his ankle. He was still in plaster when, on Friday, 30 April, at Highbury, a wonderful night was in store for football followers.

Old England, a team consisting of the likes of Stanley Matthews, Wilf Mannion, Tommy Lawton, Len Shackleton and Bobby Langton were parading their skills. They were down to play against a Young England select. The England selectors had omitted all the five forwards in the Old England line-up from selection in the forthcoming World Cup Finals to be held in the summer.

Many papers reckoned they might be forced to change their minds if this formation clicked into gear. No selection though had proved more popular than that of Mannion, the Middlesborough "Golden Boy" who had suffered because of the slump in form of his club. Wilf had served his country well in the past. He was a masterful inside-forward who might be recalled even yet.

Still, youth must be served, said some newspapers who wrote the following: "So let us not forget the Young England XI, with special congratulations to Tommy Taylor. Tommy has proved a consistent scorer in his first full season in the top division, and at Highbury we fully expect to see him book his ticket to Switzerland."

Contrary to popular belief, Tommy could not play in this game. He wasn't fit enough after the operation which obviously prevented him from taking part, though United team mates, Duncan Edwards and Roger Byrne, played. Byrne, in particular, caught the selectors' eye and he was chosen along with Taylor for the World Cup games. Though Tommy was passed fit in May and went with England in their quest for the World Cup in Switzerland, he still felt a little niggle in the ankle. It was not right, and subconsciously it affected Tommy's confidence. Many put it down to the after effects of the operation. They told the big fellow: "Don't worry. Once you get playing regularly you will be fine."

Tommy Taylor had this to say: "Well, it was a happy week for thirty-two lucky footballers. Even allowing for the traditional slip that comes betwixt cup and lip, most of the thirty-two players selected for the Football Association's May tour will soon be airborne and off to central Europe, and I, along with thirty-one others, can count myself fortunate to have a chance of joining in this great adventure. It is when you go abroad with the England players that you realise that football really is a team game.

"When I went to South America I was the surprise choice of the party. I was amazed at the way the lads settled together. Some were great individual footballers, stars in their own right but the very fact that we came away from home and were representing our country held us together like nothing else can. Drawn from various clubs, we ganged up right away, the old hands do not chum together and leave the new ones to look after themselves, but young players are always taken under the wings of the more senior players and made to feel equal. The number of caps a man could claim makes no difference at all."

Tommy was obviously pleased and overjoyed at the prospect of going to the World Cup Finals. It was and is every players dream and ambition.

He knew in his heart that he was a lucky man to be selected because of his injury, plus the fact that he had not played in the "Old England versus Young England" game, which was more like a trial match so the England selection committee could have a last look at who they wanted to travel.

Neither had he been included on the strenuous pre-World Cup programme, starting with the spring tour when England played Yugoslavia, Hungary and Switzerland. With hindsight, Tommy could count himself very fortunate having missed this particular trip. The brilliant Hungarians ran riot, blasting England 7-1. Tom Finney maintained the score could have gone into double figures for these master footballers.

Tom Finney: "Without a doubt, the finest footballing side I have ever played against was Hungary in the summer of 1954. Unfortunately, or perhaps I should say fortunately neither I, nor Tommy, played when the Hungarians came to Wembley and defeated us 6-3 during the previous season. I was a spectator, and am not ashamed to admit that I came away wondering just what game we had been playing in this country for the previous few years.

"We certainly did not play soccer the way the Hungarians did and until I actually had the opportunity of matching my skill against theirs, I felt my football education would not be complete."

England did not have a settled team; with the possible exception of two or three regulars, every position in the full England XI was open and waiting for the best players. The big problem was at centre-half, and in the three inside positions. For the previous four years the selection committee had wrestled with the centre half problem caused when Neil Franklin went to play in Bogota.

About seven or eight different players had been tried, but none could lay a permanent claim. The inside forwards in various games before selection for Switzerland were the West Bromwich Albion pair, Ronnie Allen and Johnny Nicholls while Ivor Broadis was in and out of the team.

There was no doubt the England forward line was another big headache for the selectors. After the experiment of Allen and Nicholls failed, sweeping changes followed, with Peter Harris and Jackie Sewell being given a run up front. Poor Bedford Jezzard played in his one and subsequently last England match at centre-forward against Yugoslavia. Can you imagine present day managers putting up with the sort of set-up poor old Winterbottom had to prevail under?

But that was how the England squads and teams were selected in those days. It was Alf Ramsey who changed the whole structure and system many years later when he became the England manager.

After preparing under manager Walter Winterbottom and trainer, Jimmy Trotter, on the Bank of England training ground at Roehampton, the full England squad selected for Switzerland was: Billy Wright (Captain), Gilbert Merrick, Ron Staniforth, Roger Byrne, Bill McGarry, Jimmy Dickinson, Syd Owen, Stanley Matthews, Ivor Broadis, Tommy Taylor, Denis Wilshaw, Jimmy Mullen, Albert Quixall and Tom Finney.

The squad had come in for some criticism because of Trotter's idea of playing rounders (akin to a game of baseball) after training sessions were over. Many journalist believed that the time would have been better spent working on technique and getting super-fit for the challenge which lay ahead.

Tommy himself would have relished more technique coaching. He had been a deep thinker from his days as a Barnsley player about the centre-forward role in football. Having watched Hidegkuti, the deep lying Hungarian centre-forward roaming from wing to wing and dropping deep into his own half, left a big impression on the United player. But the aerial adeptness of Hungary's main forward, Kocsis, had Tommy spellbound.

It proved an unsuccessful World Cup for England who had arrived in Switzerland just a few days prior to playing their first game. This late arrival did not meet with the full approval of the newspaper reporters. It didn't seem to bother the players who once they boarded their coach to Lucerne and settled into the Hotel Carlton they seemed happy enough. Those were the days when things were simple; no computer games or other modern toys. The players revelled in each others company and bonded friendships.

Tommy played in two games in the competition. England's first Group Four game was against Belgium on the greatly enlarged St. Jacob Stadium in Basle on 17 June, 1954. Just before kick-off there was a light fall of rain which suited England and the game ended 4-4 after extra time. Tommy's strong foraging helped to make a couple of the goals. The England scorers were Broadis and Lofthouse with two goals each. Matthews gave a dazzling exhibition out on the right.

Tommy, along with a few others, had to receive treatment for cramp after the match.

The players were trying to console poor Jimmy Dickinson who recorded an unfortunate own goal.

The historic line-up was: G. Merrick (Birmingham); R. Staniforth (Huddersfield), R. Byrne (Manchester United); W. Wright. Captain, (Wolverhampton Wanderers); S. Owen (Luton Town), J. Dickinson (Portsmouth); S. Matthews (Blackpool), I. Broadis (Newcastle), N. Lofthouse (Bolton), T. Taylor (Manchester United), T. Finney (Preston).

This was the third successive international England had failed to win which then was unique. The shock 1-0 defeat which they suffered in Yugoslavia, followed closely the 7-1 thrashing at the hands of Hungary and did nothing for morale.

Albert Quixall brought plenty of banter into the England camp, but the squad was under a great deal of pressure. The preparation for something as important as the World Cup was little more than a shambles to say the least. The selection committee were not being fair playing Taylor as the inside-forward partner for Nat Lofthouse.

Walter Winterbottom took a great deal of criticism for using this "twin" system; Taylor was after all a novice in international terms and if the selectors wanted him in the team then it should have been in his best position and that was leading the attack.

The next game was against the host nation, Switzerland. Changes had to be made. One in particular was to add years to Wolves wing-half Billy Wright's club and international career. To give solidarity at centre-half Wright was switched from his usual position to number five, but it was only made as a desperate gamble to plug a temporarily leak.

This was a much better result and performance from England, winning 2-0. This was the first time Tommy had led the England attack. He did not score, but played a storming game, the Wolves duo of Mullen and Wilshaw got the goals. Lofthouse and Matthews did not play; Nat had a sore throat and Stanley a toe injury. The Swiss defenders, like so many more, were unprepared for Tommy's aerial power and his ability petrified them. When he made his runs to meet the ball they were falling down before he rose into the sky.

The Barnsley lad received a good press for his spirited showing. He hadn't scored, but had come mighty close on two or three occasions and what impressed the likes of Charles Buchan and other worthy football correspondents was Tommy's willingness and unselfish running on behalf of the team.

Nat Lofthouse: "This was just the result England needed. Tommy played very well indeed, in fact I think he made one of the goals. Sitting on the bench I marvelled at his timing for those headers, like I said, I fancied myself when the ball was up-stairs, but Tommy was a master in the air. Tom Finney and Billy Wright were shouting encouragement to him throughout the whole game. We celebrated with a few drinks afterwards I can tell you."

This victory meant a great deal to the England party. It enabled them to qualify for the competition proper, which was now a knock-out from the quarter-final stage.

Everyone waited anxiously to hear who they had drawn in the next round; it proved to be World Champions Uruguay, who had beaten England in Montevideo a year earlier.

Taylor had played well against them and scored England's only goal. By the time the England team had moved headquarters to the Rhineland town of Rhienfelden, Lofthouse had fully recovered from his illness.

Winterbottom arranged for a friendly game with a local team to be played in Schaffhausen and the manager tried out various moves and tactics. Tommy and Nat Lofthouse were included in these practice moves, but deep down it was clear Tommy would lose out to the Bolton leader for this vital game.

Winterbottom was convinced that given reasonable luck, the duel spearhead of

Tommy and "Lofty" would in time prove a winner for England. Both put great fear into defenders and he visualized both centre-forwards scoring goals aplenty.

Nat Lofthouse: "Tommy could consider himself unlucky to drop out for this match against the World Cup holders. He had led the forward line exceptionally well in our last game, but he didn't show any resentment at not getting selected, and gave every encouragement to the whole team.

This particular game was a vitally important match for England, but we were confident that we could get a result. I believe that with myself and Tommy up front we could have caused their defence plenty of problems."

Taylor was left out because his ankle was still troublesome and England with Matthews, again playing magnificently, lost 4-2. That was the end of Tommy's World Cup dream. He, like everyone else, was disappointed, but sensible enough to know his chance would come again.

The Forgotten Centre-Forward"

In March, 1954, exactly a year after joining United, Tommy hit the headlines in the *"Daily Mirror"* when under big, bold headlines ("Forgotten Taylor Is A Winner") reporter Bob Ferrier, wrote: "In one short week and in three games, I have seen such a wealth of young football talent as would shake the Hungarians, or any other world soccer nation, right down to their very bootstuds.

A week ago, Quixall and Alan Finney at Stamford Bridge; in mid-week, a round dozen of them at Sunderland in the England v Scotland 'B' international; on Saturday, the Manchester United youngsters with Tommy Taylor."

Ferrier went on to ask if Taylor was the forgotten man of international football. "In this young footballer you will find the best of Lofthouse and Allen, (Ronnie Allen, the West Bromwich Albion centre-forward) currently the two "name" players in the position," he wrote.

"He has all the strength and speed of the Bolton man, all the quickness and skill of the Albion man.

"He has great talent and power in the air, with that suspended "float" that featured in Lawton's play. And he does it all with splendid spirit and malice to none."

On the previous Saturday, United had beaten Wolves at home, the winning goal being scored by Johnny Berry, but the talking point was Taylor's confrontation with the England's centre-half and captain, Billy Wright.

Ferrier continued: "He opposed Billy Wright, of Wolves, and although I have said harsh things about Wright in the past, and despite the general weekend comment, let me say that Wright played him very well. They had a great and manly struggle. Taylor won. With his flicks and darts and dribbling runs, and a succession of superb feints and dummies, he won but only just.

"On players such as Taylor, Quixall, Byrne and Haynes, of Fulham, our international future depends, yet Taylor is barred from a gradual transition to the full international side because at twenty-two, he already has three caps (Players who had more than one international cap were barred from playing in some other representative matches. It was a silly rule, and this was the point of Ferrier's article.) His play against Wolves illuminated the problem," concluded Ferrier.

He was right of course, but equally correct to point out that the England selectors seemed to have forgotten Tommy completely, having taken him all the way to South America, given him three games in which he had scored twice, then discarded him completely.

Strange, but we have to remember that Walter Winterbottom did not select the England teams. The selection committee did this service. No present day manager would put up with this kind of arrangement.

Did this snub upset Taylor? Not in the least. His job was helping Manchester United to regain their pride and aim for new honours. If his overall play warranted selection then all well and good, but that was not the be all of it.

John Aston: "It was rather strange the way in which Tommy was discarded by the England selectors. But that was the way things were in the 1950s. It was heartbreaking for sensitive players. But you just had to get on with your game and try and prove them wrong. There were a lot of centre-forwards around and Nat Lofthouse was highly thought of by everyone, but when one has the ability which Tommy possessed you can't be ignored for long.

Tommy missed the opening four games of the 1954–55 season due to the ankle injury with Colin Webster deputising for him. Taylor returned to the first team for the home game against Charlton on 4 September, and scored one goal. Then he missed the following two matches and despite his injury he was the team's top scorer again with twenty goals from twenty-nine games. In many ways it was a mellow season for Tommy, he did not seem to be able to shake off these niggling injuries.

Jackie Blanchflower: "I felt sorry for Tommy, he was in constant pain with this ankle problem. He played a lot of games while in agony, but never complained or made excuses to the press. Mind you, Matt thought he was exaggerating a great deal as he was never off the treatment table.

"Ted Dalton our physio, worked overtime trying everything to relieve the pain. Busby eventually took him to London, to the Queen's surgeon who twisted the ankle in every direction. Tommy screamed in pain. The surgeon X-rayed the ankle and there it was a small piece of floating bone in his ankle. Once they operated and removed it, Tommy was a different man."

"Mind you there was a really funny incident which happened concerning his injury. After the operation, Tommy was using crutches. He had to be very careful how he moved around. I was always winding him up about his inability to move freely because of the plaster cast. I used to hang my chin in front of him and goad him: 'Go on, hit that' pointing to my jaw. This went on every day, me daring him to hit me on the chin. Of course he couldn't get near me, because he was shackled by the plaster. One Saturday night we were out in Manchester city centre as usual.

"Walking down Market Street I was daring him again: 'Go on, hit me, hit me' it was all done in fun. 'Go on, hit me, you're too slow.' Wham! He hit me alright and caught me smack on the chin. Bang, I went straight through a shop's plate glass window.

"All the alarm bells starting ringing. I picked myself out of the shop window and we both scurried away. I never hung my chin out again. Mind you, you should have seen the speed of Tommy on those crutches he was like lightning."

United's first game in the F.A. Cup that season was against Reading. After a replay they won 4-1. Tommy was sidelined with a thigh injury.

"Tommy's Four-Goal Spree"

On 9 October, 1954, Manchester United faced Cardiff City, at Old Trafford. Before the game kicked-off, two daring Cardiff supporters earned the cheers of their countrymen when they "planted" a leak on the centre circle in the hope it would bring their team luck. Trevor Ford, the dashing, crashing slam-bang Welsh centre-forward put Cardiff in high glee with a goal inside the first ten minutes. It was Tommy who rescued United in the thirty-first minute.

Jack Rowley, a man of action rather than words, set the attack in motion. His pass found Dennis Viollet in the middle and as he was challenged by the tough Cardiff defenders, Viollet cleverly whipped the ball across to big Tommy. The United centre-forward was on to it in a flash, and as he was tackled by Sherwood, the Welsh half-back slipped. Taylor was round him in a flash and drove the ball past the diving Howells, the Cardiff goalkeeper.

Three minutes before half-time, Tommy put United in front with his second goal. Again the danger was created on United's left wing where Rowley was using his vast experience to the full. He sent a wonderful pass out to the advancing Blanchflower, who in turn struck an-inch perfect through ball which sent Taylor racing through the Cardiff defence to beat Howells with a rasping shot into the top corner.

Tommy was now thriving on much better support. In the first twenty minutes or so, he looked lost, as his inside forwards were trying to gain possession. The two goals saw his confidence come flooding back. United were a lot happier going in at half-time with the score 2-1 in their favour.

In the fifty-ninth minute, Taylor completed his hat-trick. He owed much of the credit to Viollet for his third goal, because the little inside-left laid on another perfect pass for Tommy to blast the ball into the Cardiff net. Viollet was playing a "blinder" and feeding Tommy some immaculate passes. Many pundits before this game had been comparing Taylor with Trevor Ford, but really there was no comparison Ford traded on his all-action, robust style whereas Taylor's game had a touch of velvet.

In the sixty-seventh minute Tommy made it a personal haul of four goals. There was a slice of luck about his last goal; he was out on the left wing, and as he ran in he tried a shot from an acute angle. It was a piledriver, and seemed to hit a defender on its way into the net.

The Cardiff players were annoyed with each other for conceding that goal, but when the game ended they were the first to congratulate Tommy on his four-goal haul.

If ever a goal inspired a player battling to hit his best form, that first one did the trick for Tommy. It gave the young centre-forward tons of confidence. It had been a heart-breaking spell for Taylor but once he scored that first vital equaliser, his sights became firmly fixed on target.

Viollet was the real architect behind Taylor's four goals, and Tommy praised his inside partner later in the dressing-room.

Dennis was shimmying his way through the Cardiff rearguard like greased lightning, and for one so frail, his shooting was awesome.

Jack Rowley also deserved credit for his contribution. Tommy was a very happy young man, he had a few drinks over the weekend to celebrate his four goal salvo. But Richard Walton writing in the *Daily Sketch*, brought him down to earth. Walton's article was headlined. "Clubmates Make It Easy For Tom."

The report went on: "Bravo Tommy Taylor, but for your sake I sincerely hope your four goals in United's 5-2 victory over Cardiff City will not mislead. For those who didn't see the game it is only too easy for them to be misled when they read, or are told, that the United leader 'must be England's automatic choice.' I say most emphatically not yet, since his ankle injury and subsequent operation Taylor has been "under a cloud" on the hard road back. After missing the last six matches of last season and the first four of this Taylor has been struggling to find the form that brought £30,000 to Barnsley. There have been periodical flashes suggesting his long awaited come-back is near complete."

Dennis Viollet's view matched that of many players: "Tommy suffered a lot with a bad ankle injury. He took a lot of criticism from some fans and a few newspaper reporters. He never once complained or made excuses. The four goals he scored gave him a boost. Tom knew that his mates were with him one-hundred percent. We were all very close in those days. Believe me, this was no bull, everyone at United were close pals. We sometimes had a verbal go at each other in training, but it was soon forgotten.

"After games we would socialize together, go to parties, and have fun. Tom and Jackie Blanchflower would get up and do a turn together. It was funny, they were brilliant with their one liners. And they mimicked Laurel and Hardy and Abbott and Costello.

"This all helped create and foster club spirit. In training we had our laughs, but Tom was the best trainer I ever watched. He put everything into training. We practised corner kicks which we put into action in games. Johnny Berry or David Pegg would centre the ball from corner kicks on the right or left.

"Tom would start his run-in from the edge of the box. He used to like me about six or seven yards in front of him, and that's where he wanted the ball. So Johnny or David would look for me, as they were about to centre the ball. I would sprint to the near post, leaving the area where the ball arrived empty until Tommy came in at full speed. I'm sure from the stands it must have been an incredible sight watching Tommy getting up so high.

"It looked as if he was ten feet off the ground. He could climb to incredible heights for those towering headers."

This is the Soccer for Me

In November, 1955, Tommy was feeling on top of the world. He was free of injury and he gave an interview in which he outlined why he was playing so well and he said; "This is the soccer for me."

"Old-fashioned centre-forward methods or the new! Give me the new every time. I have never had such a zest for the game as we are now playing at Manchester United. I have been playing the twin centre-forward role with either Dennis Viollet or Colin Webster and it has been little enough for my liking owing to injury and have marvelled at the ease with which we can slide through defences. More than that, I marvel at the fact that I get fewer knocks playing this way.

"I now find that the ball is running more towards goal for me. The plan not my own ability has helped me score seven goals in eight league games this season. I have never felt so confident. At last, I know where I'm going I feel that this is it a method which, properly played, can keep United on top and, more important, put British soccer back on its pedestal if extended. I have had the honour to be included in the seventeen strong England party which will go into special training for the match against Spain at Wembley next month.

"If I should be fortunate enough to be included in the final eleven, I shall give it my utmost no matter what I am asked to do, but I hope it will be in the manner in which I am now playing for United. That is, with me at right centre or left centre, not as a single spearhead. Honestly, I never thought that centre-forward play could be so easy as I am now finding it. To have players like Dennis Viollet taking an equal strain on the other side of the centre half, seems like something out of another world. I couldn't even pretend to tell England manager, Mr. Walter Winterbottom, what he ought or ought not to do, but if I am asked, I would most certainly tell everyone just how wonderful my present set-up is with United.

"It has had such an effect on me that each match cannot come soon enough and that goes for the rest of us at Old Trafford. There was a time when I used to hate the approach of match day. It was the worst part of the week for me. Now its all changed. Training and new tactics have become a pleasure. We're living the game morning, noon, and night. We're talking ourselves almost silly. That's what our new plan and new training has done for us.

"You can take it from me that just as Roy Paul and company knew that they had found something fresh and great last season, so it is with us United lads now. The fascinating thing about it all is that we are finding something fresh with each match we play. Kids with new toys, if you like, and as each week goes by, we are getting more and more confident about out ability to win something big.

"That is based not only on what plans our manager has laid down, but those he wants to exploit in the future. It is also based on my knowledge as an England player and what I saw in the World Cup last year. I believe in certain positions, United have better players than the Hungarians I never considered the Hungarian's defence was anything special. Our youth team, I think, is faster than the Hungarians.

"We are still training to get more speed, more agility, better ball control and certainly to perfect still more, the best team plan I have ever known. I think our methods are in fact, slightly ahead of the Hungarians in certain respects-certainly in the rapier thrusts on goal. Call me over enthusiastic if you like. But I really mean what I have said.

"That's why I have got back my confidence. I really feel we are getting somewhere now. There's no club like Manchester United for me. Life's worth living. Footballs worth playing."

Champions

Season 1955–56 saw the start of the "Busby Babes" proper in terms of maturing and playing with that wonderful flair and abandonment which was to become their hallmark. It was the start of what surely would have been continuing success for many years, on all three fronts League, F.A. Cup and the European Cup.

The club was alive and bubbling with youngsters ready to take on the world. Tommy scored twenty-five league goals and led the line with his customary zest. Some of the goals were exceptional to say the least. He thumped them into the net like a heavyweight boxing champion registering a sensational knockout!

It was if Taylor knew United were destined to win the League title that season and he was determined to make certain it happened by him getting the important goals. No player was a more fervent believer that United were on the brink of greatness than Tommy.

Because of his gregarious nature, size, and accomplishments he was highly popular with the team and though things didn't start well when he was injured in the first half of the opening game of the season against Birmingham (Tommy moved to the wing and Colin Webster played centre-forward) and Dennis Viollet scored twice in a 2-2 draw.

Tommy missed the first seven matches of the new season through injury. His first goal came against Preston.

It was Tommy's ability to out-jump anyone and everyone in Preston's packed defence that enabled United to score twice in the second half and win this match. High jumping was a prominent feature of Uruguay's training methods which they used in their preparations for the World Cup in 1954. Tommy had taken note of them and like Nat Lofthouse could turn a thrilling leap into a spectacle of rare beauty.

The ease in which he soared over a pinnacle of white shirts and deflected Colin Webster's whirlwind corner-kick past Thompson, the Preston goalkeeper, fairly brought the house down. The next time Tommy soared it was to nod David Pegg's long centre into the goalmouth to his goal poacher partner Viollet.

Colin Webster remembers: "I was banging in crosses and big Tom was getting everything. I was just about to take the corner kick from which he scored when he shouted, straight-faced 'Make sure you turn the laces the opposite side this time, will you.'

"We had a big laugh over that one. He wasn't really 100 per cent fit for this match, but his leaping was bloody remarkable. He was getting so high the Preston lads hadn't got a clue how to contain him. Those were marvellous times for everybody at the club. Jimmy Murphy was very close to big Tom, and used to boost his confidence through his talks."

Against Luton Town a couple of weeks later Tommy added a further two goals with Webster getting the other for a 3-1 victory. This was Luton's first visit to Old Trafford for seventeen years and Geoff Bent deputised well for Roger Byrne at left-back.

Against the run of play Luton took the lead from the penalty spot after Freddie Goodwin brought down left-winger Adam, for inside-forward Cummins to score from the spot.

In the fifty-fourth minute, Webster equalised and with the crowd just settling down again, Johnny Berry took a corner and Tommy sent a bullet-like header whistling into the Luton net. The speed and power of this header took spectators breath away.

John Doherty, a Manchester lad, was one of the original "Busby Babes." He was one of the brightest stars in United's soccer academy. A member of United's fabulous Youth Cup winning teams of the early 1950s John was a truly gifted forward. He had good academic qualifications on and off the field with skill, two good feet and powerful shooting many compared with Bobby Charlton's finishing power.

Doherty made his League debut in the 1952–53 season, but was troubled by a very serious knee problem which plagued him throughout his career. It led to his discharge from the RAF and later ended his brief career with Leicester. John remembers how he scored the last of his seven goals in his twenty-six games in United's senior side.

It was on 8 October, 1955, in an exhilarating game against arch rivals, Wolves seventeen-year-old Wilf McGuinness made his first-team debut in an (all-schoolboy) international half-back line. It certainly was a humdinger of a match with thrills at both ends and Tommy got two more goals.

David Pegg had put United in the lead after forty-one minutes, only for Slater and Swinbourne to edge them into the lead. In the seventy-second minute Tommy struck back to make it all square. And what a remarkable goal that was!

A pass came over from Webster and Taylor hooked the ball round a defender and towards the corner of the goal. Williams, the goalkeeper, went down for it and it bounced off the ground hitting him on the head before entering the net. It was a welcome addition to Tommy's collection.

This match always promised to be a rip-snorter. That's just the way it was turning out when Swinbourne put Wolves in the lead once again. The clock was ticking on and United seemed doomed to their first home defeat of the season. The Reds snatched the fat from the fire with the equaliser from Doherty. The 48,638 spectators packed into Old Trafford were exhausted with excitement but even more drama was about to unfold.

John Doherty explained: "I got our third goal but I scored it with my eyes closed! Tommy was prodigious and having a particular brilliant tussle with the tough Wolves defence. He was moving all over the place. Billy Wright was England's captain but he was glad to hear the referee's whistle to end this game."

Three minutes from the end of a pulsating game United got their fourth and wining goal. Everyone thought it was scored by centre-half Mark Jones, but it was the dark head of Taylor that made contact with Johnny Berry's corner-kick. Jones did go up to challenge Bert Williams with Taylor, but Mark was on his way down as Taylor hovered and smacked his header past Shorthouse who was stood on the goal line.

As the fans streamed out thousands did not know who had scored the wining goal. For many it wasn't until they saw photographs in the morning newspapers of Tommy's beautifully placed effort that they realised which United player was the hero that day. Mark Jones confirmed it was Taylor's goal. "Though I am still waiting to score my first League goal for the club my consolation is that my move upfield played a part in our dramatic victory," he said later.

John Doherty was a Tommy Taylor fan. "He was right up there in the John Charles, Tommy Lawton and Nat Lofthouse mould. He had terrific speed with a surprisingly nimble and quick stride for his size and was absolutely outstanding in the air with that ability to 'float' and remain apparently suspended for seconds at the top of his leap," says the ex-United man.

"All the great headers of the ball seemed to have this characteristic, but big Tommy seemed better than most at 'hanging' like a kite in the air. He had a powerful shot in each foot, and he was as brave as they make them, and a very intelligent player with unlimited energy."

On 22 October, 1955, at Old Trafford, Huddersfield Town took a leaf out of Matt Busby's book and introduced two youngsters to make their League entry in eighteen-year-old right-half John Coddington and twenty-year-old Ray Wilson, who in later years became one of the finest left-backs in the world.

Town were a respected First Division club in the 1950s and always produced good sides. Johnny Berry put United into the lead in the fortieth minute. Tommy was playing with plenty of dash and vigour, wandering out to both wings, but coming in for some robust tackling from the Huddersfield defenders.

Early in the second-half the Reds increased their lead. Blanchflower and Pegg helped create the opening and the winger, his path to goal blocked, turned the ball back to Tommy. His low drive had Wheeler, in the Huddersfield goal, beaten for sheer pace.

Taylor was leading the forward line with real gusto, and the danger signals went up for Huddersfield every time he bounded forward. Pegg got the third goal in a 3-0 victory and a week later Tommy led United to a 1-0 win over Cardiff at Ninian Park in a hard fought match.

On Bonfire night in November, 1955, at Old Trafford, Tommy supplied the fireworks when he equalised Lishman's opening goal. Ray Wood, was celebrating his 100th first-team appearance. Blanchflower went down the right side looking for a goal. The Arsenal defenders were guessing what Jackie intended before he passed to Viollet who turned the ball inside for Taylor to run forward. Jack Kelsey rushed off his line to challenge Tommy who dribbled round him and pushed the ball into the empty net.

On 12 November, United visited Burnden Park, the home of Bolton Wanderers. Rival centre-forwards Lofthouse and Taylor were on view with nineteen-year-old Eddie Colman was making his League debut. There was a slight mist over the ground, and in a 38,000 crowd the United supporters were in good voice.

It was a bright start for the Reds. As Byrne and Edwards broke down a right-wing thrust by Bolton, Duncan punted the ball to Berry who made a sizzling raid.

He was checked by the no-nonsense Roy Hartle, but regained possession near the by-line to swing in a centre, which Taylor, leaping higher than the cross-bar, headed into the Bolton net inside three minutes. What a truly great goal.

Nat Lofthouse said later: "This was Tommy at his best. The header he scored was world class. The angle was awkward, but he rocketed the ball into our net.

"People were making out that this was some sort of showdown between Tommy and myself. Ridiculous! We were pals. Sure I wanted to keep the England spot. Who wouldn't? There was no animosity, I assure you."

Nat had the last laugh by getting two goals in his side's 3-1 victory. This was United's fourth defeat of the season. The Manchester lads were soon back on the wining trail when they entertained Chelsea a week later. Tommy scored two, after Roger Byrne converted a penalty. Eddie Colman shimmed his way forward and cleverly lobbed the ball into the middle, where Tommy was running on to it. Robertson, the Chelsea keeper rushed out in a frantic effort to stop the United leader, but Tommy smartly dribbled the ball round him and tapped the ball in.

On 28 November, 1955, Tommy was selected as a substitute when England played a friendly against Yugoslavia at Wembley but he was not even mentioned in the match programme.

Substitutes were not permitted in domestic football during this period, but for international games a replacement was allowed up to the forty-fourth minute, though a goalkeeper could be changed at any time during the match. The Yugoslavs were a good side and had never lost here.

This game was supposedly a "pointer" for England's World Cup prospects but after thirty-four minutes Johnny Haynes, who had been playing really well, was injured in a desperate tackle from Berlin the Yugoslavian defender and had to go off the field. Tommy replaced him. It was Stanley Matthews who lifted the gloom with his wizardry on the right wing.

Tommy was trying much too hard in playing a central role then the inside-forward link job. He scored after sixty-three minutes from a Tom Finney move. Then came the second goal for Tommy. It was a carbon copy of Matthews immortal 1953 Cup Final goal-move. Stanley went straight to the bye-line, and as Taylor raced in for the inevitable cross, the crowd halted in its trek to the exits. Over sped the ball, plumb-straight, to be flicked on by Frank Blunstone. Tommy smashed the ball into the net from close range. This gave England a 3-0 victory, Tottenham's Johnny Brooks scoring the other goal.

In the Portsmouth game on 10 December, 1955, Tommy took on a roving role, moving to both wings and roving all across the front line. The goal came from one of his sorties to the left wing. Duncan Edwards, trying to get his forwards flowing, intercepted a move from the Portsmouth player Rees, out on the left "Dunk" looked up and saw Tommy; a beautiful ball was dispatched to the centre-forward who burst through the Portsmouth defence. Although both McGhee and goalkeeper Uprichard tried hard to stem the danger, Tommy scored. United went down 3-2 with Pegg getting United's second goal.

Two weeks later, Tommy was on the scoresheet again as he helped his goal-partner Dennis Viollet score a hat-trick in a 4-1 away victory over a good West Brom side. On Boxing Day, he and Viollet were plundering again, defeating Charlton 5-1 at Old Trafford. Dennis getting two more with Tommy, Roger Byrne and John Doherty also scoring in this emphatic destruction of the London team. A day later, Charlton extracted sweet revenge and walloped United 3-0!

The game against Manchester City at Old Trafford on the last day of 1955, brought scenes never witnessed before. With well over 60,000 inside the ground standing shoulder to shoulder, the gates were locked more than an hour before kick-off. Over 15,000 were locked out. The streets around the ground were awash with a human mass of heads.

"In all my years of attending these 'Derby' games I have never seen such crowds", commented Eric Thornton, in the *Manchester Evening News*. Extra police had to be called out.

City's new boy, Jack Dyson, scored after twenty-nine minutes sending Blue's supporters into raptures. But United were surging in front and it came as no surprise when, in the fifty-fifth minute, Tommy wiped out his previous failures by putting the Reds on level terms with as good a goal as anyone could wish to see.

A long ball from Wood bounced nicely for Tommy. Big Dave Ewing charged after it intending to "be first," but unfortunately he miss-headed the ball and Tommy was left clear. As Bert Trautman came out, the United leader lobbed the ball over his head.

Old Trafford was a cauldron of noise. When Dennis Viollet got the winner everyone was throwing their hats and scarves in the air.

The United forward line was full of class, flair and panache. Johnny Berry, the oldest member of the team, caused havoc on the right-wing, and was ever so dangerous when cutting inside for a pop at goal. He was brave into the bargain. On the left flank David Pegg was a free-flowing spirit and playing beautiful football. These two wingers knew how to curl those centres into the box for Tommy to get his head to.

Tommy was like a swashbuckling pirate in a slightly-built young forward line. Raw and robust, he was a centre-forward in the classic mould and one of the few players whose heading ability could be compared with the legendary Tommy Lawton or "Dixie" Dean.

Other players relied a great deal on Tommy's toughness to take the knocks and rough treatment from opposing defenders while leaving space for them to move into.

At inside-right Billy Whelan had taken over from Jackie Blanchflower. The shy, religious Irish lad, had extraordinary talent. His range of subtle skills were so extensive he would not have been out of place in Brazil! He was playing out of his skin, scoring great goals and having games veteran players would have been proud off. His distribution too was immaculate.

At inside-left was Dennis Viollet, who at times gave the appearance of just getting out of a sick bed so pale and thin was he compared to the tough, fit-looking players around him. But he was galvanised into fluent activity whenever the ball was near his feet. His control was splendid and he was the ideal ploy for Taylor. Sharp as a razor when the ball was anywhere near goal.

This forward line received exceptional service from the "engine" room. Eddie Colman, who was smaller at 5ft-6ins and even frailer than Viollet, had Bert Whalley, for one, doubting whether his skill could compensate for his lack of physique. He made up for any physical deficiencies with courage and enthusiasm. He was also one of the most popular players ever to wear a red shirt.

Little Eddie was a Salford lad, tough and sturdy with great resilience and exemplary ball-control aligned to a shimmy (body-swerve) which made him stand out even in this memorable side.

His vision helped make many a goal for his forwards, while Mark Jones was a tower of strength at centre-half.

He and Tommy's close friend, Jackie Blanchflower, contested this position with venom. Whoever was in the first team dreaded missing a game, be it through injury or international duty, because they knew they would have to wait in the reserves to get their place back again.

At left-half was Duncan Edwards, who possessed amazing physique and stamina with huge, tree-trunk legs, a barrel chest and bags of class and ability. His tackling was fair, but ferocious, leaving shaken opponents feeling as if they had been hit by a ten-ton truck. His passing over long distances matched Johnny Haynes for perfection and accuracy, finding his team-mates time after time.

Duncan was the complete two-footed player and his shooting was awesome from any distance. He was a prodigy, a unique player whom no adjectives could adequately describe.

The two full backs were Billy Foulkes at right-back, a tough ex-miner, and a fierce tackling no-nonsense type of player. Very dependable and a loyal club man, Bill must have been the only professional to play for England while still working down the pit. He played against Northern Ireland in 1955 his one and only cap.

It was rather strange really that the selectors replaced him with Ron Staniforth of Huddersfield, a player in his early thirties.

Roger Byrne at left back, was also club captain. He was the first of the "Busby Babes" a tag incidentally which he hated and although short and slightly built, Byrne's determination was formidable. He was impeccable in his play and would go to any length in the cause of his team. Roger an England regular was a highly intelligent footballer with tremendous pace which befitted his former position as a left-winger.

The goalkeeper was an unsung hero, Ray Wood. He established himself as a confident keeper who rarely inspired, but was dependable at all times. What he lacked in class he made up for in courage. He was capped three times for England and was a United regular until Harry Gregg was signed later.

The match against Sheffield United on 14 January was a stiff game for the Busby Babes after a humiliating 4-0 F.A. Cup thrashing at the hands of Bristol Rovers a week earlier. Would it affect their confidence?

The simple answer was no as Johnny Berry and David Pegg opened the scoring, but the best move came when Byrne sent a swift low pass down the left side to Pegg. A thrilling chase by Pegg, a glorious centre at speed to his centre-forward, then a great leap and a cunning downward header by Tommy and the ball was nestling in the back of the net.

4 February, 1956, was celebration day for Tommy. It was his one-hundredth appearance in the famous red shirt of Manchester United. It was announced over the loud-speakers before the match against Lancashire rivals, Burnley that Tommy

was completing his century and supporters were asked to give him a special cheer and a big round of applause. They needed little encouragement!

Tommy made certain that he didn't just receive applause at the start but also throughout the entire match and at the end. He had a "cracking" game, giving wing-half cum centre-half Jimmy Adamson a real roasting on the slippery turf. Tommy scored and strike partner Dennis Viollet got the other in United's 2-0 victory.

United's match at Wolverhampton was of vital importance to both sides. Wolves were challenging strongly for the First Division championship and had to be beaten convincingly if the Red Devils were to be taken seriously as potential Champions. On 18 February, 1956, United played on a three-inch covering of snow in front of over 35,000 fans. They had an added incentive to win Mark Jones had become a father a couple of days earlier and the team wanted a victory as a gift for the entire Jones family.

After half-an-hour United took the lead Billy Wright, racing out to United's right wing, tried a short inside pass. It was immediately intercepted by Viollet who, in a flash sent a glorious ball through the centre for his partner, Taylor, to latch on to. Tommy beat both Stuart, the Wolves right-back and Shorthouse, their left-back before driving an unstoppable shot into the roof of the net.

It was brilliantly taken but England captain Wright must be blamed for allowing him the opening Tommy added a second goal in the second half to give United a big boost in a 2-0 victory. United had a scare in the thirty-sixth minute when Hancocks the right-winger, missed a penalty after Edwards was alleged to have handled the ball.

It was during this season that Tommy was selected to play for the England "B" team and his first game was against Scotland "B" at Dens Park in front of only 11,500. With barely three minutes left of a dreadful match in which the English side were tipped to roll over the Scottish team Tommy surged through the defence like a tidal wave and saved the day for his red faced colleagues.

Credit for this face-saving must go to Tommy. The final touch was made by John Atyeo, who was described thus: "The most anonymous performer in the most anonymous international performance I have ever seen. It did not even have a printed programme," wrote George Follows.

Tommy, covered in mud through his first half brilliance put in a titanic finish. He was playing the Scotland defence almost on his own and scored his goal in the forty-third minute when he raced through and drove an unstoppable shot past Brown, the Scottish keeper.

"The England forwards were just a bunch of airy-fairy footballers apart from Taylor. He made mistakes, but one goal scored, one goal made, two headers just over, two shots brilliantly saved he was everything that really mattered. His match-saving effort was magnificent. He collected a throw in, beat Rea, rebuffed Glen with a mighty shoulder charge, swerved past Malloy and gave Atyeo his scoring chance," wrote Follows.

A Century of Golden Goals

When Manchester United travelled to Huddersfield Town, on Saturday, 31 March, 1956, the team was playing like a well oiled machine. The day before, Good Friday, they had thrashed Newcastle at Old Trafford, 5-2. They were on course to lift the First Division Championship.

The defence was solid and dependable with captain Roger Byrne, and Bill Foulkes and either Mark Jones or Jackie Blanchflower at the heart of it, while the midfield was full of power and class with little Eddie Colman and powerhouse Duncan Edwards spraying lovely long and short passes through to the hungry forwards.

This was a tough match. Huddersfield, though struggling against the threat of relegation, had taken ten points out of the last fourteen, more in keeping with a team going for the Championship! It was a game in which the full qualities of Tommy Taylor were seen in full flowing majesty. United needed the front line leadership of Taylor to steady them down.

No cause was ever lost when he was playing. He would miss chances (like all other forwards) but he would never let his head drop, never brooded about the ones that got away. He would just be more determined to score when the next opening came his way.

Tommy was hoping to get on the scoresheet because he had scored ninety-eight goals during his career so far (twenty-seven of them with Barnsley). His target was 100 league goals. There were thousands of United fans in the ground and they knew in their hearts this United team was something special; they also felt that these young players would become even better with experience and the passing of time. It was a wonderful atmosphere.

There was much niggling all over the field. Huddersfield seemed desperate, their tactics to kick the ball as hard and as far as they could, hoping United's defence made mistakes.

There was much more method and culture about the Red Devils play and after great inter-play between Taylor and Viollet, Dennis sent in a terrific shot. The Town goalkeeper, Fearnley turned the ball for a corner.

In the twentieth minute the League leaders went ahead after a brilliantly executed move which saw Viollet lob the ball over the Huddersfield centre-half's head. Taylor, was on the ball in a flash.

He unleashed a rocket of a shot which Fearnley turned aside; Berry came thundering forward and let fly and there was United's leader to apply the finishing touch for the ninety-ninth League goal of his career. Then came Tommy's 100th League goal and what a marvellous one it was! Berry took a high corner and Tommy was positioned outside the eighteen-yard box. He soared, met the ball flush on his forehead and it went like a bullet past the 'keeper and into the roof of the net, arguably one of the best headers ever seen at this ground.

Even the Huddersfield supporters rose to acclaim it. It put United firmly on their way to victory and on course for the League Championship.

Harry England: "I can remember that goal as if it happened yesterday. It was the best headed goal I have ever seen. Tommy left tickets for myself and three other mates of his from Smithies. Town were a damn good side in those days, but United had these young kids, and they played lovely attractive football.

"When little Berry centred, I watched Tommy's movement. He was outside the box, and made that run of his, sprang up and the power he put into that header was like one of Duncan Edward's rocket shots. Even the Huddersfield fans stood and clapped, that's how good that goal was.

Two days later, United fought out a goalless draw with Newcastle at St. James's Park. Five days later they were due to face Blackpool at Old Trafford. Victory here would see them crowned as First Division Champions.

In the final run-in towards their championship success Busby took his men for regular week-long stays at the Norbek Hydro, in Blackpool. The players enjoyed this welcome break from normal routine and it helped to break the monotony. Tommy in particular loved running on the sands with the wind blowing through his hair.

Open up the Lord Mayor's parlour, lay down the Red carpet, break open the champagne. On 7 April, 1956, the Busby Babes were crowned First Division champions for the second time since the war. The gates were closed some time before the kick-off with over 62,277, (a post-war record) jammed inside Old Trafford and several thousand locked outside.

Youthful exuberance was evident and there were traces of nerves in United's ranks as Stanley Matthews throw-in went straight to Jackie Mudie, his inside-forward partner, who, immediately turned the pass inside for Durie to head a good goal.

A few minutes after half-time, Tommy had to leave the field for attention to a bad cut over his right eye and Wright, the Blackpool defender, also required treatment. After an hour's play (while Taylor and Wright were off the field) United drew level.

Berry sent John Doherty through the middle, Farm, the Blackpool goalkeeper, bowled him over. Roger Byrne, who normally took the penalties, asked Berry to take it and he made no mistake from the spot.

John Doherty: "Its funny really, Roger told us before that match that the night before in our hotel he had dreamed we were awarded a penalty which we missed!"

In the eightieth minute Tommy put United ahead and sealed the championship victory. Thousands of joyous United followers swarmed across the pitch as the game ended. They stood in front of the main stands shouting for Byrne . . . Taylor and every other hero in turn.

In the dressing room it was champagne and cheers as Busby's bubbling youngsters celebrated. The only regret was that Matt Busby was not there. He was in Glasgow because of a family bereavement, but followed United's title clincher by telephone on his return journey. After phoning Matt was told his side were a goal behind and when he 'phoned again from Lockerbie discovered his "Babes" were winning 2-1. He was beside himself with joy.

More stops and a few more phone calls to Jimmy Murphy provided a full match report.

There was wild and happy rejoicing throughout the city with tributes from many former United players and other celebrities. Busby was overjoyed for his team had achieved this honour without the help of older experienced players.

Matt Busby: "How I wish I could have been in Manchester tonight to congratulate the boys. It was a great blow to miss the match in such unhappy circumstances, but I never doubted their spirit or ability to pull through. It would have been a tragedy in football had they missed the title after playing so well through the hardest months of the winter.

"I have never known a spell so tense and hard, but this young team has done me proud. I am proud indeed of all my young players, right down from the First Division side to the colts. Our senior side is one of the youngest ever to represent United, and our Central League team skipper Jack Crompton excepted it looks likely to be the youngest ever to win the Central League championship, too.

"Two or three years ago, at the annual meeting of the club's shareholders, I said that United had youthful potential worth tens of thousands of pounds. I'm proud the boys have proved me right.

I have, too, a grand board of directors, for which I am truly thankful; a wholehearted colleague in secretary Walter Crickmer; fine coaches in Jimmy Murphy and Bert Whalley and front-line bulwarks in trainers Tom Curry and Bill Inglis. Ted Dalton, our physiotherapist, has also worked wonders on injured players.

"How eagerly United's younger players like Ian Greaves, Eddie Colman, Mark Jones, Duncan Edwards, Billy Whelan, John Doherty, Dennis Viollet and David Pegg have stepped-up and taken their chances. And Tommy Taylor, who is only twenty-four, could be England's centre-forward for years to come!"

Roger Byrne: "To say I am a proud captain tonight is to put it mildly. I can hardly realise the championship trophy is really ours and that the months of tension since we took the lead last December are over. Blackpool were worthy opponents.

"We never underrated their challenge and could not take anything for granted.

We were not only fighting for the title to-day. We were all pulling out our best for the man who has done all the scheming and worrying for us all — our manager, Mr. Matt Busby. What a pity he couldn't be with us to share this hour of triumph!"

Allenby Chilton: "Though I left United just over twelve months ago, I still look for their result first. I am very proud of United. They have proved every bit as good as the 1948 side. I thought it would not take them too long to win the championship because they have so many great young players. I shall be having a double celebration, with United winning the League and my own team, Grimsby Town, promoted to the Second Division."

Johnny Carey, United's former captain, was overjoyed too and phoned Matt Busby to congratulate him and the two old friends spoke about United's title win in 1952. Carey had promised his wife that he would be home for a certain time, but with the speeches and celebrations after the game he was late arriving.

When he did arrive his wife wanted to know why he was so late. His dinner was spoiled. Two hours after winning the Championship he was washing the dishes as a penance for being so late home. All the players concerned in this latest championship victory had joined the club while Carey was still at United, and he had followed their careers with great interest since their first timid steps across the threshold of Old Trafford.

Johnny Carey: "The first time I met Tommy Taylor was at London Road Station. Matt Busby and I had gone to welcome him. As the train jerked to a halt, a big, athletic figure, hatless jumped from the train, and strode along the platform with hands dug deep into his raincoat pockets. Under one arm was a brown paper parcel, and the imprint of the studs clearly indicated they were the Taylor football boots. Thus, a £30,000 footballer arrived in Manchester.

"Several photographers got us posed for a picture. I suggested Tommy put the parcel down, and so, I learned later, spoiled what would have been a 'photographic scoop.' What an inspired signing Tommy has proved to be for my old club. He is a remarkable centre-forward, completely different to the normal swashbuckling type.

"Tommy does so many things simply. Matt Busby has many seeds in the garden of his Soccer academy. They are planted in fertile soil. How gratifying to see them flower so radiantly!

"Like a true gardener, he will tend them carefully."

The Lord Mayor of Manchester, Alderman T. Regan sent his best wishes and said: "I am very proud that Manchester United have won the championship so clearly and have made sure of it well before the end of the season.

"Manchester has certainly been in the forefront this year and I sincerely hope that after United's outstanding achievement Manchester City will make it a double event by bringing home the F.A. Cup."

The Mayor of Stretford, Councillor J.M. Maxted, said: "The triumph they have achieved has been brought about by the wonderful team spirit which so obviously exists within the team, and by the co-operation of each team member, along with the hard training which they have to put in."

Sir Stanley Rous, F.A. Secretary: "I am sure that members of the Football Association would wish me to offer congratulations to United on winning for the fourth time the championship of the Football League. It was obvious that their early dismissal from the F.A. Cup by Bristol Rovers was not allowed to disturb the morale and spirit of the team."

Manchester United's old boys were quick of the mark with their congratulations. As was City's manager, Les McDowall and a host of other celebrities.

Henry Cockburn, (who was playing for Bury): "It is a wonderful performance and a triumph for that happy blend of youth and experience. I haven't seen United much this season, but I gather they are not quite as good as the side in the late 1940s! On the other hand, United have a great stock of reserves and in a few years they should have one of the finest teams of all time."

Johnny Aston: "My playing days are over, but my watching days at Old Trafford are just beginning. What a great side this United XI is going to be! And what magnificent youngsters are also coming up. I heartily congratulate my colleagues on their success. They have won the championship in a canter."

Stan Pearson, (playing for Bury): "I'd like to add my congratulations to Matt Busby and his men on a splendid achievement. They have shown great determination, particularly in this last vital period, and in view of the accent on youth and the tremendous reserve potential, United can be a real power for many years to come."

Jack Rowley (with Plymouth Argyle): "United have proved beyond all doubt the truth of the saying that the strength of a team lies in its reserves. By careful coaching and 'nursing', United's youngsters have made tremendous strides and this, allied to the experience of the slightly more mature men, has produced a great combination. I see no reason why United should not maintain their proud position for a long time".

Charlie Mitten (with Mansfield Town): "Former United players all over the country will be anxious to pay tribute to the men from Old Trafford. Some were privileged to see the side in the making, and it was obvious that the honours could not be long delayed. One has only to look at this season's success at all levels to realise that the future will surely bear the stamp of Manchester United".

Les McDowall, the City manager: "Well done, Manchester United! Winning the League Championship at any time is a fine performance, but to have the title safely in the bag with three weeks still to go is a magnificent achievement.

"Having seen little of Matt Busby's boys in action this season, I have not been in a position to argue with the niggling comparisons of the present team and the one which lifted the championship in 1952.

"If ever there was a case of comparisons being odious this is it. The perfectionists forget that the team which won the title in 1952 consisted of mature, experienced players who had been team mates for years.

"They had developed a wonderful understanding and there is no doubt that their football was really attractive to watch. Yet, with all due respect, I am bound to point out in defence of the present side that the 1952 team topped the table with fifty-seven points.

"This season United have already equalled that total and are almost certain to pass it. And today's team, it must be remembered, has been 'born' during the transition period from the old to the new.

"Many are youngsters of scant League experience compared with their 1952 predecessors, yet they have held their place at the top of the table for half a season and have won the title with time to spare.

"United have proved themselves a good side beyond doubt and those who would detract from their great title feat by making invidious comparisons must be mighty difficult fans to please."

There was a reception in Manchester's Town Hall on Saturday evening 21 April, 1956, following the last game of the season against Portsmouth, a 1-0 victory with a Dennis Viollet solitary goal. When the final whistle blew, thousands of supporters converged onto the pitch eager to hail the new champions. The Police were powerless to keep them back, but this was a joyous crowd who merely wanted to show their appreciation for their team. The whole ground was a sea of heads and faces. A truly amazing spectacle!

Thousands more people lined the route and congregated in Albert Square as the team bus brought the triumphant heroes to Town Hall. You would have thought royalty was descending upon the city, so great and pulsating were the emotions. There were sporting celebrities from the city's community among the more than 450 representatives present.

What do you do when you have scored the winning goal which makes your team champions of the First Division and you have an attractive lady at your elbow?

Well, Tommy celebrated by drinking champagne from her shoe! Sat in the Midland Hotel at the celebration party to mark United's winning the title, Tommy was with eighteen-year-old Ann Sutton of Denton, and Roger Byrne and his girl friend Joyce Cooper. Both Tommy and his captain were sporting patches over their eyes which was a legacy of their battle against Blackpool in their "match of the season."

United's title success sparked off the busiest period for many months and requests simply poured into the club offices for players to appear in benefit or

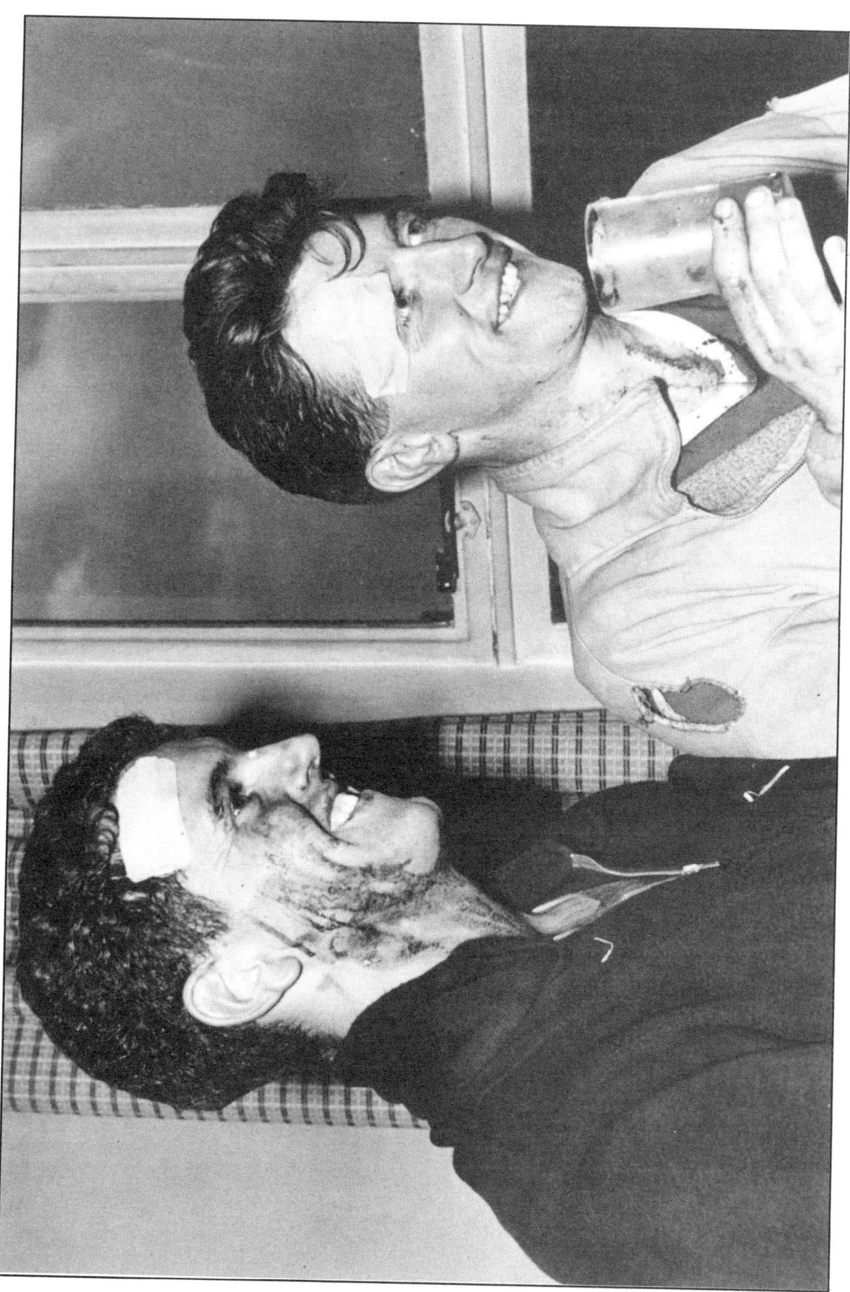

Tommy and Roger Byrne, both complete with battle scars, celebrate Championship victory.

charity matches and the like. It was good that the club and players were in such demand, but much as the players wanted to oblige, they simply couldn't. It was impossible.

Matches against Home Farm in Dublin had already been arranged. Then the Johnny Aston testimonial was fixed for Old Trafford. The Football League was to oppose the Irish League in Belfast; Tommy, Roger Byrne and Duncan Edwards had been selected as travelling reserves for this match.

Then Byrne, Tommy and Mark Jones were booked to appear at Altrincham in a Ken Grieves's cricket benefit. Coming up was the Brazil game and the close season United and England tours.

The end of the season is usually a happy occasion as everyone is looking forward to the summer break, but for players released by clubs it became quite sad. Just before the United staff finished for the season and various players went on international duty or with the club on their close season continental tour Tommy was training at Old Trafford along with Laurie Cassidy whom he got to know quite well.

Laurie Cassidy: "When we finished our stint, Matt Busby called a few of us into another room away from Tommy and the other players. Beside myself there was Cliff Birkett, Noel McFarlane and Johnny Scott. When he had bad news to relay, Matt would cough and clear his throat before continuing.

"The directors have informed me that I have to release you players, he told us." It was obvious he didn't like this task, and he always said it was the directors who had made the decision. I accepted his explanation. He had youngsters coming along and he needed to play them. I'd had a good run and I was teaching.

"As I came out of the meeting, Tommy was outside doing something or other and I must have looked a little dejected. "What's wrong Laurie," he asked. I explained what I had just been told by the boss, and Tommy was about to tear into the room to confront Matt about the club releasing me until I stopped him. It was a lovely touch and I have never forgotten his gesture.

"The other lads of course were soon fixed up with other clubs. But to this day I often think about Tommy's spontaneous reaction to my being released by United. He was a thoughtful, caring person. I watched his career take off and was delighted when he received the praise he received. He was the best centre-forward ever."

After getting changed Tommy was still upset about Laurie Cassidy. Waiting outside Old Trafford with his autograph book in his hand was a tall, gangling youngster who would in later years join Manchester City, feature in their successful Youth team and serve them for many years.

He also made a bigger name for writing some brilliant, witty, hilarious books on football and for his business acumen and after dinner speaking.

Fred Eyre: "I was outside the players entrance at Old Trafford and I wanted

Tommy's autograph. He was a God to me. I idolised him and thought he was the best thing since sliced bread. Anyhow he came out and looked upset about something. I rushed forward and pushed my book in front of him. Usually he was smiling and would sign at the blink of an eye lid but for some reason he wouldn't sign.

"I followed him as he walked home. As we got near his house and with me badgering him to sign he turned to me and said: 'I've told you a hundred times already, I'm not signing anything, now go away.' I persisted as only a true, dedicated autograph hunter would.

"I knew he was absolutely fed up with the sound of my north Manchester accent and the incessant wailing. Just as he was going to go into the house I said in my cheekiest voice: 'Well if you wont sign your autograph, just scribble on my book.' Tommy turned around and walked toward me and as I held out the book he scribbled lines all over the page.

"I looked shocked and I shouted 'What are you doing?' He broke into a grin for the first time and replied: 'Well you did say scribble, and I have scribbled.' We both burst out laughing. A press photographer snapped the both of us laughing outside his digs. I held no animosity toward Tommy over this incident, because I had constantly over the past years shoved more pieces of paper and pictures and books at him than most. He had always obliged. He seemed to have a perpetual smile and we kids never upset him in any way. What a player he was though, I thought he was tremendous."

Around about this time calypso music was all the rage. Cedric Conner had recorded a song called the "Manchester United Calypso." It was a witty, catchy number very popular with United followers for obvious reasons and was featured on radio stations and request programmes quite a lot.

Happy Memories

With only three games left of the "Busby Babes" first Championship winning season, Tommy buoyant and delighted at scoring his 100th senior goal, and the manner in which United's play had caught the public's imagination discussed his career so far, and his worries about his ankle, his improved play, scoring goals and the team spirit at Old Trafford.

"When I reached Old Trafford in March, 1953, as a raw youngster of twenty-one, Manchester United were in a transitional stage. That famous team which won the F.A. Cup in 1948 and the league championship in 1951–52 season was breaking up, he reminded fans.

That happens to all clubs, so I was not altogether surprised when in my first season I played only eleven League games United finished in eighth position, the lowest in post-war seasons.

"They got back into fourth place in 1953–54 and were highly placed last season. Now we have topped the League for so long I think everybody was ready to accept that the Championship would come our way when we concluded our Easter programme with five points from six.

"It has been a season of happy memories. I have had my best scoring season with twenty-four to my credit before the Blackpool game. (Tommy scored the winner in United's 2-1 victory over Blackpool.)

"What is equally gratifying is that these goals have come in thirty-one matches, as against my twenty-two goals in the 1953–54 season from thirty-five games. Last season I played in only thirty League games and got twenty goals. A week ago at Huddersfield I scored my hundredth league and cup goal in senior football. What a thrill that was!

"I doubt whether I shall succeed in beating Jack Rowley's record for United of thirty goals in the season 1951–52, but I feel I have a great chance to do it in the future.

This is said in no spirit of bravado. It is intended to convey an honest opinion of the magnificent team spirit that exists at Old Trafford. We do not care very much who scores so long as we get more than our opponents.

A centre-forward is naturally expected to hit the target more frequently than his inside or wing forward colleagues because he is a spearhead. Dennis Viollet has scored nineteen goals this season, so it is obviously no one man band." (Viollet made it 2-0 in the last game of the season. A 1-0 victory over Portsmouth.)

"The season has not been without its worries. Remember a couple of seasons ago an ankle injury nearly ended my career? The symptoms were so difficult to trace that I nearly lost heart. Then by a chance examination, a specialist literally put his finger on the trouble just under the ankle.

Things turned out all right, and I would like to pay tribute to all the people who helped me recover, particularly our manager Mr. Matt Busby, who's words of encouragement helped me so much.

"United are a great club. We are a young side too, and we are gradually eliminating the faults most footballers possess. I know for instance that my own work has been speeded up considerably since my days with Barnsley.

First Division football is very fast and to dwell on the ball is to invite trouble. These are aspects of the game I have learned the practical way at Old Trafford. I have also been fortunate in playing for England and England "B," where I have been able to improve my general style.

"I am still learning, and that should be the desire of all footballers, whether senior or junior football. Profit from your mistakes. Be a team man first, and play football all the time, and you are bound to get reward in the end."

Tommy's Greatest International Game

Winning the First Division Championship in 1956 was a splendid achievement for this young and still developing team. They were a fine advertisement for Manchester all over the world. But what did the new season hold in store for them?

Having brought off a magnificent "treble" the First Division and Central League titles and the F.A. Youth Cup (for the fourth consecutive season) the club had set themselves a tremendous yardstick.

Every member of the Red Devils staff was excited at the prospect of playing against Europe's finest teams. Tommy received an overdue call-up by England because of his outstanding form for United. He was awarded his sixth cap when the England selectors chose him to play against Scotland in the home International match at Hampden Park, Glasgow in April, 1956, in front of 134,000 fans. This would be the first time the United centre-forward had worn the white shirt of his country in the British Isles.

Albert Scanlon: "Though Tommy was honoured to play for his country in any position, it was a little unfair to select him out of position again. He was asked to play inside-right as a poacher and provider, alongside Nat Lofthouse. This wasn't his style as everyone at Old Trafford knew. In six matches for England only once had he been picked in his true role . . . centre-forward."

The match ended in a 1-1 draw with Johnny Haynes netting a goal with less than thirty seconds remaining after Graham Leggat had put Scotland in front. The United pair of Roger Byrne and Tommy set-up the chance for the Fulham man.

Byrne inspired the goal. Moving up the left-wing, he crossed for Tommy, who left George Young, the Scottish centre-half floundering, and rose like an eagle to flick the ball into the path of Haynes, who scored from twelve yards.

Naturally the critics were as one in requesting changes and a new system up front for the prestigious game against Brazil at Wembley on 9 May, 1956. They were calling for heads to roll. Many wanted to discard Stanley Matthews and Tom Finney.

Shortly before playing for England against Brazil Tommy willingly and freely gave his services to aid the cause of raising much-needed cash for the Barnsley players Benefit Fund. Barnsley played an All Star XI team which consisted of ex-Barnsley players.

The previous day Tommy had represented the Football League against the Irish League in Belfast. Though tired after playing in his fourth game in the space of ten days he gave a good account of himself after being made captain for the night.

Danny Blanchflower, Sam Bartram and Mark Jones also played. The makeshift team won by 6-0. Later Tommy had a few drinks and relaxed listening to Blanchflower's and Bartram's hilarious stories.

Brazil were on the threshold of the greatest era in their footballing history when they came here to oppose the "Old Masters," England, for the first time.

The foundations were there for the team that would go on to win the World Cup in sensational fashion in 1958 and retain it four years later. They had outstanding players of flair and unbelievable skill like Didi the brains of their midfield. The two unrelated full-back partners Djalma and Nilton Santos, goalkeeper Gylmar, Zozimo, central defender Pavao and other stylish players throughout the side.

Nilton Santos, was famed for his attacking flair as a full- back. He was as excited as a schoolboy when told he would be marking the forty-one-year-old Stanley Matthews. Santos was not as happy after the match.

Neither was central defender Pavao, who was about to find out why Tommy Taylor was being hailed as "The new Tommy Lawton."

England's team lined up as follows: Reg Matthews (no relation to Stan); Hall, Byrne; Clayton, Wright, Edwards; Stanley Matthews, Atyeo, Taylor, Haynes, Grainger. Brazil's team was: Gylmar; Djalma Santos, Nilton Santos; Zozimo, Pavao, Dequina; Paulinho, Alvaro, Gino, Didi, Chanoteiro.

Tommy was in the thick of the action from the first loud blast of the referee's whistle when he brought the flashy Brazilian goalkeeper to his knees with a quickly taken rocket of a shot in the opening seconds. This was just the start and moments later, Tommy the "Tank," moving at terrific speed on to a through ball, left Pavao standing. A sudden burst of acceleration saw him drive a low shot past Gylmar into the back of the net.

The classy Brazilians were well and truly shaken by this explosive start. They had not recovered from Taylor's opening goal when Colin Grainger cut inside to plonk the ball into the net to make it 2-0 for England. Stanley Matthews was showing the Brazilian team why his name was still magic, waltzing past Santos time and time again. All this was within the first six minutes or so!

Ronnie Clayton, the cultured Blackburn Rover's right-half, who was to serve England well over the coming years and who built up a terrific understanding with

United's Duncan Edwards, remembers the Brazil game with fond memories. He was an admirer of the Tommy Taylor style of elegant centre-forward play.

"In the opening few seconds of the Brazil game we were under a bit of pressure in our half. Tommy dropped back and picked up a loose ball and set off on one of those high-stepping runs of his with a pack of Brazilians chasing after him. He beat about five or six Brazilians and sent a rocket of a drive only inches over the cross-bar. If that one had gone in the net, it would have been the goal of the century."

Didi completely baffled goalkeeper Reg Matthews early in the second half to score a cracking goal with one of his famous "falling leaf" free-kicks. Paulinho showed that he, too, could bend the ball when he scored with a cross shot from fifteen yards.

Then the Brazilians went completely haywire. In amazing scenes tempers snapped when French referee Michel Guigue awarded a disputed penalty. The Brazilian players threatened to walk off.

When peace was restored, Gylmar saved big John Atyeo's spot kick, but minutes later, Tommy scored England's next goal. Then a second penalty was awarded to England. Roger Byrne, usually very meticulous on such occasions, shot wide, but this was a magnificent team performance from the whole England team.

Without a shadow of a doubt though, Tommy Taylor was inspiring England to greater heights. There was an air of majesty about his game. His jumping was awesome and the Brazilian defenders were puzzled, even mystified, as Stanley Matthews floated over those tantalising centres.

The ball was hanging in the air, putting Gylmar in a quandary of whether to go for the ball or leave it for his defenders to clear. Then there was Colin Grainger's fast, hard, driven crosses.

Tommy's running off the ball was another factor which upset the classy Brazilian's composure. He was like a Sherman Tank, bursting through the middle and England eventually won 4-2, but one could see Brazil had the makings of a cracking team for the future.

Johnny Haynes said: "This was one of the best England teams I have ever played with. Colin Grainger and Tommy Taylor were brilliant and did the business for England. I personally enjoyed having Duncan Edwards and Roger Byrne behind me, while Stanley Matthews gave a great exhibition of wing wizardry."

Tommy Taylor: "Matthews gave us the inspiration to lift our game. You could see that the Brazilians were terrified every time he got the ball and they were so busy worrying about him it gave the rest of us more space in which to work."

Jackie Blanchflower: "I would have to say that was Tommy's best game for England. He was magnificent. Those Brazilians were world class as their record later revealed, but Tommy was their equal. He loved these type of games, because he could pit his wits against defenders who were reputed to be the best in the world."

Jimmy Greaves: "Taylor had real class and quality and can be bracketed with Tommy Lawton and Nat Lofthouse as the best of England's post-war centre-forwards. He had excellent positional sense, he was strong and determined, and difficult to knock off the ball."

Blanchflower: "When England played Brazil, Tommy was in sparkling form. He was very proud when selected for England. Against these superb players Tommy stood out.

"It was only a matter of time before these Brazilian wonder boys became World Cup winners. They were agitated every time the ball was centred high into their penalty area. Tommy was lethal, like a viper, getting his head onto everything. I would count this as his best match for England." England played the first match of their foreign tour without either Finney or Matthews the first occasion for many years this had happened.

The match against Sweden was a bitter disappointment, after the scintillating victory over Brazil. It was quite obvious that the England players were suffering some kind of reaction after their Wembley vintage showing. United had five players in this England squad. Tommy, Edwards and Byrne, Johnny Berry and Ray Wood.

A 0-0 draw was not very distinguished. Berry played outside-right in the Swedish game, but hardly received any service. Virtually the whole team played badly, on a very bumpy pitch and a strong wind and glaring sunshine didn't help.

The team pulled itself together for the game against Finland, beating them 5-1. Tommy had a nasty looking boil on his arm and just before half-time, after a collision with the Finnish goalkeeper, Hurri, he was replaced by Nat Lofthouse, who scored twice taking his England tally to twenty-eight one more than Steve Bloomer's forty-five-year-old record.

At the banquet after the match Colin Grainger, who was a fine singer and later went on to become a night-club entertainer, gave a brilliant impersonation of Al Jolson, the famous "Mammy" singer. The Finnish centre-forward played the piano and the whole party had a wonderful time.

The most important match of the tour, and the most difficult, was the third and final game against reigning World Champions West Germany in Berlin, on 26 May. The England squad trained for this prestigious match at a German State soccer school at Barsinghausen, near Hanover. What a sumptuous training camp it put our sparse facilities back in England to shame. It was situated in lovely grounds, with facilities for every possible sport, outdoor and indoor. The food was excellent and the added bonus was the beautiful weather.

England were put through their paces by Walter Winterbottom and his staff. Tommy was struggling to get fit and dearly wanted to play against the champions.

Tommy scoring against Brazil at Wembley in May, 1956.

Tommy again goes close against Brazil.

After a vigorous stint of sprints the United goal machine was declared fit.

Hitler's impressive Olympic Stadium was brimming over with 100,000 people, a good half of them British soldiers. It was a dramatic atmosphere and England scored a great victory beating the World champions 3-1 with goals by the scheming genius Johnny Haynes, Grainger and a memorable solo effort from Duncan Edwards.

He broke through to score with a thunderous and unstoppable shot from the edge of the penalty area. After the game the soldiers from the Berlin garrison overwhelmed the players with requests to celebrate with them. Tommy and the United lads had a great time. With the England tour finished the players went their separate ways.

It had been a fairly successful trip with Walter Winterbottom trying hard to form his team for the future. Roger Byrne, big Duncan and Tommy seemed to form the backbone of his planning along with Billy Wright and one or two others.

Nat Lofthouse: "It was a grand tour, we were undefeated and everyone played reasonably well. Don't forget we had just finished a long hard season back home. Tommy was preferred to myself for the centre-forward spot and I had no complaints whatsoever.

"I came on as substitute against Finland when Tommy was injured and was fortunate to score two goals and set up a record. I must be perfectly frank and say that I had the feeling that big Tommy would overtake my record number of goals for England. We had a really wonderful time in Germany, our troops were cheering and yelling like mad.

"Germany were a bloody good team though, so our win over them was a fantastic achievement. How can I ever forget big Duncan's goal? It was like a cannon-ball hitting the net, the Germans were frightened to death of him. Tommy had a smashing match and was unlucky not to get a goal or two."

Blazing the Trail into Europe

The idea of a European Cup competition was first mooted in 1927 when Henri Delaunay, the secretary of the French Football Federation, put a proposal to the executive committee of FIFA.

It all came to nothing because. It was felt that there would be problems due to these additional fixtures. Later, with the advent of improved air travel which would reduce the time element, plus the arrival of floodlighting, the idea was suggested once again when a French sporting magazine, *L'Equipe*, revived the possibility in an article in 1954.

They received an encouraging response. The magazine proposed that the champion league club of each European Football Association should take part in a championship of champions. In April, 1955, representatives of clubs from sixteen nations met in Paris at the invitation of L'Equipe to launch the competition to be played in the 1955–56 season.

It was a wonderful idea and just what was needed, especially for English clubs. After winning the league in the 1956–57 season, Matt Busby was determined to take his young team on to the playing fields of Europe.

There is no secret that the Football League management committee were totally against the English champions playing in any competitions not under their jurisdiction, especially matches against the top European teams small minded thinking by the management committee at that time!

The previous years champions, Chelsea, after originally entering the competition, conceded to the Football League's wishes not to enter this brand new competition. United, however, were going for the unique treble. English football had been shocked to it's very foundations.

It had also been knocked out of its complacency by the Hungarians in 1953, when England were overwhelmed and beaten 6-3 at Wembley and six months later, losing 7-1 in Budapest. We needed a re-think about all aspects of our game. Matt Busby and his staff were revolutionaries. He had seen the need for change years before the Hungarians thrashed the living daylights out of us.

Manchester United were far sighted. The club defied the Football League and duly entered the European Cup in 1956. It was a bold, brave decision which United took, playing a key role in widening the horizons of our football and improving the game in England. They were the pioneers of change, and would go into the record books as the first English club to play in the European Cup.

Tommy Taylor had some of his finest games for the Reds in the European Cup competition. The club and the fans looked forward with anticipation and baited breath to the Wednesday night matches. The city of Manchester took on the role of ambassadors when playing host to our European neighbours on those nights.

The entire British Isles was focussed on the club's experiment. Manchester United's first game in Europe was to be played away against the crack Belgium team, Royal Sporting Club of Anderlecht, who were coached by former Blackburn Rovers' player, Bill Gormlie.

Anderlecht had won the Belgian championship seven times since 1946–47, a record easily qualifying them as their country's outstanding post-war team. There was widespread interest from leading sportswriters and fans throughout Belgium concerning United's game against their champions who were ably captained by Jeff Mermans, who had played in fifty-seven internationals.

The momentous date was 11 September, 1956. There was a crowd of 35,000. The disappointment of losing Duncan Edwards through injury was put aside, Jackie Blanchflower taking the young giant's place and having a "blinder!"

The "Busby Babes" were undefeated in the league coming up to the game against

Anderlecht and seemed on course to retain the Championship, though there was still a long way to go of course. At this early stage of the season Tommy had netted four goals and his partner Viollet was also in sparkling form with seven. On the previous weekend, they had drawn away with Newcastle United, Billy Whelan scoring their only goal.

As the match against Anderlecht got under way United had a fright when Mark Jones gave away a penalty (for handling). Mermans, their international centre-forward and captain, hit a post with the spot kick. Bill Foulkes cleared the rebound and then little Eddie Colman made the goal for electric heeled Viollet to score United's first in Europe. The team were overjoyed and captain Roger Byrne barked instructions to "calm down" and concentrate on not giving away a goal.

Tommy scored the second goal. David Pegg raced down the left wing and on hearing Taylor's shout floated an inch-perfect centre into the goalmouth Tommy's forehead met the cross perfectly and Whoosh, it hit the back of the net. Tommy arms stretched to the heavens was congratulated by his team mates. This goal was a "cushion" to take back to Manchester for the return leg a fortnight later.

Mermans who spoke perfect English stated: "I was most impressed with United's form. I have seldom seen such a wonderfully headed goal as that by Tommy Taylor. How does he manage to jump so high?"

United received a great press for their performance. Not even Arsenal, in their palmiest days, received such high praise. Six sports journalists from Manchester were in the official party along with two from London.

Without exception the reports were very flattering, especially concerning Taylor's jumping feats and all round distribution of the ball.

After the celebrations in their hotel after the match, Busby and Murphy were planning for the following Saturday's game at Old Trafford, against Sheffield Wednesday. The Football League management committee would be looking very carefully for any signs of tiredness or lack of commitment from the Reds. They need not have had any worries on that score.

Berry, Tommy, Viollet and Whelan made sure that the Reds stayed on course for their second Championship with a resounding 4-1 victory in front of over 48,000 fans.

One of the fears of the Football League management committee was that all the travelling to and from these European destinations would have an adverse effect on the United team so that they would not be able to give of their best domestically.

The team's form would suffer, in their opinion, and the League was much more important. But these youngsters answered these short-sighted officials by winning. Bracing themselves for the return leg against Anderlecht to be played at Maine

Road, United beat their neighbours, City at Old Trafford, 2-0, Whelan and Viollet getting the goals. The team were playing attractive and exciting football. They were getting better and better with experience. Every player was fighting to keep his place in the team. There were only three players who could be regarded as almost certain of their places if fit Roger Byrne, an ice-cool captain, Edwards, because of his special talents and Taylor for his goals and his leadership of the United attack. 26 September, 1956, will go down in the record books for ever. It was the Red Devils first ever European cup-tie on home soil.

United's own floodlighting system was not in operation at this time, so they had to play the second leg at Maine Road. There was great speculation in the press and on the radio as to whether the fans would turn out in sufficient numbers for such games. Originally this game was scheduled for an afternoon kick-off at Old Trafford, but it was felt a later kick-off would enable more spectators to see the game. The answer came with the attendance which was 43,635. Busby and his chairman, Harold Hardman, a former England international, were delighted at the large attendance and full of enthusiasm for this new and exciting venture.

There was a strange kind of magic about competing in European competition. A cold, brisk winter's night, sell-out crowds, playing under the new invention of floodlights the atmosphere at fever pitch and with strange foreign names in opposition. Plus, there was money to be made, big money. It rained heavily all day. There were puddles all over the pitch.

But this didn't dampen supporters spirits who were thrilled and excited at the chance to see their team take on the might of Europe. Yes, there was a special kind of buzz in the air on this night with the Beswick Prize Band doing their best to entertain the crowd.

Excitement was high as the teams made their way out to thunderous applause. Anderlecht really believed that they could wipe out the two-goal deficit as the teams got to grips with the sodden conditions.

It was clear United were fired up for this occasion. Duncan Edwards was back for this game, though Blanchflower had played excellently in the first leg. The team were raring to go, none more so than the dark-haired, good-looking left-winger, David Pegg.

After only nine minutes, United scored one of the best executed goals ever seen on any football ground in any part of the world, let alone Europe. Roger Byrne sent a peach of a pass down the wing to Pegg. It was the sort of pass that any forward dreams of receiving. This was Byrne's forte, brilliant quick interceptions then a beautiful pass to one of his forwards.

Down the wing Pegg sped, rounding the full back as if he wasn't there and looking up he saw Tommy running toward the Anderlecht goal. Pegg knew just where the big fellow wanted the ball and obliged! Water sprayed from his boots as Taylor rose head and shoulders above everyone else and a very powerful downward header was dispatched into the corner of the goal, sending raindrops flying from the net. It was a simple, but beautifully worked goal, involving Byrne, Pegg and finished off superbly by Taylor.

The crowd loved every second of this game, especially the majestic style of the entire United team. Every player was a hero in the atrocious conditions, but the football from this young team was simply breathtaking. When the referee blew for half-time everyone apart from the Anderlecht team were disappointed.

They wanted the show to continue even though they were soaking wet through. The Belgians, five down at half-time, through two Taylor goals and a hat-trick from Viollet, faced a hopeless task. The team they were trying to contain were playing superlative football at a blistering pace. United, magnificent all through, might have been forgiven if they had taken their foot off the accelerator and cruised through the reminder of the match, but that was the furthest thing from their minds.

After all, had we not watched the Hungarians show no mercy when thrashing England twice? English football took a hammering from the foreign press after those disasters. Now here was our chance, through the Red Devils, to answer them back. Viollet and Pegg were monopolising the game, and Colman, with his body wriggles and hard running was causing havoc.

Billy Whelan was brilliant and Tommy completed his hat-trick after a muddle in the Anderlecht goalmouth. He got the seventh, then Viollet got his fourth goal from a Byrne move. Little Johnny Berry scored, every player was trying to set-up Pegg to get him on the score sheet. Could they get double figures? The answer came from Whelan and 10-0 was the incredible score.

This Anderlecht team were no little club from Iceland or Malta. Certainly not. Belgium was a very strong football nation. Indeed, as they are today, and Anderlecht were more than worthy champions.

On their previous visit to England, the Belgians had beaten the mighty Arsenal at Highbury. This indicates how good they were. They had also played against the best teams from Hungary and Russia, and never been beaten the way United had defeated them. Take nothing away from the Reds, this was a marvellous team performance.

Mermans, the Anderlecht captain asked: "Why don't they pick this whole team for England? (He did not know that Billy Whelan was Irish) The best teams in Hungary have never beaten us like this. United were awesome. A brilliant all-round team. Why did we lose? The answer is simple; once Tommy Taylor scored that first goal our defenders couldn't believe that any man could jump so high, but once his header went into our net, there was no holding the team.

"The wet ground did not suit us. We have nothing to be ashamed of in being beaten by such a team."

Busby was beaming at Merman's remarks and was even more delighted and proud when the Anderletch captain told the press he had played in many countries against the finest teams and he believed that neither the great Hungarians nor the Russians could teach Busby's boys anything.

Everyone at Old Trafford knew of Busby's admiration of the brilliant skills and teamwork of the Hungarian team. So for the Belgium captain to compare his babes with those world-class stars was the icing on the cake for him. This was a once-in-a-lifetime showpiece. In the match officials changing room, the dapper figure of Welsh referee, Mervyn Griffiths, was exhausted as he peeled off his sweat-soaked shirt.

Mr. Griffiths a Cup Final referee and the man in the middle for dozens of internationals, had shared with Anderletch the exhausting task of keeping up with this super-charged young United team.

Mr. Griffiths: "They couldn't pick an England team to beat this side. I am glad the Football League allowed me to carry on refereeing for another season if only to have seen this game."

Leo Horn, the Dutch official who had refereed the first leg in Belgium, was determined not to miss the return match. He had booked a ticket in the stand-and brought forward by a week a textile business trip to England.

Leo Horn: "Manchester United are the finest side in the world. The whole team was superb. I never expect to see the like again. Individuals? Well Taylor's leaping was out of this world and Pegg! What a winger. But why discus individuals when United won so convincingly by excellent Teamwork."

So Manchester United's determination to go into Europe was fully vindicated. The result, the large crowd, and the goodwill from the foreign press all boded well for English football.

The Football League couldn't have any arguments about United's decision to go against their wishes and enter the competition

The club had given the whole country its pride back and people from all over Britain were now eagerly waiting for their next venture into Europe. A new breed of Manchester United supporter was being formed.

Three days later Busby's youngsters travelled to London to face Arsenal, beating them 2-1 with Berry and Whelan the scorers. This was a vital win for the Reds and once again the performance was magnificent. Busby and his staff were pleased; they, more than anyone, knew that players could not perform brilliantly week in and week out and particularly after what had been for all concerned "a journey into the unknown."

In the next round of the European Cup, (on the 17 October, 1956) and again at Maine Road in front of 75,598 spectators Borussia Dortmund were the opponents. Everyone was looking forward to another soccer showpiece. Bert Trautmann, the

City's German-born goalkeeper, told Matt Busby what he saw of Borussia having seen the championship play-off, in Berlin a few months earlier. In short they played in a style similar to United's.

They were a very experienced side, and a team much older than United so a very interesting struggle was anticipated. Viollet scored two goals in twenty-seven minutes to give the Reds a 2-0 lead, before an own goal made the scoreline 3-0.

The Germans fought back, and claimed two late goals following silly mistakes, giving the youngsters of United a 3-2 victory. In the return leg in Dortmund on 21 November, 1956, in front of a 45,000 sell-out crowd (many of them British soldiers stationed in that area) it was a no-score draw on a frozen solid pitch. United's defence won all the honours and the Germans were slightly unlucky not to score, but Mark Jones had a storming match and kept them at bay. Tommy was out-numbered and fought a lone battle up front, but the visitors were safely into the semi-final and ready to face Atletico Bilbao.

"I'm Santa Claus"

Taking time off from his duties with Manchester United Tommy was selected as a substitute for England's match against Yugoslavia in a friendly at Wembley on a dreary, chilly winter's afternoon. He was not even mentioned in the official programme.

The Yugoslavian's were a good side and had never lost to England. Although substitutes weren't permitted in domestic football, in internationals a replacement (up to the forty-fourth minute) was allowed, though the goalkeeper could be changed at any period of the game. Johnny Haynes, who was having a very influential game, was hurt after thirty-four minutes and replaced by Tommy, who was expected to play centre-forward and inside-left at the same time.

Only Stanley Matthews shone in a boring match which England eventually won 3-0, Brooks of Spurs having given England the lead after twelve minutes. Every member of this England team seemed to be trying to convince the selectors that they should be included in the following Wednesday's World Cup qualifying match against Denmark.

Under difficult conditions, Tommy burst on the scene by getting two brilliantly taken goals, but instead of acclaim, he was rubbished by the press.

Ronnie Clayton: "It was a game full of pressure for all the players. The selectors were watching the game carefully with a view to our match a few days later against Denmark. Tommy took Johnny Haynes place, Tom Finney was centre-forward and Johnny Brooks the other inside forward, with Stan (Matthews) on the right wing and Frank Blunstone on the left. It was obvious that Tommy should move into the middle and lead the attack thus allowing Tom Finney to play inside-forward.

"Tommy scored after about an hour's play, Finney and Brooks set him up. Stan made the second goal for Tommy when he dashed down the wing with the driving sleet in his face, he went straight to the bye-line and as the crowds were making their way to the exits, Stan put over a beautiful centre, Blunstone got to it first and he flicked it on to Tommy who was racing in for anything that fell loose and he smashed the ball into the net. I thought Tommy played well. He had scored twice and adapted himself well when coming on for Haynes."

A few days later, 5 December, 1956, to be exact, at Molineux, Tommy scored a hat-trick while playing for England in a preliminarily round of the World Cup in which England won 5-2. Duncan Edwards was drafted back into the England team at inside-left in place of Blunstone.

Finney moved to the left wing and the United pair, Edwards and Taylor, netted all five England goals in this first tentative step towards the World Cup with final stages to be held in Stockholm. Duncan received praise in every newspaper the following morning. His goals were blockbusters, but Tommy, who had scored five goals for his country in the space of just over a week, was again pilloried by the press.

One well-known reporter, Roy Peskett, wrote: "Now what about Tommy Taylor, the first England player to score a hat-trick since Roy Bentley's three against Wales. There is quite a connection between the two occasions. When Bentley scored his goals I was taken to task by readers for saying: 'That's all he did.' *This was also true of Taylor's effort last night. If he had not scored Taylor would have had a terrible game.* Now his hat-trick will keep him in the running for the next four months until the team is chosen to play Scotland."

"If Tommy Taylor Is England's Best Centre-forward, Then I'm Santa Claus." was the headline to the *Daily Express* article written by Henry Rose the next morning.

People all over the British Isles thought the Henry Rose report was quite funny and laughed while reading the article. But it was a cruel, spiteful piece aimed at a brave and honourable player and totally uncalled for. Outwardly Tommy shrugged his shoulders, smiled when asked for his comments and tried to get on with his career. But United's staff and supporters were incensed and very angry by the verbal assassination of their favourite centre-forward.

John Doherty: "I felt very sorry for Tommy. People forget that players are only human. Criticism hurts them and, more importantly, their families. I was disgusted by what was written about Tommy. People since have said he wasn't hurt or upset by what Henry Rose wrote. How do they know? I have been asked several times if players can hear taunts or abuse from fans while playing. During the heat of a game a player is aware of the shouting and cheering or booing, but he is much too engrossed to take much notice of what individuals might shout, But reading an article in a newspaper is a completely different thing entirely."

Rose apologised to Tommy because of the sackful of mail received at his office. At United's next home game he appeared in the press box wearing a Father Christmas outfit! Matt Busby and Jimmy Murphy let Rose know in no uncertain terms that his article had been uncalled for.

It's a Wonder they ever got their Breath Back

There are many historic games in the history and legend which has built up around United over the years. They are an exceptional club in many respects, but without doubt the quarter final games which they played against Atletico Bilbao, the Spanish Champions from the industrial Basque region, were arguably the greatest games the Busby Babes ever played.

"Travel To Sunny Spain" said the posters in travel agencies all over Manchester in the fifties. This was the start of an adventure in foreign holidays for young people in Great Britain who had been used to the family holiday in Blackpool or Clacton.

When the United players left for their first leg match in Bilbao they were bubbling with excitement, expecting to see sunny beaches and palm tree's littered along the roads and streets, and a bit of sunshine. Nothing could have been further from the truth when their plane finally touched down in Spain.

They had a harrowing flight in an old Dakota, with Jones and Whelan very ill during the journey, and Edwards, never the best of travellers, looking forlorn. The heating on the plane had been accidentally turned off, and the whole party was freezing. Harold Hardman, United's seventy-five-year-old chairman, suffered a mild stroke which resulted in him being rushed to hospital, thus missing the match.

As the plane circled Bilbao through the clouds, the pilot, Captain Riley, had a difficult task in landing on this small airfield. He asked everyone to keep a lookout for the runway not calculated to inspire confidence in the green-looking travellers. Little did they know that the airport had been closed because of the poor conditions.

It was the British assistant consul, who heard the aircraft flying overhead and raced down to the airport and got it re-opened. The plane landed in a freezing blizzard. It was just like Manchester. There had been days of torrential rain and on the drive to their hotel, instead of seeing palm tree's, the team saw nothing but millions of umbrella's being held by the residents.

"It's just like being in Manchester," said a laughing Tommy, looking at the unbelieving faces of the United party. The food in the hotel did not suit the players either and Tommy was ill with stomach trouble after eating some fried rice, but he kept quiet until after the match.

Because of the incessant downpour Busby had doubts that the match would get started, let alone finish. He tried to keep his players spirits lifted and the usual banter prevailed, but they were there to qualify for the semi-finals of the European

Cup. The United boss had watched the Bilbao team play the crack Hungarians Honved, in their second leg-tie in Brussels.

Honved had those masterful inside forwards, Puskas and Kocis, in their line-up. This was about the time of the historic uprising in Hungary when the crack Honved team fled their country and went into exile. The first leg was won by Bilbao in Spain 3-2. Busby always maintained that had Honved been allowed to play Bilbao in their own country, then they would have scored the goals necessary to take them through to the quarter-finals, but in troubled Hungary at that time, there was no time for soccer.

As it was, they only managed a 3-3 draw after a terrific game which saw their 'keeper carried off and left winger Czibor, who was limping badly, took the goalkeeper's jersey. Bilbao played like an English team, something akin to a Wolverhampton Wanderers, quick on the ball and searching for the most direct way to score goals.

They did not play the brand of soccer we in England had come to expect from these Continentals with their "flashy" flicks and tricks. Bilbao had only lost one game on their own ground for over three years.

They had beaten the famous Real Madrid who were the holders of the European trophy, to first place in the Spanish Championship the previous season. They had five current Spanish internationals in their line-up in goalkeeper Carmelo, centre-forward Arirta and the complete half-back line of Mauri, Garay and Maguregui.

For most of the United team it was a case of treading new fields on the Spanish trip. Only Byrne and Edwards had ever played in Spain before, in the England side which drew 1-1 in 1955.

In the San Mames Stadium, Bilbao, the rain had turned into huge snow flakes which were falling like sheets. Inspecting the pitch, the United party were horrified. It looked like a swamp and none of the markings were distinguishable and conditions were vile.

Roger Byrne declared these were the worst conditions he had ever played in. It looked highly doubtful, if played, the game could be finalised. But the match officials declared the pitch playable and both teams set out to entertain the 45,000 spectators, who had braved the elements.

The Spanish champions, in their familiar red and white stripes, showed their class and skill by tearing after United like a dog after a bone, taking a 3-0 half-time lead. The ball was so full of mud and heavy that both 'keepers ceased trying to bounce it. Soaking wet, a dejected United team, in royal blue shirts, trooped into their dressing room. What could anyone say to them?

Busby talked to them in that soothing, calming tone of his, and as he moved away that fiery Welshman, Jimmy Murphy started his "sermon." He was inspiring and uplifting, using his voice and hands. The "preacher" of Old Trafford had the eleven players jumping off the benches only too eager (and seething) to get back on the field to pull back those three goals.

"Remember lads, wear those shirts with pride," were his parting words before they ran back out on to the pitch.

Many soccer pundits say goalscorers hunt in pairs. That certainly applied to Tommy Taylor and Dennis Viollet. When these two were flowing, they were unbeatable! And it was these two who, through the tiresome mud and slush, pulled the game back to 3-2.

The fighting spirit of the entire United team was commendable. A deathly hush fell over the hitherto vocal crowd. Tommy showed his fighting heart and spirit in this game; he never ceased trying.

The snow flakes seemed to get bigger as the weather deteriorated further. The referee gave the Spaniards some mysterious free kicks, but like all great sides Bilbao surged back and due to mistakes and errors in the Reds defence got two further goals.

The amazing thing was that four of those goals were scored from headers which was not the Continental players greatest strength. Tommy who should not have been playing due to his stomach ailment, was charging all over the place in an effort to snatch goals. His tussle with the massive Jesus Garay, at centre-half, was absorbing to say the least.

Tommy was extending the formidable Bilbao pivot to the limit of his powers. These two asked nor received any quarter. United were three goals behind with the minutes ticking away alarmingly.

Busby and Murphy were ashen-faced when Billy Whelan showed just why he was regarded as a world class inside-forward by United followers. With five minutes left the slim Irishman took a pass from Edwards and set off on a run from his own half with the ball never more than inches from his feet and gathering mud as he moved towards the Spanish goalmouth.

Tommy was moving up too, taking defenders with him. "Pass, Pass, Pass" came the shout from the bench and his team-mates. Still Billy ploughed through the clinging, tiring suet of a pitch; he did a pirouette past one player before beating three more Bilbao defenders who had moved after him with bad intentions.

Busby and Murphy nearly had heart failure as Billy resisted parting with the ball. As he got nearer and nearer the Bilbao goal Busby buried his head in his hands as Garay fiercely determined that the Dublin lad would go no further, left off marking Taylor and charged after Whelan.

Everyone thought Billy had overrun the ball, but he hadn't. He was absolutely determined to score and he did, lashing it in the top left-hand corner. It was a phenomenal goal. A goal in a million? Puskas, Di Stefano, Pele, or any other world class forward has never scored a better individual one in snowy Spain on 16 January, 1957.

The United party was delirious. They were now only two goals behind for the second leg in Manchester and they fancied their chances! Bilbao laid on a beautiful banquet after the match at the sumptuous Carlton Hotel. It was a lovely "spread" but it was their genuine friendship which shone through more than anything else.

Soccer was indeed a great ambassador in the world. Without football how would Tommy and his team mates have visited South America, the U.S.A., Denmark, Sweden, Germany, Belgium and Spain and made so many friends? United's problems though were not yet over. The party had to get back to England for their game against Sheffield Wednesday the following day.

The whole of the Basque country was snowbound. The Dakota had been left outside during the blizzard as the hanger at Bilbao airport was full. A ground engineer had flown from England to service the plane. The pilot took one look at the covering of ice and snow and proclaimed flying was out of the question. However, United were determined to get back to England in order to fulfil their League fixture.

In desperation the United officials got the airport staff, players, supporters, and even the press party helping to clear the snow and ice from the wings and fuselage of the frostbound aircraft to enable it to take off. It was a sight to behold watching these famous Busby Babes with brooms and shovels.

Can you picture modern day players doing such tasks? Less than fifty miles out to sea, on their way to Jersey for refuelling and lunch, they were flying in beautiful sunshine. Tommy remarked; "It was a great experience, and one that I shall always remember, The Spanish players were very fair and sportsmanlike. I had a few skirmishes with Garay, their centre-half, but it was all in the heat of the game and we shall be trying like mad in the return game in Manchester."

The Greatest Sporting Performance Of All Time

The return match was at Maine Road on 6 February, 1957, in front of over 65,000 frenzied spectators whose hearts pounded on a night anyone fortunate to have been present will never forget. It was a memorable occasion which had gripped the whole of the British Isles whether they were interested in soccer or not. These young ambassadors from the cotton city had caught the nation's heart strings and even old ladies were asking: "Can They Do It" while out shopping.

Could the young Red Devils wipe out that two-goal deficit? That was the question everyone was asking. One thing was certain and that was no soccer competition had whetted the appetites of the public as much.

Wherever one travelled on the Continent, the European Cup took pride of place in the thoughts of the fans. No team could have been given a greater welcome or such generous hospitality on foreign soil as United received on their three trips to meet the Champions of Belgium, Germany and Spain. United had proudly carried the flag of British football and achieved more to bolster our prestige abroad than could possibly have been the case in any series of foreign friendly matches.

The demand for tickets was overwhelming. United secretary, Walter Crickmer, said that he could have sold between 300,000 and 400,000 tickets. It seemed everybody wanted to be able to say: "I was there." What promised to be an historic night of rousing passion never before witnessed in Manchester or elsewhere.

In an absorbing match at Maine Road on the previous Saturday United had run rampant, beating City 4-2 in front of 63,872 fans. Edwards, Whelan, Viollet and Tommy getting the goals.

Ken Barnes: "What a terrific match this was. We didn't play badly at all, but United were superb. Someone said to me before the game. 'Don't worry Ken, they'll be saving themselves for Bilbao.' He could have fooled me. Tommy scored a goal against us for which no blame could be attached to Bert Trautmann. I forget who crossed it, but from about six yards range he soared up and powered a downward header which was moving like a rocket and appeared to pass through Bert's legs."

Roy Clarke: "It was a pulsating game, and we played exceptionally well. But let's face it this "Busby Babes" side were something else. Yet we matched them all through the ninety minutes. The difference was their forward line-plus big Duncan. He was like a sixth forward. Tommy Taylor had been roaming along the line and doing those decoy runs which he was brilliant at making. Then he appeared out of nowhere as a ball was centred near our penalty spot. I thought 'Oh dear,' and bang! The ball was in the back of our net."

Matt Busby had taken his team away a few days before the European match to their favourite training location, Blackpool, where the players were in good spirits laughing and larking about.

Busby gave his lads a post lunch talk about the importance of the game and then motored from Blackpool to Goodison Park the home of Everton. The reason for his visit was his Youth team had a first round F.A. Youth Cup game against Everton's Youths. This game was nearly as important to the United manager as that against Bilbao that evening. In the Manchester dressing room, the banter was toned down by the players themselves as they changed and readied themselves for what lay ahead.

Tommy was flexing his muscles with a bit of stretching, his eyes giving away his fierce determination. They had beaten their neighbours City, 4-2 the Saturday before and were in whirlwind form. At the first shrill blast of referee Albert Dusch's whistle they launched ferocious attacks on the Spanish Champion's goal.

But these Continentals knew what to expect. They were past masters at putting up the shutters and frustrating teams whose sole intention was to attack. What's more, they had the satisfaction of what they thought was a very secure two goal lead. They showed great defensive calmness and tried to take the pace out of the game. Their manager Ferdinand Dauik, a former Czech international had said: "At the very worst we will have to play-off in Paris. No team can beat us by three clear goals."

Within the match itself, another personal duel developed between Tommy and the giant Bilbao centre-half, Jesus Garay, one of the best of his type in modern times. This tussle alone was spell-binding.

They had of course clashed on the snow covered Bilbao ground and though that was a wonderful contest of skill and sportsmanship, this confrontation under the Maine Road floodlights was bewildering. This was Tommy Taylor at his finest. He loved playing against foreign defenders because he could pit his ability against their technique.

It wasn't just a physical challenge but also a "thinking" one into the bargain. He was hyped up and bouncing around the field. The roar of the crowd could be heard for miles around. The intensity inside the ground was heart-stopping, we were all willing them to get the two goals needed to at least make it a draw.

But the minutes were ticking away faster and faster with little hint of a goal from the Red Devils. The yelling got louder and the nerves tighter. Then it happened. Just before half-time Duncan Edwards surged through the middle leaving opponents in his wake like skittles and he let fly with one of his "specials."

The ball hit Garay, and spun away from him to that ace snatcher of half-chances, Dennis Viollet. He reduced the leeway of two goals and the roar from around the ground split the heavens.

During the interval, Busby spoke calmly, reassuringly to his team, telling them to keep playing the way they had done for the previous forty-five minutes. The crowd became drenched in emotion as the drama unfolded. The players could hear the bedlam coming from the terraces. It was a frenzied and emotional pleading message: "Come On, You Reds!"

The players looked at each other. How could they let such fanatical followers down? There was an extra determination as they stood up to leave the dressing room. On leaving, Jimmy Murphy winked at big Tommy and said: "Come on son. You can do it."

Viollet and Billy Whelan both had the ball in the Bilbao net, but both "goals" were disallowed for offside. Fans, long since at boiling point, bubbled over. They roared their disapproval at the linesman who had flagged. Many were fainting with the tension, Fifty minutes, sixty, seventy-one . . . Tommy hit a post and the groans were heard everywhere, but before the vast crowd had recovered from their agony, the stout-hearted Taylor put his team level with a shot from his much-criticised left foot after a quick Eddie Colman free-kick.

The big centre-forward gave the massive, magnificent Garay the slip; selling the perfect dummy and pivoting like a ballet dancer before racing forward and thundering a totally unstoppable shot into the Bilbao net. The hoard of frenzied supporters were delirious. Thumping each other on the back, shaking hands with complete strangers, crying and laughing at the same time, jumping up and down, yelling and screaming.

John Doherty: "Tommy's left leg was like a jangling of old bones whenever he lifted it and shook it. I think it was due to an earlier injury while in the Army. We used to have a laugh with him about the noise coming from his knee. Yet he scored that all important goal with his dodgy left foot. He took some ribbing about that later from all the lads."

"UNITED . . . UNITED . . . UNITED . . . UNITED!" That was the chant which rang around Maine Road. Eighty minutes, eighty-five . . . Yes, with just five precious minutes left of a totally fascinating game, a replay in a neutral country looked on the cards. But these United lads were inspired. They wanted nothing to do with replays.

The Spaniards were nervous now, their composure gone, when Tommy and Billy Whelan combined once more. Tommy, his black hair streaming in the wind, sprinted out to the right wing with Garay scrambling after him trying to force him out wide.

The "neglected" Johnny Berry moved into the centre-forward position. The atmosphere was electric as big Tom accelerated past the Bilbao player as if he didn't exist, cut inside looking for an angled shot at goal. Berry was screaming for the ball as Tommy paused for a moment, suddenly changed direction and flicked a beautiful pass to the little winger who, without hesitation, smashed the ball into the net.

The heavens erupted. Busby, a man of impeccable social behaviour, jumped from his touch-line seat, grabbed Jimmy Murphy, and both were doing a dance near the pitch. There had been nothing like this before in the history of football in the whole of the British Isles.

Men in the stands were joyously shaking hands with each other and clapping hoping for the final whistle. The United lads were magnificent to a man. But without a shadow of a doubt, this match belonged to Tommy Taylor, he was superb throughout the ninety minutes.

Tommy and United had given Britain its pride back. One might say that there was little in English football the Hungarians, Bilbao, Real Madrid, Barcelona, Brazil or any of the other great foreign teams couldn't better.

In the main one would be right, but in learning the game so fast these great footballing powers forgot one exciting facet of the game or deliberately decided to dispense with it.

In trying to emulate these wonderful Continental teams we had almost forgotten the one thing (or deliberately disregarded it) what made us famous . . . heading . . . the ability to climb high and put the ball in the back of the net. The fact is that while South America and Europe had produced superb ball artists in Di Stefano, Puskas, Didi, Pele and Kopa, they had never had a Dixie Dean, a Tommy Lawton, a Nat Lofthouse or for that matter a Tommy Taylor.

The foreign coaches replied that because they played their football where it should be played on the ground they did not need one.

This perhaps was true, but even the best European wingers and the Brazilian flank men had to cross in the air occasionally and because they never had a Dean, Lawton or Taylor they were missing out on one of football's greatests possibly the greatests of thrills. There is little more exciting than to watch a player rising like a bird or diving full length to rocket the ball into goal with his head as hard and as accurately as most could with their feet. Such men are matchwinners.

They make goals from nothing and throughout the history of the game, have never been in abundance even in Britain. Without any hesitation Tommy Taylor was "King of the Air" in England.

Jimmy Murphy: "Tommy was fantastic. He gave Bilbao plenty to worry about with his long, raking stride and superb heading ability. This was Tommy's match. Although he was a lethal finisher, he was completely unselfish and the way he casually flicked the ball for Berry to score proved this point."

Wilf McGuiness: "Whew, what a game! And what a noise the crowd made. I have never experienced such a night when emotions were so high and clearly visible. Grown men were crying with sheer relief. I think that deep down many thought the lads couldn't pull it off, but this was Tommy's finest night. He was absolutely sensational."

Everyone at Maine Road on an unforgettable night was exhausted and practically speechless after an hour-and-a-half's bewitching, pulsating, stamina-sapping and splendid entertainment. There are people in who said that they could never live through such heart stopping drama again.

It was a wonder that they ever got their breath back. "Greatest Victory In Soccer History" was the headline to Henry Rose's report in the *Daily Express*. "My hands are still trembling as I write. My heart still pounds. And a few hours have passed since, with 65,000 other lucky people. I saw the greatest Soccer victory in history. ninety minutes of tremendous thrills and excitement that will live for ever in the memory.

"Manchester United brought off one of the greatest sporting performances of all time. Take your curtain calls Manchester United. Take an extra one, Tommy Taylor. Santa Claus salutes you, beard and all."

"My heart still beats like a Tom-Tom, as I endeavour to describe the greatest match I ever saw, which was cheered by the greatest crowd I ever heard and starred the greatest centre-forward exhibition I ever saw. It was Tommy Taylor's game and the game of Tommy Taylor's lifetime. But Manchester United, led by the six foot and thirteen stone of fighting fury that was Taylor, just gobbled them up on their way to the semi-finals of the European Cup," wrote George Follows the following day.

On the following Saturday, at home in front of over 60,000 people against Arsenal, where it was felt the Reds would just about muster enough strength, after an exacting week, to contain the "Gunners" this amazing team ran riot.

Winning 6-2 with goals from Berry (2), Whelan (2), Edwards and Tommy, his matchless headwork again was sheer magic. He vied with little "Snake-Hips" Eddie Colman for the man of the match award. What stood out like a beacon was his accurate judgement in heading the ball to colleagues better positioned to cause damage.

Superstitions

In February, 1957, after beating Everton at Goodison in the fifth-round of the F.A. Cup in which Duncan Edwards scored the only goal of an exciting ninety-minutes, United felt mighty relieved as they were taking their bath.

Earlier in the season Everton had thrashed the Babes 5-2. As they bathed there was a knock on their dressing room door. In walked Peter Farrell the Everton captain to say: "Thanks, lads, for a good clean fight. Best of luck on the way to Wembley."

Many sceptics had wondered about the United team's stamina and physical strength in standing up to their triple bid for honours, but captain Roger Byrne told everyone all the players owed it to themselves and the team as a whole to keep in peak condition all the time. He admitted that from a mental viewpoint, the strain was indeed being felt by all concerned. Asked about personal superstitions, match "gimmicks," and lucky omens. The deep thinking skipper admitted his colleagues were near the top of the list in that respect.

The week previous, Busby's free-scoring team had beaten Charlton Athletic 5-1 with Tommy getting two goals while nineteen-year-old Bobby Charlton had four good reasons to remember his first League appearance in London.

Three of them, of course, were provided by his brilliant hat-trick, and the other because young Bobby did the trick in a pair of borrowed football boots!

By some oversight Bobby's boots were left behind on the trip down to the Valley, Charlton's ground, so he used a spare pair of Byrne's boots.

At the beginning of the season Byrne went on record stating that the Champions were not only aiming to retain the League title, but were setting their sights on the F.A. and European Cup targets too.

Roger Byrne: "Last year, for instance, I wore the same suit before every home match. The longer our run without defeat the more I became convinced that the suit was bringing us luck. But the spell was broken when we lost to Everton last October, after twenty-six games without defeat. The suit was immediately cast-off!

"In international matches I always try to go out last carrying a ball. I have done it in every appearance at Wembley and so far I have not been on the losing side there yet. Ray Wood perhaps has the funniest superstition. He always follows Mark Jones on to the pitch. He says if he follows a forward the player carrying the same number in the opposing team invariably scores. That is why we all pull Mark Jones's leg and say it is the reason he has occasionally scored an 'own goal' for the opposing team!

"Tommy Taylor, who is having such a brilliant season at centre-forward, credits his success to the fact that he has dispensed with wearing shinguards. For a centre-forward in League soccer to do that is quite an achievement, but Tommy says he feels less hampered and he is certainly more mobile than ever. We have all tried to dispense with these little 'idiosyncrasies' at some time or another, but they are all part of a footballer's make-up."

With the second successive Championship virtually sealed, the United team was progressing well on all three fronts. Reaching the quarter-final of the F.A. Cup against Bournemouth, they also had their European Cup semi-final game against Real Madrid coming up.

But once again tragedy struck. Tommy unfortunately suffered another troublesome injury which was to spoil his otherwise perfect season. On 18 February, playing against Charlton, Tommy was hurt badly after a heavy tackle. He had to leave the pitch to receive treatment to his shin bone, but returned to score twice. He played in the following match against Blackpool, but was not really fit.

A few minutes after a burst of running, Tommy began to feel the effects of the previous week's injury and moved out to the right wing. At half-time he received further medical attention, but returned at outside right. Back in Manchester it was revealed Tommy was suffering from a cracked shin bone, a particularly painful and irksome injury. The pain stretched from his knee down to his ankle. He obviously missed both the games against Bournemouth, and the semi-final against Birmingham played at Hillsborough, and the following five League games. It was a frantic race against time to try and get Tommy fit again.

On 6 April, at home to Tottenham, he returned and adjusted fairly well in the 0-0 draw. The following week at Luton, he got back on the score sheet, Freddie Goodwin received a pass from Edwards and instantly lobbed the ball over Kelly's head, for Tommy, who was unmarked, to breast the ball down and blast it into the back of the net. Fouled out on the right wing, Tommy brushed himself down, signalled to the worried looking bench that he was alright, and moved into the middle. Johnny Berry ran over and took the free kick and with an orthodox centre floated a great ball into the goalmouth.

Tommy with plenty of space in which to run and leap, selected the corner and smashed the ball wide of Bayham's left hand and as he was falling to the ground watched his header nestling in the corner of the goal, but United looked tired in this game.

Matt Busby was worried. He knew Tommy was a most important player for his all star team. He pondered on what he should do if he had to replace the gifted Taylor. He could move Duncan Edwards to centre-forward or put Colin Webster in the number nine jersey, but wanted to keep the shape of the team intact. He conferred with Jimmy Murphy and decided to use one of his brilliant youngsters from the Youth team.

But before anything was done on that problem, more important matters lay ahead. In the shape of Real Madrid!

Murder in Madrid

Jimmy Murphy said on many occasions, that Taylor played some of his best ever games in the European Cup. These games brought out the "it's us against them situation." The vast throngs who witnessed those Wednesday night matches were always full of anticipation and excitement.

Because the games were two-legged affairs different tactics had to be adopted. For instance, the home team had to try to score as many goals as possible in order to give them a "cushion" for the away game. This meant that the visiting team would undoubtedly put up the shutters and defend to the last man.

And who was better at defending than these Continental teams? It was sheer hard graft for a spearhead, especially in the away matches. Bravery was the number one priority. None were better equipped or more courageous than Tommy Taylor. English defenders are tough, but the sly, devious tricks some of the Europeans used were cynical, calculating and highly dangerous.

It was very rare for Tommy to lose his temper, but when he did he would take retribution in his own way, quietly and usually without prior warning. There would be no demonstration, or appealing to the referee for protection. He would become the "Silent Executioner".

Ian Greaves: "We all knew Tommy could look after himself. We had heard that he had been a boxer. I don't know whether that was true or not but defenders would only be allowed to go so far with their foul tactics against him. Then he would let them know in his own way that they couldn't take liberties. He was a very placid type of fellow. It took a great deal to get him angry, but boy, when he did, look-out! He was as hard as nails."

Manchester United's young team came of age when they faced the mighty and marvellous, Real Madrid in the 130,000 capacity wonder ground called the Bernabeu Stadium, in Madrid on 11 April, 1957. Looking at the size of this stadium for the first time took one's breath away. It was a truly magnificent setting a home fit for kings. This Spanish team were brilliant, and each player outstanding in their own particular position.

They beat the majority of other teams with exceptional team work and individual skills. Against United's young team they showed an ugly and cynical side which brought a great deal of criticism.

Tom Jackson of the *Manchester Evening News*, had visited the Madrid training camp just before their previous game in Nice, set in glorious country in the picturesque hills. Di Stefano and Frenchman Raymond Kopa, both told Jackson how much they were looking forward to playing against United and mentioned Tommy Taylor specifically.

Matt Busby also watched Real play the French Champions, Nice, in the previous round and was overwhelming in his praise and admiration for a team which gave the French Champions a 6-2 drubbing. He was in raptures about one player, Alfredo Di Stefano, Madrid's Argentine-born deep-lying centre-forward.

When briefing his players on the exceptional virtues of the Spanish champions, Busby could hardly contain himself. He was so enthusiastic it was almost unbelievable, but United's players did not believe a team existed that was clearly their superior.

Tommy was still recovering from his shin bone injury and it was a race against time to get the big fellow fit and sharp for this vital European semi-final.

A few days before leaving for Spain, Tommy was given a run out in the mid-week Central League game against Derby at the Baseball ground. The pitch was icy and rock hard. It was Tommy's first full game since the injury and Matt Busby and his first and second lieutenants, Jimmy Murphy and Bert Whalley, scrutinised his performance. They were well pleased after watching their man hit a power-packed hat-trick, and Tommy gave them the thumbs-up sign. His goalpartner, Dennis Viollet, who had been under an injury cloud throughout the season due to groin trouble and missed quite a few games, was also included in the game against Derby Reserves, and scored a brace of goals.

Murphy winced within the first fifteen seconds of the kick-off as Tommy went into a charge-cum-tackle with Derby's heavyweight centre-half Mike Smith. But United's centre-forward came out of the challenge with an A1 ticket. He was alright. Tommy beat the Derby 'keeper Colin Moorhen by sending him the wrong way for his first goal. Then roaming out to the wings and back in his own half, using a burst of speed, a pause, a quick change of direction, little delicate flicks, Tommy was like a foal trying out its legs for the first time. He had not attempted any jumping on such a bone-hard surface, but just when the Derby defence heaved a sigh of relief at the prospect of not going up with him for the high centres . . . Bang! He scored with two headers!

Steve Richards, a sports writer, attended the floodlit match at Derby and after watching Tommy score his superb goals, declared: "After watching Taylor come out of that heart-tilting rush in the opening seconds in his first game since chipping a leg bone in February, he convinced me fifty yards away in the stands that

Manchester United will win the dream double and can now play Real Madrid the best way they know how . . . The Taylor way."

Matt Busby: "I was very pleased with Tommy. We have got to wait in case there is any reaction to his injury, but so far so good. I am hoping he will be alright, but at week-end we play Spurs and right now I cannot say definitely whether he will play. Dennis Viollet also came through the game alright, and he should be ready for the weekend."

To say the United boss was happy at his two ace marksmen's performances was putting it mildly. He was absolutely glowing, because with a fit, sharp Taylor and Viollet in his team he knew no cause was lost. He badly needed both of them for the important matches coming up. Tommy and Dennis were rated two of the deadliest scoring forwards in the First Division and a very important cog in Manchester United's engine. With these two fit and sharp, no cause was lost.

Tommy Taylor: "I could not have picked a worse pitch for my first match or should I say better pitch? It was bone hard and looked risky, but I realise now that it gave me a thorough test. I'm thrilled about the goals and felt great chasing around again. After spending the next few days resting I should be perfect for the weekend."

Tommy did indeed play against Tottenham. Though rusty and missing a few chances he was delighted to be back in action once more. He knew that there was a vast difference from the Central League to First Division football.

United were overjoyed that he was back in action. He gave the whole team added spark. And they knew that with the big fellow in their starting line-up against Real anything was possible. The staff were happy as they set off for Madrid wearing their trilby hats and gaberdine raincoats. These European excursions were a relief from the at times tedious League programme. It gave players and staff a change of scenery and a chance to compare the two soccer systems. The players were all friendly with each other, in fact one journalist likened them more to a youth club than a First Division club.

Wilf McGuinness: "I was taken along on this trip, though I wasn't going to play. We flew on a BEA Elizabethan. I think it was called the Sir Thomas Gresham. Flying in the 1950s wasn't like it is today, where you just get on the plane and fly direct to your destination. In those times the aircraft would have to stop say in Jersey and refuel before travelling on to its destination, but it was a great adventure for me. Tommy and the lads were always having a laugh. Tommy had only had a couple of games prior to this important semi-final with Madrid. I don't honestly think he was 100 per cent fit. Yet he never complained about anything."

Come on, Referee, be Fair

For nearly an hour of the match against Real, it seemed the young United side were right to think that they were the equal of team in the world. Real might have been a goal down at half-time, because Taylor missed the best chance of the match, but Madrid showed their true potential after the interval.

Gento, the stocky, flying speed merchant on the left wing produced a centre for Rial to head into United's net from close range and then the great Di Stefano scored after showing some brilliant touches. This man showed why he was the idol of the Latin and the paragon of Continental footballers. His ball control was sleek and furtive, and the sudden, darting acceleration from a standing start was a sight to behold. There was no doubting this fellow's artistry or class. His little side-steps and dummies along with his other tricks were exquisite. He was an artist.

Real raised their game and the spectators were making a waterfall of noise from the towering stands. United's players had never heard such noise, not even at Old Trafford. It was the kind of experience which most of this young team had never tasted. United responded with renewed vigour and pressure. It was here that Tommy's qualities came to the fore like a beacon on a foggy night. He fought for any little chance which came his way, he was driving himself on and on. He just would not be thwarted by the downright viciousness of Madrid's malicious and disgraceful fouling tactics.

Tommy was having a hectic battle with the whole Spanish defence and pulled a goal back with a scrambled header to give his team some sort of hope.

It looked like United might snatch a moral victory from this disaster until Gento and Rial combined for Mateos to score. The Babes believed that the tie could be retrieved again at home as they had done against Bilbao.

Unless the forwards could play better than they did in Madrid then they could wave good-bye to their hopes of winning the triple crown seemed to be the overwhelming consensus of opinion from all the newspapers and football critics. Though forwards such as Viollet and Whelan were brilliant individual players, they were certainly not the robust or challenging type of inside-forwards. In this red-hot, hostile kind of environment they struggled.

United lost 3-1 in the European Cup semi-final first leg. "Let me say right now that I doubt if United's attack will ever play so badly again. The real trouble was that the forwards stood still instead of going in and challenging for the ball. They were too slow running into open spaces and Tommy Taylor was left without any assistance from either Viollet or Whelan. It was not until the last fifteen minutes, in fact, that the United attack functioned," wrote Alf Clarke, of the *Manchester Evening Chronicle*.

"The lion-hearted Taylor hit the crossbar with a typical rasping header, but never has the Barnsley lad stuck to a bitter task with finer courage. He was kicked, pummelled, elbowed, shoved, held by the shirt, and generally man-handled in a way completely foreign to English notion. If this sort of stuff is repeated at Old Trafford and the referee has described this as a "friendly game" remember then

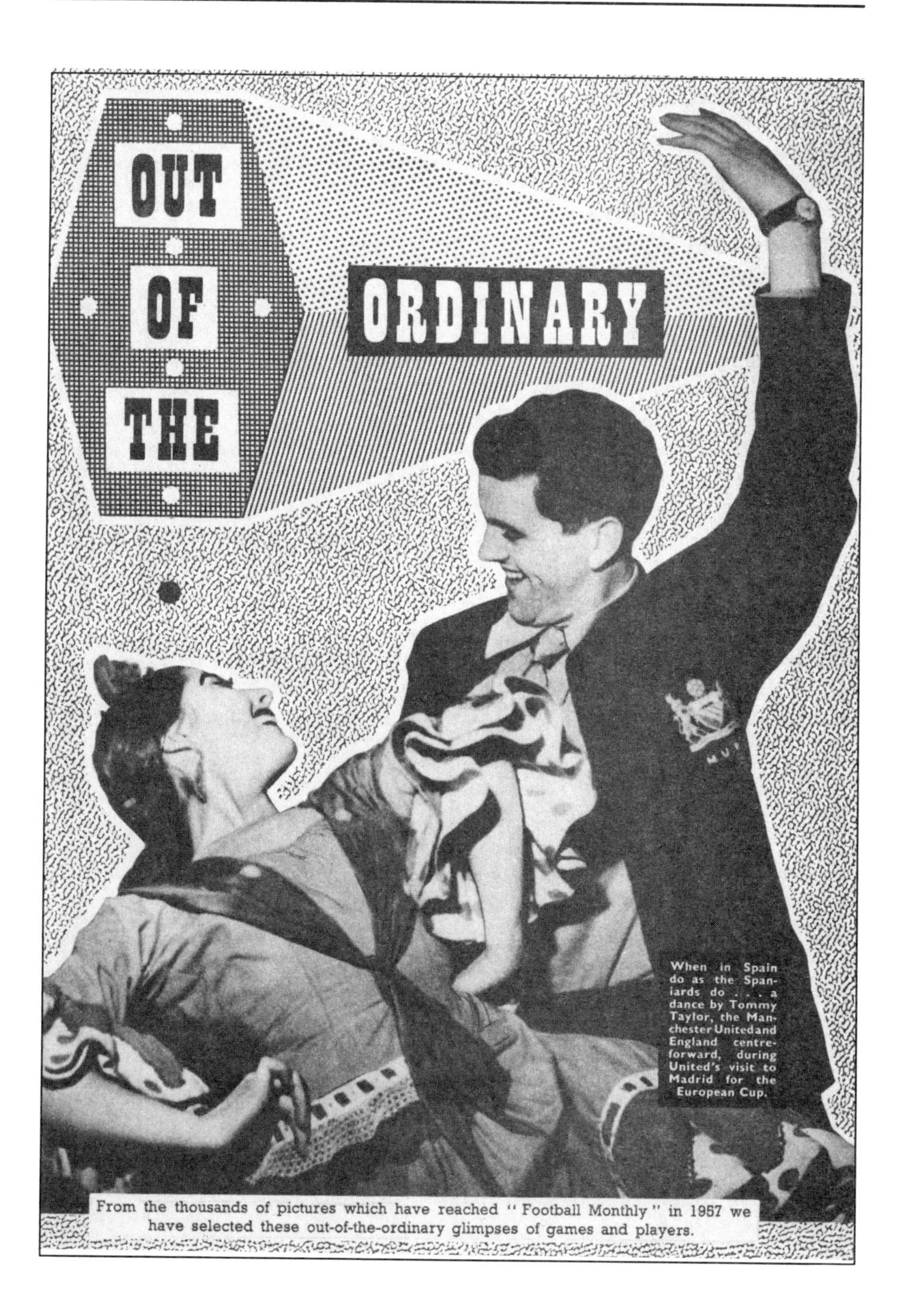

When in Spain do as the Spaniards do . . . a dance by Tommy Taylor, the Manchester United and England centre-forward, during United's visit to Madrid for the European Cup.

From the thousands of pictures which have reached "Football Monthly" in 1957 we have selected these out-of-the-ordinary glimpses of games and players.

the spectators may prepare themselves for something novel in the way of friendly football," said Old International in *The Guardian.*

George Follows, a reporter for the *Daily Herald* had never seen such blatant behaviour on the football field. "Centre-half Marcos "Marquitos" Alonso, justified his reputation as the champion clogger of Spain. He slashed Tommy Taylor off at the stocking tops. He nudged, jostled or obstructed him at every opportunity. Real Madrid got away with murder.

"They hacked, slashed, kicked and wrestled their way to victory. Some of their forward play was fascinating, but their defenders committed nearly every crime in the football calendar to extract the venom from the Red Devil's attack. Referee Leo Horn, from Holland, weakly allowed the Soccer skulduggery to continue to the truly bitter end."

Wilf McGuinness: "The lads were terrific. They played their hearts out. But this Real Madrid side were the tops. Tommy took unmerciful stick from big Marquitos, but fought for the ball like a terrier."

It was said by the national press that Real Madrid got away with fouling on every occasion where there was the slightest sign of danger to their goal. They committed acts of violence which should never have been permitted. No player came in for more punishment than the brave-hearted Taylor, who for most of the game battled single-handed with the ruthless Real rearguard. After the game, the United party sat down to dinner with the players and officials of Madrid, in one of the leading hotels in the city. Each member of the British party received a watch.

Don Santiago Bernabeu, the Real Madrid president, raised his glass and toasted them and said: "English footballers have always been masters in this sport, and Spaniards are their best pupils."

Jose Villalonga, the tall fair-haired Spanish manager said: "It was a great game and the tension never let up. Manchester United fully demonstrated that their fame is well deserved. Your Tommy Taylor and your outside right, Berry, are in my opinion the best and most dangerous men in the English team."

Marquitos: "I felt very worried before the game started, but now I think I was able to neutralise Tommy Taylor's activity. He was moving around a lot and was excellent when the ball was in the air. But I felt I got the better of 'our' match."

When these comments from the giant centre-half were translated into English, the United players all smiled and looked directly at Tommy, who smiled and looked straight at Marquitos, winking at the Spanish tough guy, and grinned. His time would come . . . back in Manchester! There was a bullying sadistic quality about Marquitos.

This was the perception people had of him, and he never mellowed until he came to Old Trafford. There was surely no way he could get away with his aggressive play when he came to Manchester. If the referee didn't see to it, then Tommy certainly would. Sports writers in the Madrid newspapers described the match as a truly magnificent game, but failed to make any mention of the roughness and alleged foul tactics which marred the game for the English reporters.

Nor was there the slightest criticism of the match officials who had allowed the Madrid team to get away with unfair tactics.

Alf Clarke: "I was very disappointed in the refereeing of Leo Horn, of Holland. He was very much a "homer" and he should have awarded United a penalty when Berry was brought down. He should also have been more severe with Di Stefano when he deliberately kicked at Blanchflower of all people. Taylor, too, was pushed, shoved and elbowed time and time again."

Roger Byrne: "Real are a good team. We never played really as a side until we were two goals down. I still feel, as I did with the Bilbao return match, that we have a chance of turning the deficit into success."

Tommy Taylor: "I expect to come in for some tough treatment, but this was way over the top. The first time Marquitos kicked me he caught me right on the spot which I damaged six weeks ago. I was surprised I walked off the field after this . . . I thought I was going to be carried off."

After the official reception, the players headed for the night spots. Tommy and David Pegg and a few more of the players visited a few bars and downed a few drinks in order to relax after such a torrid game. The local Senoritas were more friendly towards the handsome Taylor than the Spanish defenders had been earlier!

Jackie Blanchflower recalled later: "Tommy frightened their defence. He was getting up to everything which was crossed in the air.

"Their defence wouldn't get away with the kind of treatment they handed out to Tommy that day. It wasn't just one of them. It was three or four, grabbing his shoulders, pushing and holding him around the waist. He got his goal through pure persistence. This goal gave us a chance. Di Stefano was something extra special, a completely different type of centre-forward to Tommy. He flowed through the game, dropping back in his own half to pick up the ball then dispatching it exactly where he wanted it to go. Yes, he was class. Mind you, he committed a foul on me which should have seen him sent off.

"But I will never forget the way Tommy kept on trying to score and create openings when everything seemed against him on that particular day. They talk about lion-hearted fighters, my God Tommy had guts. He would just pick himself up whenever he was brought down. He never complained to the referee, but just got on with the game. Those defenders would put the frighteners up 99 percent of opposing forwards, Tommy was that one fellow who they couldn't intimidate no matter what foul tactics they used. The amazing thing was they were so skilful that they didn't need to do these cynical deeds. They were all comfortable on the ball and could play themselves out of trouble."

Dennis Viollet: "I remember the game well. Matt was in raptures over what a great, great team they were. This was, of course, before we played them. He had been over to France to watch these Spaniards. He was so excited about the likes of Di Stefano, Gento, and in fact the whole team that he could hardly contain himself.

"We respected his views obviously, but our lads fancied our chances against most teams, not in a big-headed manner mind you. They were indeed a wonderful side and on a par with the great Hungarian team which thrashed England twice. They had individual skills, great world class players, but as a team, they were one unit. Brilliant! But those defenders, oh, they were something else. If ever people wanted to know about how brave Tommy was, I would refer them to this particular game, because he took unmerciful punishment from the Madrid defence.

"I always admired Tom's bravery and whole-heartedness. But in this match he should have been awarded a red badge for courage and tenacity. The Spaniards realised early in the game that he was a threat in the air. It was like watching a mugging when Tom made his runs to get up for the high balls. There were three or four of them surrounding him, and they were not saying hello I assure you. I feared for his safety."

The United party flew back to England and went straight to Luton for their game against the "Hatters." Would United be battle weary after their physically torrid tussle in Spain seemed to be the question on every reporters lips? Tommy gave the perfect answer . . . Two brilliant goals. United remained undefeated in the League for the remainder of the season. Tommy starred in a 4-0 victory over Sunderland, getting an eighty-ninth-minute goal after Billy Whelan got a brace and Duncan Edwards a third.

This victory secured the League Championship for United. Tommy was suffering the impact of so many games over the past few weeks, but Busby needed him desperately five days later, because this was the return game against Real Madrid.

This match was the first European Cup game played at Old Trafford. The new floodlighting system had been installed. The United lads rolled up their sleeves and got down to the task of trying to salvage this game. They were hoping to do a Bilbao on Real, but this was almost impossible.

The Spanish soccer masters cruised to a 2-0 lead with goals from the French international forward, Raymond Kopa, another brilliant ball player who also was an outstanding goalscorer and a player of great vision. Byrne had kept him fairly subdued in Madrid, but because of United's all out attacking, Kopa had more freedom.

And that man Di Stefeno again scored making the Red Devil's task hopeless at 5-1 down on aggregate. If the volume of noise could have pulled United through then they would have been home and dry. Unfortunately, Real were much too wise and experienced for the young "Busby Babes". In the second half United, inspired by Tommy Taylor's gritty swashbuckling performance equalled the score in this game to 2-2 with goals from Tommy and a fresh-faced teenager, Bobby Charlton, who had replaced the injured Dennis Viollet.

Tommy had a torrid and absorbing tussle once again with Marquintos the Real centre-half with the shoulders of ox and the roughness of Rocky Marciano. With the tempers of both the crowd, and players red hot after continued malicious tackles on Tommy by this giant, the referee was very lenient toward Madrid.

The Barnsley man then decided it was time to take some kind of retribution. As the United centre-forward and his opponent, went up for a high centre, Tommy got that touch higher, flicking the ball on to a team-mate. As play proceeded, the giant Spanish defender was lying prone on the muddy pitch. Nobody was aware of what had happened to the dark eyed hulk of a man laying prostrate on the pitch.

John Doherty: "Tommy wasn't frightened of anyone, I'm not just saying that in a blase fashion, because he wasn't. No defender could put the frighteners on Tommy. Plenty tried, I can assure you, but usually they came off second best. I remember him saying during some games: 'Have a breather. I'll pull them all over the place'. What he meant was that he would get the defenders looking for him by constantly switching positions."

United's young kids stretched every bone and sinew in their young bodies to perform as they had done against Bilbao, but as Jimmy Murphy said: "It was a world-class, experienced side packed with internationals, against a young, up and coming world-class team. Our kids did us proud. We will learn from playing against these of teams. And our lads will reap the benefit."

An interesting little story to relate about the great Di Stefano. A couple of days before the match against United, Alfredo was walking in Manchester city centre and thirteen-year-old John Donohue, on his way home from school, spotted the great player from the bus window. With extreme haste young Master Donohue jumped from the bus and chased after the Real Madrid man.

Upon reaching his idol, John produced his school homework book politely requesting the Argentinian to sign his autograph. In an amazing fit of Latin temperament, Alfredo threw the book to the pavement in full view of onlookers.

This act of petulance brought forth scorn from the press. John was heartbroken and bitterly upset at Di Stefano's reaction.

After scores of complaints, a Real official through the newspapers, asked for the schoolboy to visit the Midland Hotel where the team was staying. Along went John and Alfredo shook his hand and said: "Please forgive me, John," he said in broken English.

"Please be my guest at Old Trafford for the match against United. John said: "He's a good fellow, but I don't think United need to worry to much." The thirteen-year-old John Donohue, now into his fifties, has done a great deal of research for this book.

The Black Prince of Old Trafford

About this time, Matt Busby was talking about how he firmly believed United were better equipped than most for further glory and honours. He cited his current Youth team who would win the F.A. Youth Cup for the fifth successive year. The future looked very promising indeed.

Soccer's searching spotlight had been turned full glare on United's first team this season. Their bid for the game's major honours on the home front and their tremendous tussles in the wider field of the European Cup had really captured the imagination.

But there was another aspect of the club's activities which had provided a great deal of encouragement and satisfaction over the recent months and this was the splendid successes of United's reserve team which had shot up the Central League table so rapidly over recent weeks that a repeat of the previous season's Championship achievement was now within their grasp. Busby mentioned six young hopefuls who he maintained would, with normal development, become better players and help United in the not to distant future.

One of the players mentioned by Busby was starring in the United Youth team at this time. A crashing, bashing, bull-necked, old-fashioned type of battering ram centre-forward who had a penchant for finding the net. A diamond in the rough, a Scot who had attended the same school in Aberdeen as Denis Law, but who had represented England as a schoolboy, because his father, a trawlerman, had moved the family down to Hull, while the lad was just eleven years old.

Alex Dawson became known as the Black Prince of Old Trafford, and a bright future was forecast for this tank of a lad.

Dawson joined United's groundstaff in 1956 and a year later he signed professional forms with his beloved club. There were plenty of classy forwards on the clubs books in those days, players who, perhaps, were more gifted than big Alex.

But none were more committed to getting goals than this swarthy dark-haired all-action fellow. He was one of the most exciting and fearless youngsters in football. As a sixteen-year-old, Alex was netting a hatful of goals against tough, hard-bitten experienced opponents in the Central League.

Alex was a mere fourteen years old when a former Liverpool playing colleague of Busby's, Eric Patterson, who had settled in Hull, 'phoned and recommended that he took a look at Dawson, saying: "He looks a natural to me."

The United staff kept Alex under constant observation, these being the days when League clubs could not approach boys until they left school. The reports Busby got from his staff were very impressive.

Jimmy Murphy was sent to watch Alex play for Hull schoolboys against Barnsley Boys. Alex was playing on the right wing, but getting up tremendously high for any centres or high balls from the left flank.

After just twenty minutes, Murphy said to Bert Whalley who had accompanied him on his mission: "Come on Bert, let's go I've seen enough." Alex Dawson was considered Manchester United material. It was Murphy, of course, who first recommended Tommy Taylor to Matt Busby.

Matt Busby commented: "Many United supporters have already seen many of our younger players. Lads such Alex Dawson, who has a footballing brain and physique far beyond what is expected from one so young. Alex, is one of United's jewels, and I'm sure a future international."

Alex Dawson said: "I loved every minute of my time at United. When I joined them there was an air of optimism about the whole place. It was vibrant. The first team had just won the Championship and the other teams at the club were all successful.

I was a right-winger when I first played in the colts and the A and B teams. Tommy Taylor was my idol. What a graceful forward. One game in the A team sticks in my mind. Kenny Morgans was playing centre-forward, and he got injured. I was on the wing when Bert Whalley told me to move to centre-forward. I got a hat-trick and after the game Bert turned to me and said: 'Alex, you're a centre-forward from now on.' Though I admired and respected Tommy as a player and a person, my style of play was more in the style of Nat Lofthouse.

"In April, 1957, the club were going strong for three trophies. The first team was a settled side and Bobby Charlton and Albert Scanlon and a few others were considered for first-team duty before the likes of myself, though, the boss did blood several of us younger players from time to time.

"On this particular day I was lapping Old Trafford when big Duncan Edwards fell in beside me and said: 'Alex, I think you'll be playing against Burnley.' I thought he was pulling my leg until he said: 'Tommy is injured and I think the boss is going to select you to take his place.' Well, I was floating on a cushion of air from there on.

"I ran that little bit faster, jumped a fraction higher, and my practice shooting was so much harder. Nothing happened. The boss never said anything to me about playing in the first team. In fact, I went home to Hull for the Easter break.

On Easter Monday morning I caught the train back to Manchester. As I walked from the train, Bert Whalley was waiting on the platform. 'Hurry up Alec, the boss is having a team talk, you're playing in the first eleven this afternoon.'

"I felt ten-feet tall. When I ran out at Old Trafford to face Burnley there were forty-odd thousand spectators in the ground. All the lads were offering me encouragement. No, I wasn't nervous or frightened. How could I be when the likes of Duncan and Roger Byrne were behind me. I scored on my debut, and we won 2-0. Colin Webster got the other goal.

"Later in the week after making my debut, I bumped into Tommy as he was going in for treatment on his injured shin bone. He smiled, and told me how pleased he was that I had scored and told me to keep up the good work.

"He really was a great man; he always seemed to have a smile on his face. Nothing ever seemed to bother him.

"I played in the last two games of the season and got a goal in each one and we won the League Championship again. Yes I was pleased with my performance, but like I said, playing in that team was easy because of the type of world-class players we had in every position. In practice Johnny Berry and David Pegg would swing those high crosses or corners over, and I got on the end of them. Bert Whalley helped me a great deal in my early years at the club. I had studied Tommy making that little run of his to meet the centres and used it in my game.

"But I could always get up high, even as a schoolboy, though I must admit that having watched Tommy in action he made it look so graceful. He was always pulling my leg. One day we were lapping the Old Trafford pitch, he caught up with me and said: 'If you give me your wages, I'll step down and let you take my place. I think they were playing Shamrock Rovers in the European Cup. He was joking of course. Tommy Taylor was the best centre-forward I ever saw."

"Double Tragedy"

After the Real Madrid game, Busby and his staff and players analysed their position. The dream of the treble was of course now finished, but the whole club set their sights on the double, a feat no other club had managed to achieve in modern times. It was last achieved by Aston Villa sixty years earlier in 1897.

Their second League Championship had been secured five days before they faced Real Madrid. This was the game when they beat Sunderland at Old Trafford 4-0. The points total of sixty-four was the best in the First Division since 1931 when Arsenal managed sixty-six.

The Barnsley lad had to miss the final three games of the season in an all-out effort to be fit and ready to face Aston Villa at Wembley in the F.A. Cup Final on 5 May, 1957. Sat in the lounge of the Hendon Hall Hotel, United's headquarters before the Cup Final, Tommy was thinking how fortunate he was to be selected, having had a race against time to prove his fitness after suffering a nasty injury.

No player wants to miss a Cup Final, and Tommy was no exception. Appearing at Wembley was every players dream for the League was one hard slog through the autumn and then the muddy and icy conditions of winter.

But the F.A. Cup with all its glitter and razzmatazz, splendour, pomp and ceremony with Royalty present was what all youngsters, older players and veterans alike hoped and prayed for. Tommy Lawton, that great centre-forward, cherished an F.A. Cup Final appearance. It was one of his biggest regrets never to play in a final.

United had trained at their usual training headquarters in Blackpool staying at the Norbrek Hydro. They had been filmed on the beach by the BBC in their new white strip with red edges, and they looked very smart. It was a good atmosphere with everyone doing their stint briskly. They were like a well oiled machine by now.

The whole of Manchester was Cup Crazy. Electrical shops did a booming business selling television sets for the forthcoming Cup Final. Streets had buntings hung across them, pubs and clubs had mementoes on their bars, and festivities arranged for after the game. Dustbin vehicles had cardboard cut-out F.A. Cup's on the front of their radiators as did hundreds other vans and lorry's. Rosettes were in shop windows along with slogans imploring the Red Devils to victory over Villa.

It was like one big festival of enjoyment. Unlucky Dennis Viollet was declared unfit to play due to niggling groin trouble. Dennis had striven in vain to recover his form and sharpness; he had not scored since 6 February.

The nineteen-year-old, rocket-shooting soldier-boy Bobby Charlton, took Viollet's place at inside-left. (Viollet failed a fitness test just twenty-four hours before the match). Bobby, during this period, was famous for the number of goals he scored and the sensational manner in which he scored them. He was two-footed, moved like greased lightning and yet was only a reserve player in this galaxy of a world class playing staff.

The teams were: United: Wood, Foulkes, Byrne, Colman, Blanchflower, Edwards, Berry, Whelan, Taylor, Charlton, Pegg;

Aston Villa: Sims, Lynn, Aldis, Crowther, Dugdale, Saward, Smith, Sewell, Myerscough, Dixon, McParland.

Without any bitterness whatsoever, United were robbed of the chance of completing the double when, after barely six minutes of play, Peter McParland, the Villa dangerman, headed the ball into the United 'keeper's hands. There was absolutely no danger.

Ray Wood was looking who he could kick the ball to when the Villa player, strong and robust threw himself at the United 'keeper. There was a fearful crack and the United man ended up with a smashed cheek bone and double vision. Wood had to be carried off.

This act by McParland made a complete mockery of this Cup Final. Charlton was ready to go in goal where he often performed during kick-abouts, but Roger Byrne signalled the versatile Jackie Blanchflower to take Wood's jersey and he played magnificently. Edwards had to take over at centre-half with Billy Whelan dropping back to take Duncan's place in the half-back line. Substitutes were not allowed in those days.

It seemed a travesty of justice when McParland scored both the goals to put Aston Villa 2-0 in front. The Villa forward emphasised why he was one of the best matchwinners in football, but nothing would convince the United team, along with millions of people watching, that his charge on Ray Wood was not a foul!

In the dying minutes the valiant Red Devils, playing in their white jerseys with red edging and with poise and class, the ten men hit back with everything they could muster, and forced a succession of corners. From one on the left, and with barely ten minutes remaining, Duncan Edwards brushed everyone aside and took the kick himself.

It was driven like a cannon ball into the Villa goalmouth. Tommy made his run from outside the box beating Dugdale, and soared magnificently into the heavens and his header powered past the outstretched hands of Nigel Sims. What a fantastic header!

Immediately Busby waved Ray Wood, who had been on the right wing as a passenger though suffering from double vision, back into goal so as to release Blanchflower in an attempt at a last gasp equaliser. In a rousing, exciting and memorable finish, which saw Whelan also put the ball in the net "GOAL!" screamed the Wembley crowd and millions of television viewers. The referee disallowed it for an offside infringement with three minutes left.

The Manchester attacks continued, but all to no avail. Busby's men understandably were not at their free-flowing best. Blanchflower, Byrne and Edwards were United's heroes in adversity and most spectators were convinced that without the injury to Wood, the Red Devils would have completed a fabulous double.

Tommy Taylor walked sadly off the Wembley turf, head down, shoulders slumped in that familiar way of his.

Gone forever was the opportunity to create a record unlikely to be beaten. There would be no second chance for Tommy or some of his team-mates. It was too late for them. It was sad that the greatest centre-forward of that time could not have added an F.A. Cup winners medal to his two Championship medals.

He had not yet hit his peak, but already he was as chilling a finisher as "Jack-the-Ripper." He was also prepared to shed sweat and blood for his team. Tommy had become one of the great match-winners of those times.

He was all about undiluted passion for his profession. He loved the game, and the thrill of scoring goals. More important, he loved pulling on the red jersey of United or England. He raised the role of centre-forward to an art form the deadliest, most productive striker in Britain.

Though heartbroken by the disappointment of missing out on the double, Matt Busby told his players in the dressing room: "You did wonderful lads, magnificent. We are all proud of you. Don't worry. We'll be back at Wembley again next season." He never spoke a truer word!

The players themselves all firmly believed that they were good enough to get back to Wembley the following season. This was a young, vastly improving side. Tommy had his moments during the game, scoring with his breathtaking header and also getting another headed goal which was disallowed. His duel with the Villa centre-half Jimmy Dugdale was rough and tough with the Villa man edging it on the ground, but coming a poor second when the ball was in flight. Tommy was still feeling the effects of his injury though.

It is extremely doubtful whether any English club had ever had to withstand the pressure, tension and overwhelming drama which these young Busby Babes had to undergo during those hectic weeks of April and May, 1957. They had secured their second successive League Championship winning twenty-eight League games, and had been beaten in the semi-finals of the European Cup by the greatest club side in the world, Real Madrid, while battling their way through to the Cup Final. Tantalisingly near to making the record books for this team was due to become legends.

"Booed at Wembley"

Five days after the bitter disappointment of losing in the Cup Final and missing out on that hard fought for "double," Tommy was leading England's forward line at Wembley. This was the first of England's World Cup games to be played during May.

The opposition the Republic of Ireland. Tommy was treading the hallowed turf of this famous stadium and was back to his sharpest. This was a different Taylor who had moved like a ghost through most of the previous Saturday's Final, due mainly to his rustiness in missing United's three previous games before Wembley because of injury.

In the ninth minute, Billy Wright broke up an Irish attack and swung a lovely ball up to Stanley Matthews. Stan put a long ball up the touch-line to the lurking Taylor. Tommy was on to the ball like a greyhound after the hare and beating West Ham's Noel Cantwell before slamming the ball past young Eire keeper Alan Kelly to score England's first goal.

The crowd were on their feet yelling and cheering this beautifully worked and executed goal. The chant went around the stadium: "We want goals." The England supporters were anxious for their team to reach the World Cup finals and got behind the team. England were on form and on full throttle. England's second goal in the nineteenth minute was a thing of sheer beauty has slick a move as one could hope to see in a full season.

Duncan Edwards flicked a ball through to Johnny Haynes. Marked tightly, he rolled the ball back to Roger Byrne. Tom Finney signalled for the ball. The ever alert Byrne delivered a lovely short ball to the Preston player's feet. Finney pushed it inside to big Tommy, who was through in magnificent fashion, running twenty-five yards, beating the Irish centre-half and dispatching the ball neatly in the side of the net.

The Wembley crowd, sensing a goal glut, were good naturedly chanting for more goals. Things were looking rough for twenty-year-old Kelly in the Eire goal and they were about to get rougher. He complained about the treatment he received from Taylor. John Atyeo, recalled for his first international of the season, got another six minutes before half-time. Amazingly, just a minute later, almost directly from the kick-off Tommy scored England's fourth and his own hat-trick. The third goal was from a Finney corner-kick one of Tommy's magnificently glided headers, which went like a cricket ball past young Kelly, who was hurt in the process. After treatment Kelly was able to continue and ponder what had been a fine opportunist hat-trick. Taylor's first two goals were the result of his own individual break-throughs, throughout Tommy wandered intelligently across the forward line.

Though the Irish supporters booed Tommy lustily every time he got the ball, the United goal-machine was back on top form. He moved into position with all his uncanny anticipation and had his sights on goal the whole time. With club-mates Roger Byrne and Duncan Edwards moving up at every opportunity to help their zestful leader, Tommy had a storming game.

Alan Kelly said later: "Taylor fouled me many times. He also fouled me when he scored England's fourth goal. It was one of the roughest matches I have ever played in."

It has to be said Kelly was one of the slightest, most boyish-looking goalkeepers one would find in international football. Certainly he got buffeted often by the big pair of Tommy and John Ayteo, but this was a World Cup qualifier. The wild booing by the Irish fans aimed at Tommy in the second half was uncalled for and Johnny Carey, the Eire manager and one-time United captain did not complain.

Johnny Carey: "The boos were unfair. Taylor went for the ball every time. I have no complaints about his treatment of our 'keeper."

With a minute left Ayteo made the final score 5-1 in England's favour. The England team, apart from Tommy, came in for plenty of criticism from the critics. Matthews and Finney, in particular, received a roasting, but it was poor Atyeo, despite scoring twice, who took the brunt of the scorn.

The England team flew to Copenhagen to play the return game against Denmark. Copenhagen was one of Tommy's favourite places. This was another World Cup qualifier. The Barnsley goal king was on top form again getting a brace in England's emphatic 4-1 victory.

The final qualifying match was in Dublin against the Republic. England battled hard and Tommy's club-mate and fellow Tyke, David Pegg, won his first and sadly only full cap for England. The result was a 1-1 draw, with England now qualified for the 1958 World Cup finals in Sweden.

On 24 May, 1957, Milan's Internazionale Soccer Club denied they had offered Manchester United a substantial amount of money for Tommy Taylor. "We haven't made a bid for Taylor or any other British star lately," said a club spokesman. The rumour started with a report in the Copenhagen morning paper, *Politiken*, which said an Internazionale representative had approached Matt Busby after United's victory in a friendly match in Copenhagen on the Tuesday night.

True or not, the story brought a couple of weeks of transfer stories which was never off the back (and sometimes) front pages of every newspaper in the British

Isles. It was big news. Tommy was never out of the headlines regarding the speculation.

"Taylor can't resist £10,000" was the headline in the *News Chronicle* on 29 May, 1957. The report stated Taylor wanted to follow John Charles into Italian football to get rich quick. "In Manchester yesterday, envoys from Milan's fabulously rich Internazionale club offered him £10,000 'pocket money' to join them."

Eric Thompson wrote in the *Daily Express:* "Tommy Taylor, Manchester United and England centre-forward, looks like following John Charles, of Leeds United, into the soccer export market." Thompson went on to say that the Italian club would use the same technique used by Juventus in breaking down the resistance of Leeds by offering the player a small fortune!

"When Charles received a similar offer he said. 'I simply can't refuse it.' "And Leeds United said: 'We couldn't possibly deprive the player of money like that.'"

"It's such a fantastic temptation that I can't really resist it any longer," said the England centre-forward, Tommy Taylor. "Boloney," countered United chairman, Harold Hardman. "No director has yet been approached by Internazionale. As far as we are concerned, the matter ended when our manager, Matt Busby, turned down a £55,000 offer last week. As far as our players are concerned, money means nothing. We want to keep them."

"The offer is so tempting I simply cannot resist it. I couldn't earn such money if I stayed in English football for life," Taylor told the Express. But what was the truth behind all this transfer speculation and fuss? Had the Italians made a genuine offer for Taylor's services. Or was it a load of nonsense as the United chairman and Matt Busby stated?

When England played Denmark in Copenhagen in May, 1957, the big spending Italian clubs were out in force. They had been keeping an eye on the form of Taylor and were especially impressed by his centre-forward display while representing England. They launched an all out attempt to sign Tommy.

First, it had been reported that the Italian Football Federation had offered Matt Busby a £100,000 contract to tempt him to accept an unprecedented post as their new Manager Supremo . . . in charge of all players, managers and clubs in Italy!

There was a soccer crisis over there since the three crushing and humiliating defeats suffered by the Italian National side over the previous two weeks.

"The Italian offer, though very flattering, does not interest me in the least, no matter how much they offer me," said Busby from the Zurich Hotel where he was staying with the United youngsters competing in an international youth tournament in Switzerland. The truth of the matter was that the Italians had never made any such offer. It was pure speculation and rumour spreading on their part and later Busby made a statement. "I don't know how these stories start, but I've never received any offer from Italy. You can't refuse an offer that's never been made."

Busby was first approached by the Italians while over in Denmark watching the England match. They made it crystal clear that they wanted Taylor and were prepared to hand over a large sum of money to United for his signature. After playing in the England game, Tommy flew back to Manchester, but was contacted by the persistent Italians without Busby's permission.

Busby was angry and extremely annoyed with officials of Internationale, who, behind his back, had made an illegal approach for Taylor and taken the England leader to a Manchester hotel, wined and dined him and asked Tommy for his services. Meanwhile, Taylor was taking the line that John Charles took when offered a £10,000 signing-on fee from Juventus. "Well, what would you do?"

They promised Tommy anything and everything, painting a rosy picture of life in the land of song and sunshine. Then there were the promises of a big monthly salary and huge bonuses. They were making promises which would turn any youngster's head and which did in fact at one stage have Tommy reported as saying he had agreed to move to Italy. Busby was hopping mad. It did not take the wily United manager long to put an end to that kind of speculation as soon as he arrived back in Manchester.

"We are not selling Tommy Taylor to Italy or to anybody else," said the United manager. "And that is the end of the matter." Busby intended speaking with his directors on his return to Manchester, advising them to turn down any offers for Taylor or any of his other stars. In fact he was thinking of reporting the Italians to FIFA.

Matt Busby: "I could easily have accepted the Italian offer for Tommy Taylor. I could have done what Leeds and Spurs did, accept their big fee and sit back, but that would not have been the end of the matter. They would have come back for Duncan Edwards, Eddie Colman, Billy Whelan, David Pegg or any other of our players. The big clubs are seeing their best players spirited away to foreign shores just when top-class players at home are in short supply. We at Manchester United have worked hard to build up a whole club full of first class, exciting young footballers. This has taken us years to build and we are not going to see them leaving because these Italians wave a big cheque.

"Several thousand of pounds in the bank would be nothing compared to seeing the best side in England playing in a foreign country. These Italians are experts at getting newspapers to print headline stories in order to cause unrest at our clubs."

John Charles had moved from Leeds to Juventus a couple of months before, and big John had become an "idol" in the land of the lira. Tottenham had also allowed their captain, the young England wing-half, Tony Marchi, to join an Italian club. Both Leeds and Spurs took the line that it was unfair to the players if they stopped them cashing in on their soccer ability.

The maximum wage was still in force in England. The Football League Management Committee were adamant that the maximum wage restrictions would stay in force. Busby had spoken out and campaigned persistently about this unfairness to players earning capacity in England. "Let us pay these players the sort of money they deserve," he said.

The Italians had been thrilled watching big Tommy soar up to the skies heading United and England to success. They envisaged the United leader plundering through those tight defences in Italy and becoming as big an attraction as Charles had become if they could lure him over. Tommy was, of course, flattered by the Italian interest. What young ambitious footballer wouldn't?

Tommy's mother said: "Even at those fancy figures it's going to take a lot of enticement to get our Tommy away from home. Four years ago when United came for him, he didn't want to leave Barnsley. He threatened to go back to the pit rather than leave his home town. I don't fancy the Continental people much. So if he were to ask me, I would try my utmost to persuade him to stay."

There was of course, another reason for Mrs. Taylor's disapproval. She and her husband, Charles, watched Tommy play every time they got the chance. "He hasn't got a 'steady' girl friend, and it was me who went to the Cup Final as his guest. If he did go abroad we should be very disappointed, because we could not watch him play," said Mrs. Taylor. So Tommy stays with United. He will stay in the lodgings in Old Trafford near the cricket ground, instead of the promised villa in sunny Italy.

But what was the real truth behind the £65,000 price tag the Italians had placed on Tommy's head? Was it true? Would Taylor have moved to Milan? Matt Busby had told his centre-forward absolutely nothing about the offers made for his services by Lajos Cseisler, Internationale's representative. He heard of the approach from a Daily Mirror sports reporter.

"Who is this fellow, Cseisler?" Tommy asked the reporter, and seemed stunned when the "Mirror" man explained. Tommy did not speak for several moments, but made no criticism of Matt Busby. "No, I don't reproach him," said Taylor. "All my loyalty is to Manchester United. The team has the right to me until I am not useful to it any more."

After Busby heard that the Italians had spoken to Tommy without permission and saw that the newspapers were having a field day with stories about the proposed move he immediately phoned the young centre-forward, and ordered him to go into hiding and told him not to speak to any reporters until he arrived back in England.

Tommy was booked into the thirty-room, unlicensed Towers Hotel, in Trinity Square, 100 yards from the promenade at Llandudno, in North Wales. The press were running all over trying to find Taylor. This transfer saga ran for a couple of weeks, but after staying hidden in the hotel for two days, Tommy just had to get out. Looking like a holidaymaker, he went with the hotel manager, Ernest Pearson, to a local county school sports meeting.

But even Welsh schoolboys could recognise an England centre-forward. They mobbed him. Then some of them trailed him back to his hideout. The secret was out.

Mr. Pearson: "I have had definite instructions from one of United's club officials, who is a personal friend of mine, not to let anyone speak to Tommy. This hotel was United's headquarters for Cup training five seasons previously. These instructions were passed on to me from Matt Busby. Tommy will stay on here. If anyone comes here from the Milan club, they will be wasting their time."

One keen fan, fifteen-year-old Peter Owen, of St. Mary's Road, Llandudno, slipped into the hotel to get Tommy's autograph. He spotted him in a telephone booth. Tommy obliged the lad and had a short conversation with him. Meanwhile, Matt Busby, on hearing the news that Tommy's hideaway had been rumbled, sent further instructions that Taylor should stay indoors until he came back from Switzerland. Tommy stayed in the hotel and watched the Test match on television!

Speaking to a *Daily Mail* Correspondent in Zurich Busby said: I have had no information about the latest developments at home, but as far as I am concerned it is still no," adding: "I shall take up the matter with my board of directors as soon as I get back to Manchester on 8 June."

Busby was really seething and extremely angry at the continued saga, but he replied diplomatically to the question about an alleged meeting which took place between him and representatives of the Milan club. "No meeting took place."

Competent Swiss Soccer observers took a somewhat cynical view that Busby's "No" referred to the amount of money offered by the Italians. Was it considered insufficient? Internazionale, it was pointed out by the Swiss, were one of the Continent's richest clubs, and would be able and willing to make a substantially higher bid if hard pressed.

Were United holding out for more money and a similar deal which took Mark Hughes to Barcelona many years later. Only they know the true answer. Once back in Manchester, Busby sent for Taylor and straightened out a few things.

Busby then announced: "Tommy says he is happy with us and would abide by our decision. So he stays." On 8 June, 1957, Tommy broke his ten days "silence" and told a *Daily Mail* reporter: "I will be playing for United next season, but if I had my own way I'd still be off to Italy. I saw the 'Boss' today, and he repeated the club's first words to me when they first heard of Internazionale offer for me: 'We won't let you go'. But I would have gone if it had been left to me! You can't shrug off £10,000 in your pocket every day."

Harry England: "I was the only person who knew where United had sent Tommy to hide away. I had reporters knocking on my door at all times of the day or night.

"They offered me money to reveal where he was staying, but of course I never told them. Would he have gone to live and play in Italy? I don't honestly know but he always said that if he had gone he would have taken me with him!"

But perhaps the last words on the unsavoury business was from John Charles who from his Turin hotel said: "There has been a great hullabaloo over here about the signing of so many overseas stars. I have been told by Signor Agnelli, president of my new club, Juventus, and by other Italian officials, that I shall definitely be the last overseas player to sign for an Italian club.

"I understand the Italian Federation are dismayed by the showing of the Italian national team, and there is a big move to encourage home players. There is to be a ban on imported players. The scheme comes up for ratification by the Italian Federation in a few days. There is no chance of Tommy Taylor or any other lads being able to cash in over here. Everyone I speak to is adamant about this". At this news, Matt Busby and his staff heaved a sigh of relief.

But would Tommy have gone to Italy if given the chance? "Yes," he told Harry England his close friend from Smithies. Jackie Blanchflower, though, thinks Tommy would definitely not have gone to Italy, stating that it was hard enough to get him to leave Barnsley for Manchester. We will never know the answer to that question.

Tommy's Last International Appearance

Before England played France, at Wembley Stadium, the newspapers were rife with rumours about who would be selected for the national team. All the why's and wherefore's were gone into in fine detail. It was Tommy Taylor's impending selection which seemed to invoke all the controversy.

Poor old Tommy. He just couldn't win. Should he be selected to lead the England attack? This was the main topic of conversation in workshops, factories, pubs and clubs, on the bus or train, to and from their jobs. In fact anywhere football supporters met and discussed the game. Taylor seemed to be at the heart of the debate.

On 18 November, 1957, Frank Taylor wrote: "It's about time someone beat the tom-tom for Tommy Taylor . . . and I'm doing so this morning. It's about time someone wrote the truth about Tommy Taylor, and I say this: It will be a shabby business if England leave out the laughing boy of British Soccer from the line up to play France at Wembley.

"Hold on there. I didn't say Taylor was the finest footballing centre-forward in the land. I'd rate Tom Finney and Ronnie Allen higher. But Taylor has been put through the mincing machine by people who have not given the lad a chance to play his normal club game. England's selectors meet in London today to name the side for the match with France. They don't need to spend much time over the defence. It's the forward line which causes the worry".

Taylor went on to say we should scrap Walter Winterbottom's twin-centre-forward system. "It has misfired every time it has been tried. Put it in the waste-paper bin where it belongs, gentlemen.

"We have tried any number of permutations; Lofthouse and Mortensen: Lofthouse and Sewell: Lofthouse and Taylor: Lofthouse and Wilshaw: Taylor and Atyeo: Taylor and Kevan. It's the plan that's wrong. Not the players."

Mr. Taylor give his views as to how best England should use Tommy's attributes for the sake of the England attack: "Let's get this straight. As a grafter, a man ready to play until he drops, as a centre-forward challenging for every ball and ready to let rip, then Taylor has no equal. You either take Taylor for what he is, or you leave him out.

"They could try Taylor again . . . and who? If Dennis Viollet, his clubmate, was match fit, I'd plump for Viollet. We must give Taylor support. That's why I beat the tom-tom for Taylor. I'm disgusted at the raw deal he has had in the white shirt of England. Fit him in the right line and he won't let England down."

When England's selectors eventually named the team, Tommy was to lead the attack. Frank Taylor wrote in the *News Chronicle*: "It may be the last chance for the England leader." Frank went on to say that he applauded the selectors for not rushing to panic stations.

"Many thought Taylor's head would roll . . . Not so I make no apology for banging my own drum. I was right all along the line.

Taylor In . . . at centre-forward, but, this could be Taylor's last chance to prove to the football world he is not so bad as some of his England performances have suggested to television viewers. This time big Tom, of Manchester United, has Bobby Robson, a sharp, darting type of player, along side him. This will be Robson's first cap."

He displaced the big blond-haired Derek Kevan. Many impartial observers were asking "What about Dennis Viollet?" Tommy's clubmate was having a storming season. These two were the deadliest duo in the whole of the Football League. It would have been fairer to Tommy too, to have along side him a player who instinctively knew where the big fellow liked the ball played. Besides giving England another goalscoring forward!

There was much speculation seventeen-year-old Chelsea scoring sensation, Jimmy Greaves, might be drafted into the England forward line, but this was dropped because as Frank Taylor wrote: "It's no reflection on Greaves, but his style would clash with that of Haynes."

Tommy outwardly never bothered about the criticism which he had to endure before and after the England team was chosen. One must understand the anticipation football supporters held in store for when National sides were chosen in those days.

The fans today treat things differently. There is not the same interest in the national team.

Just before leaving to join up with the England party Tommy opened his heart on the subject of the criticism from the press and a certain section of the fans.

"I don't mind criticism when it's fair, but these critics make me wild," said Tommy after a tirade of abuse about his selection. He could not understand why the critics would not give me a break. He was tired of constantly being panned before, during, and after a game. "I can't do anything right for some people!

"I knew before the England team was chosen that if I was in it the selection would come in for a hammering. I've been so worried that I asked Mr. Busby what I could do about it, and he said: 'Pay no attention. As far as I'm concerned you're playing well.'

"I have never complained before. It's no use pretending that criticism doesn't affect me because it does. I'm admitting it's very upsetting. It's not that I can't take it or anything like that because after all in this game you've got to recognise you'll have poor games as well as good ones, and there'll be criticism.

"When your selection is hammered *before* a match, it's an entirely different matter. I keep wondering what I've got to do to please some folk. Now, when I go out on to the field at big matches I look up at the stands and terraces and think to myself: 'I hope everything's going to be all right and I can get a break from everybody.'

"A player should not have to worry like that before a match, but I do although today I'm feeling a bit better because of Mr. Busby's support. Generally, I'm just a quiet fellow, but some of my critics make me wild, and I can tell you that instead of feeling very happy about my selection at breakfast-time, after reading and hearing the criticism I was thoroughly upset."

But all his United colleagues were 100 per cent behind him. As were the legion of United's supporters. Dennis Viollet, in particular, knew how deeply Tommy was hurt by the stinging and unfair criticism by the press. Tommy bottled his feelings up inside and was for ever laughing and joking, but he would tell Dennis of his disappointment by certain reporters articles concerning his England selection and performances.

Bryan Douglas, the brilliant little Blackburn right-winger of the 1950s and '60s was selected to play his third international against France. He was Tommy's roommate in the England hotel and has vivid memories about Tommy's cheerfulness and seeming couldn't-care-less attitude to his critics.

Bryan Douglas: "I was in the same room as Tommy. He was a good laugh. He had a dry Yorkshire wit and was always smiling. He relaxed me because he was so easy going. I had never encountered him before meeting him for this match against France. Blackburn, being in Division Two, we never came into contact. I had of course seen him and that great United side play quite a few times. I well remember reading and hearing about what France were going to do to England. Tommy was not concerned with what they had to say.

"He was under a tremendous amount of pressure about his selection. Nat Lofthouse was another cracking centre-forward, who was unlucky that he wasn't selected. Then there were other centre-forwards, Derek Kevan and Ronnie Allen, and one or two others. It must have been upsetting to keep reading the newspapers and listening to the wireless and hearing that the so-called experts considered other centre-forwards better and more deserving of the England position than Tommy himself, but he never seemed to let it bother him.

"Mind you, he gave all the critics his answer on the field where it really mattered. He scored two brilliant goals and led the line cleverly. The best of this fellow was yet to come. He was so agile and good on the ground, and in the air just terrific.

"The thing which I always remember him for though, was his exuberance and smiling face. Just after the Munich disaster I was speaking to a French journalist who was marvelling about Tommy's aerial power and all round play. A great player and a wonderful, kind human being."

His clubmates, Roger Byrne and Duncan Edwards, who were also selected to play against France, were annoyed at this press assassination of their team mate. "One thing was certain though, when the chips were down, Tommy could be relied upon to come up trumps," both players reasoned.

"Tommy Taylor will not only be England's centre-forward against the Scot's at Hampden Park next April, but also lead our attack in the World Cup in Sweden next June. That's looking forward a good while, I know, but he's got the full confidence of the selectors and is also backed by team manager Walter Winterbottom. There had been doubts about his continuing ability after mediocre shows against Wales and Ireland, but he was more like his old self against France.

"Those who remain critical should remember that although he missed three good chances the two goals he scored were magnificent ones," wrote Eric Thornton.

Tommy did come up trumps, scoring two thrilling goals and causing mayhem throughout the whole of the ninety minutes. This was to be Tommy's last appearance for his country.

"This Is Harry Gregg"

When England played Northern Ireland at Wembley on 6 November, 1957, it would mark only the second time that the United centre-forward would play on a losing side for his country. The Irish beat England in a shock 3-2 result. It was a glorious sunny day, but there was a sparse crowd inside Wembley to watch Ireland gain their first victory over England on English soil for over forty years.

Harry Gregg, who played for Doncaster Rovers, had a "blinder" in the Irish goal. Tommy was facing his clubmate and close friend, Jackie Blanchflower, who played a superb game at the heart of the Irish defence. Roger Byrne, had been writing a weekly column for a newspaper and he headlined his article that week. "Who will be the Best Man on Saturday." He was referring to the fact that Tommy was to be the best man at Jackie's wedding!

Jimmy McIlroy missed a penalty for Ireland, hitting a post with the ball rebounding and hitting Eddie Hopkinson's shoulder before trickling over the line for Ireland's first goal. McCrory shot the Irish into the lead again after A'Court

Tommy "encounters" Harry Gregg.

had equalised for England. Simpson put Ireland further into the lead before Duncan Edwards, with one of those exquisite goals in which he specialised, tried to rally England, but Ireland ran out winners. Edwards and Ronnie Clayton were raining shots at Gregg, putting the English forward line to shame.

Tommy and Kevan came in for plenty of criticism from the press. Back in Manchester, Tommy and Jackie were discussing the game while having a pint or two, when the conversation got on to the goalkeepers.

Ireland's in particular, Gregg, who was playing for Doncaster at this time. Jackie was laughing about Gregg's antics between the posts.

Jackie Blanchflower: "Tommy Taylor was fearless. There was never a defender who frightened him. Honestly, he was never feared of facing any of the many tough guys knocking about in those days. And I never once heard him say 'Oh, I don't fancy playing against so and so.' So I had to laugh when we were discussing Harry Gregg. Tommy asked me: 'Who the bloody hell was that mad goalkeeper you had? He was playing centre-half most of the time. He even headed a high ball which I was going up for.' You can well imagine Tommy's face when Harry was signed by Matt Busby, and introduced to the players."

"Strikers Hunt in Pairs"

Tommy Taylor was the leader of United's forward line from the moment he arrived in March, 1953, until his life was cruelly snuffed-out in February, 1958. He was never dropped from United's first team.

It was said by many that when Busby selected his senior team, the first name on his team sheet was that of Tommy Taylor. During his five years as the spearhead of the "Busby Babes" attack, Tommy had several inside forward partners. In his early days he had the benefit of the "brainy" Stan Pearson, one of United's great stars of the past and a Cup and League winner.

Pearson made a big impression on the soccer scene after the war. A consistent scorer himself, he could also spray out some marvellous sweeping passes. In over 350 games for United, Stan scored 160 goals. He was a truly brilliant schemer.

Pearson joined United as a professional in May, 1936, from the Adelphi Lads' club. Taylor only got the benefit of Pearson's wonderful knowledge for a short period, because within a year of Tommy joining, Stan was on his way to Bury. Jack Rowley was another of United's "greats" who partnered the Barnsley boy in his early days. And there is no doubt whatsoever, the youngster learned a great deal from Rowley. Jack could be very cantankerous at times, but he certainly advised Tommy on when and where to move on the field.

There was little finesse about Jack's play, but he worked with directness and opportunism. He was dubbed "The Gunner" by the more fanciful critics, because of his searing, cannon-ball shooting. Rowley joined United in October, 1937, and left in 1955 having appeared in 425 League and Cup games, scoring 220 goals. There were several other players who were tried as Taylor's inside men.

Eddie Lewis, Jackie Blanchflower, John Doherty and Colin Webster, but without doubt the player who gained most from his partnership with the big man, was the quick-silver Dennis Viollet. Indeed, every former United player who was interviewed for this book, stated without reservation that Viollet was the most successful partner Tommy ever had.

Dennis Viollet is spoken of with respect and admiration by older followers of United who witnessed his many sparkling displays. His name to them is already a byword because of his example, both on the field and off. He has done the game of football great service and has won a deserved place in United's gallery of immortals.

His was an exceptionally brilliant career, which made him one of the greatest inside-forwards in the game. Viollet turned professional with United in September, 1950, after two years in the clubs junior ranks. A former England schoolboy he was a compelling performer with good ball control, a deceptive swerve and a powerful shot. Indeed, it was Viollet who succeeded Stan Pearson in the League side in the 1953–54 season, making his League debut at Newcastle in April, 1953.

John Doherty: "Dennis Viollet was the best partner Tommy ever had for club or country. People today talk about certain players being 'great.'

"That is an over-used word, but Viollet was 'great'! He linked up brilliantly with Tommy."

Dennis Viollet was a prolific goalscorer at the highest level. In 259 League games for the club, he notched up 160 goals.

In fact, Dennis scored 204 in all games for United, including thirteen in twelve European Cup-ties and five in eighteen F.A. Cup matches. It is a fact that he still holds United's League scoring record with thirty-two goals, scored in the 1959–60 season. Here was a player who snapped up the half-chances at a terrific rate.

He won League Championship medals with United in 1956 and 1957. He represented the Football League in the late 1950s and was capped twice by the full England team in 1960 and 1961. He was unlucky to be awarded only two caps. He deserved much better than that.

But Viollet was the silent type of goal-scorer, in as much has he never boasted about what he could do. He simply did it. Believe me, this fellow was in the same mould as the Jimmy Greaves, Brian Cloughs, Ian Rushs and Garry Linekers of this soccer world, with perhaps a little bit more to offer! He was awesome, among the best for sure, and was absolutely lethal in the eighteen-yard box.

One has only to check the goalscoring records at Old Trafford for his pedigree. From making his League debut in 1953, until leaving for Stoke in 1962, he scored ten goals or more every season for the first team. He wasn't the flamboyant sort who waved his arms about, shouting and arguing with opponents or officials.

In fact, that was his trump card and may well be the reason he scored so consistently. He drifted into scoring positions like a ghost. He was an intelligent, articulate player of the highest order.

Billy Whelan, was born in Cabra, Dublin. Billy, or Liam as his family called him, was a tall, ball playing inside-forward of the highest calibre who could read a game superbly. He joined United in May, 1953, after playing for the Home Farm club, in Dublin.

Billy made his first-team debut against Preston at Deepdale less than two years later going on to play in seventy-nine First Division games and scoring a remarkable forty-three goals. In six F.A. Cup ties he got four goals, and in eleven European Cup matches grabbed five goals.

He went on to become a Republic of Ireland International, winning four caps. "He's a great player, make no mistake about that. But how do you make him believe it?" The object of this particular admiration was Liam 'Billy' Whelan, and it was Matt Busby who asked this pertinent question of his right hand man, Jimmy Murphy. These two canny, soccer wise-men knew they had a solid gold nugget on their books in Whelan.

"Watching Billy Whelan in play was like watching Johan Cruyff, but without the tantrums, or George Best. They were all alert, masters of the ball, and supreme footballers. Billy had this leisurely gait, too. All great players had this trait and Billy was a great, great inside-forward," said Jimmy Murphy

In this phoney era, when the standard of football decreased as rapidly as transfer fees increased, Whelan was as good as any South American footballer. He was a vital cog in the United team, often dropping back deep to pick up any loose balls, then, looking up, he would dispatch it to Tommy. Like Viollet, he was the "silent" type of goalscorer.

Tommy Taylor: "Dennis Viollet was the best partner I ever had. We had a telepathic understanding. I made the runs and nine times out of ten Dennis would find me. I would have loved to have had him alongside me when playing for England. We were a great double act for United."

Dennis Viollet: "I had the privilege and pleasure of playing alongside big Tommy. I also watched him when I was out of the team through injury or whatever. It's an old cliche, but never-the-less perfectly true, I honestly can't praise him enough. He was the greatest and loved the game of football, Manchester United . . . and playing for his country. And what a heck of a fellow! The memory is still clear. He used to thunder those headers in, scoring many, many spectacular goals, and there were so many which were carbon copies. For some reason I don't know why I remember his greatest headers coming from corner kicks on Johnny Berry's side.

"That's not to knock David Pegg and say he couldn't take corner kicks, but it stands out in my memory the ball coming in from Johnny's side. If Tommy didn't get them on target, I used to turn around and look for anything, the bits and pieces and maybe get a little flick or whatever and maybe score a goal from one of Tommy's attempts at goal. I'm sure when people talk about Taylor that has got to be one of the things they remember. A wonderful, intelligent header of the ball not just from corner kicks from crosses into the box and Tommy had a far better shot than he is given credit for. He had a rocket of a shot in his right foot.

"I recall him blasting an unstoppable shot from well over twenty-five yards against Pompey. He was no slouch with his left foot either. I have so many happy memories of playing alongside Tom. One of his many outstanding attributes which was unbelievable was what is now termed 'work rate'

"They used to say Tommy lead the line superbly. This is something you don't see these days. Tom had this great gift of not only playing this very demanding role on his own, but he also had this fantastic workrate. His movement of the ball was again really unbelievable.

"One minute he would be on the left side of the field and the next second he would be over on the right. Always looking for the ball, checking his stride and he wasn't a sprinter by any means. He had a terrific, powerful burst of speed and was a lot faster than many defenders thought but wasn't a flyer by any means.

"He was built like a race horse with big, powerful, shoulders and tremendously strong-legs. I emphasize again his work-rate, because it was absolutely phenomenal. We were a perfect blend really. Tommy was the power-house and so strong he could hold defenders off; I was the fellow with the speed and agility.

"Many, many of the goals I scored for United were the direct result of what Tommy did by his unselfish running and taking defenders away from the area's. I remember many occasions Tommy getting up to head those high balls and flicking the ball over the top of defenders. Then it was up to me. I was blessed with speed and many times I used to get on to these knock-ons and hopefully get goals.

"I did this on some occasions because of the sheer hard work done by Tommy Taylor. He was very unselfish and his movement had many of us breathless. Many's the time he has been in a position to have a shot at goal, but if he saw a teammate in a better position, then he would slide the ball to them. This again was just another example of his many great attributes. He loved banging in the goals.

It didn't matter to Tom how he scored with his feet, head or if the ball bounced of his shin or his backside and ended up in the net he was quite happy. But like I said, he made many, many goals for myself and other members of United's team and also for England, I well remember him helping set up chances for his England colleagues and I'll tell you something I would have hated being a defender playing against Tommy.

"I saw defenders with fear in their eyes after watching Tom soar up to head the ball and watch it go rasping into the net. His marker must have been the most tired player on the field at the end of ninety minutes. I can still see Johnny Berry and David Pegg moving inside taking up space in the middle which Tommy had created by taking defenders away from those area's.

"We had many players who could and indeed did capitalise on this ploy of Tom's. It wasn't just me getting goals from his delicate but accurate flick-on's. Johnny and David and Billy (Whelan) scored a great number of goals because of the work done by Tommy. He was one of those players who never got the credit he deserved."

Wilf McGuiness, Dennis Viollet, Mark Jones and Tommy Taylor.

"Strive For Perfection"

Matt Busby never tired in his praise for those wonderful Hungarian footballers of the 1950s and their immaculate style of play. He used to tell Tommy Taylor and his other players about the total dedication of that master forward, Puskas, who emphasised that having reached his peak he then sacrificed everything to stay at the top. That was the United manager's lesson to all his players.

They did not need much reminding. They only had to study their second team's achievements and also the club's youth team to realise that the challenge to first-teamers was knocking louder every day from the number two dressing-room at Old Trafford.

Harry Johnston, an England international who had been a dedicated and loyal servant to Blackpool, found himself along with two other seasiders' internationals playing in their reserve team at Old Trafford one weekend. United's second string hammered them 4-0. Afterwards Johnston confessed that it was just like chasing shadows trying to cope with the supercharged United youngsters. The United side was captained by Jack Crompton.

Jack Crompton was one of United's most loyal and valued stalwarts. Jack joined United in 1943 making his debut in 1944.

"Mr. Dependable" played in over 250 senior games, having his last game in United's Championship winning team of 1955–56 when he deputised for the injured Ray Wood. He retired in the summer of 1956, to become a coach with Luton Town. He returned to Old Trafford in 1958 to help Jimmy Murphy rebuild the club after Munich. Jack was a member of the very first United team ever selected by Matt Busby.

"I remember Tommy Taylor joining United very clearly. Myself and Allan Chilton, Jack Rowley, Stan Pearson, and John Aston had played in the 1948 Cup winning side. That was some team but as happens in football, we were getting older and certain aspects of the game were changing. When Tommy came he was no more than a youngster himself, but adapted well and settled down very quickly. Myself and the older players knew that Matt had signed a good forward after his debut and by watching him train. What I noticed about him mostly was that he would listen to advice and try and act upon what had been suggested. His bubbling personality put us all in good spirits."

Taylor v John Charles

During the middle 1950s John Charles was considered the best header of a ball in the entire Football League. Comparisons were made as to who was the better header of the ball, big John, or big Tommy? His club, Leeds United were in the Second Division when United played them at Elland Road in a friendly match.

Opposing Tommy was Jack Charlton, who's younger brother, Bobby was United's star inside forward in their all conquering Youth team. Jackie was having a much harder task against Tommy, than young Bobby was having against Newcastle United's Youth side at Old Trafford. For this game against Leeds, played in very muddy conditions, both teams showed spectators how top class football should be played.

Jack Charlton was marking Tommy and was having a hard task trying to pin down the elusive United leader. John Charles was leading the Leeds attack against Mark Jones, who was a little apprehensive having always wanted to play against Charles. Roger Byrne had played against the Welsh giant twice and maintained that it was always a privilege to oppose him.

Roger Byrne: "In all my six years in professional football I can say I have not come across a more considerate player than 'Big John' I have yet to see him resort to a deliberate foul surely one of the hallmarks of greatness for one so young. His quickness on the turn, his speed off the mark, and his heading have to be seen to be believed. Yet, it is to Mark Jones's credit that he played Charles as effectively as I have ever seen him played.

"To my mind Charles's best position is undoubtedly centre half. I should hate to think of Wales playing without him in defence. His command of the penalty area is unbelievable, and one day I hope to see him oppose Tommy Taylor. For he has mastered England's Nat Lofthouse in the air, but I have yet to see Tommy bettered by any centre half. In my opinion, these two are the best headers of a ball I have ever seen. It would be a match worth going a long way to see. Who would come out best? I wouldn't care to say.

"Will eighteen-year-old Bobby Charlton be as good as his brother? Well, that's a difficult thing to say. Bobby has yet to make his debut in League football while Jack is already well established. Perhaps the easiest way to answer that question is to say that of the two I would prefer to have Bobby in my team!"

The Final Season

As season 1957–58 approached, sceptics were asking if the struggle of going for the treble had taken its toll on the young United team. It was one of Matt Busby's dearest wishes that his "Babes" would triumph once again by winning the League for the third consecutive time. In preparation for the coming season Busby took his Red Devils to Berlin and Hanover for warm-up games for their assault on the League, F.A. Cup and the European Cup.

Bobby Charlton: "I thought we must have a very good chance of winning the League title for a third time in succession, as well as having another good run in both the European and F.A. Cup competitions. Our team was getting better and better as it approached a peak which should have been reached in 1960."

Matt Busby: "Manchester United's number one priority and what we are aiming for is the First Division Championship for the third successive season. This has to be our number one target. This would be a wonderful achievement for the club. Our young players are maturing after the experience of last season when we came ever so near to winning the treble."

This feat, of course, would have emulated what Herbert Chapman did at Huddersfield Town and Arsenal. It was a hard task and nobody knew that better than Busby and Murphy. But these two wise old birds knew full well that their Youth team had a new influx of stars ready to challenge for first-team places. Lads such as Kenny Morgans, Mark Pearson, Alex Dawson, had already been blooded in the first team.

United started the campaign well enough, with eleven points from the first six matches. Tommy notching four goals. Against Leeds in early September, United routed the Elland Road team 5-0 with Johnny Berry netting two, Dennis Viollet one and Tommy also scoring a brace of goals. The "Babes" got four second half goals in a shattering nine-minute spell.

Tommy's first was a gem. Whelan sent a ball straight into the centre-forward's path, and Tommy, with a fierce drive, found the corner of the net. Viollet and Whelan were in tantalizing form, running the Leeds defence ragged. It was these two who were instrumental in Tommy getting his second goal and United's fifth when they threaded a ball through and Kerfoot, the Leeds defender, failed to clear. Tom drove the ball home. Roger Byrne was annoyed and upset at criticism of him and his team-mates when they refused to take part in a training film which was to be shown to millions on BBC television.

The Beeb offered Byrne and his team-mates a £10 all-in fee. What a storm of controversy their refusal caused! Immediate reaction was to label United a team of "big heads" and some folk suggested that it was high time they were brought back down to earth. The BBC allowed Roger two minutes in front of the cameras to explain his team's reason for not appearing in the film.

Byrne responded: "Two minutes in front of the cameras was hardly long enough to explain. I had not been prepared for the questions which I was asked to answer, but No! We're not big heads. It is not a crime to 'cash in' on whatever talents we may posses or on the success which has come our way. Do you blame us for trying to secure our futures after our playing days are over by reaping a few extra rewards?"

The overwhelming majority of football supporters in the 1950s honestly believed that soccer players were getting "big" money. They knew, of course, what they read, that all players were on £20 a week, but many fans thought the players were getting "back-handed" payments, especially the Manchester United stars. After all, they were entertainers drawing thousands of people to watch them perform.

"Good-luck" to them seemed to be the general consensus of opinion. They, of course, thought that the players were similar to film stars and crooners or show-business personalities and as such deserved the "big" rewards that went with the status.

The background to the United player's side of the story was that the previous season they appointed a committee consisting of Dennis Viollet, Ray Wood, Johnny Berry, and Mark Jones. Call it a finance committee, if you like.

Their job was to be responsible for pooling any cash which came in for signed articles, public appearances, and from advertising for the benefit of every player who had figured in the first team over the past two years. At the end of the season the "pool" was shared out according to each players first-team appearances.

Roger Byrne; "Our reason for not accepting the BBC's £10 'facilities' payment was not because we have suddenly become money-grabbers.

"It involves a principle. If anyone is interested enough to make a film of us for commercial purposes then they should be prepared to make a reasonable payment. We did not want the money just for ourselves. In fact, we had agreed that if the £10 offer was stepped up the cash could have gone to the National Football Player's Benevolent Fund. I can add that I have received messages from other player's and clubs applauding our stand.

We also had a telegram from the BBC saying that they appreciated our point, there was no hard feelings, and wishing us all the best for the new season."

The Red Devils waited with eagerness for F.A. Cup holders, Aston Villa, to visit Old Trafford, and on 5 October, 1957, with over 43,000 inside the ground the atmosphere could have been cut with a knife.

"Now we'll show Villa what would have happened to them last May in the Cup Final, only for that injury to Ray Wood. Villa will play the 'real' Manchester United," said one supporter outside the ground to a radio broadcaster. United thrashed the Cup holders 4-1 and the Brummies were put to the sword from the opening whistle.

Billy Whelan laid on the first for Tommy and throughout he gave Dugdale, the Villa centre-half, a roasting.

It was HIS persistent worrying of the shaky Villa pivot which resulted in Dugdale slicing the ball into his own goal, putting the Reds 2-0 in front. Pace pulled a goal back before Pegg got United's third with Tommy again on the mark for the fourth goal.

Wilf McGuinness: "I played in place of big Dunk, and we played Villa off the park. Everyone was buzzing and especially Tommy. He got two goals, but should have been credited with a hat-trick because he was the cause of Jimmy Dugdale scoring an own goal. Jimmy was a big, strong, robust centre half. I think he was a Liverpool born lad, but he was absolutely delighted to hear the final whistle because of the roasting Tommy gave him. He could not get anywhere near Tommy when we pumped those centres into their area. This was Tommy at his best."

Tommy missed United's 3-0 defeat at Portsmouth. He was leading the attack for England against Wales at Ninian Park, England winning 4-0 but did not figure on the score sheet. Johnny Haynes, who scored two, Tom Finney and an own goal giving England victory after Taylor's superb hat-trick against Villa a few days earlier in the F.A. Charity Shield match.

Tommy was next on the goal sheet against West Bromwich Albion. He would gladly have forgone his two goals in exchange for the two points United dropped in a thrill a minute game. After eight minutes Tommy seized an opportunist goal. Bobby Robson, who years later became England's manager, equalised, only for Tommy to restore United's lead.

Berry hit a fast free-kick into the eighteen-yard box, out jumped the massive West Brom defenders and thumped a ferocious header into the back of the net. Robson scored again and Tommy's rival for the England number nine shirt, big Derek Kevan, added a further goal. Ronnie Allen notched West Brom's fourth while Billy Whelan made it a respectable 4-3 though Berry missed a penalty. This was one of the best attacking games ever witnessed at The Hawthorns.

Freddie Goodwin had taken over the right-half position in the first team from Eddie Colman and the Salford born wing-half asked Matt Busby for a transfer. In a topsy-turvey situation, a couple of weeks later, Colman was restored into the first team and Goodwin then requested a move.

Freddie Goodwin: "Tommy scored five goals in two games and I saw what an ace marksman he was. But more than his goalscoring exploits, what stood out was the way he could skyrocket upwards and nonchalantly head the ball into the net. This was a fabulous skill for a forward to have and United were fortunate in having such a player as Tommy Taylor.

"These people are worth their weight in gold. Later, when I became a manager myself, I'd have given anything to have a similar type of centre-forward in my teams. Mind you, every manager would be blessed if they had a Tommy Taylor in their teams, but during my first-team games with United he was ever so helpful to me."

But then United were thrashed by Bolton 4-0 and by mid-December they had lost seven matches. It was as if the strain of the previous season had caught up with the team, and they were certainly losing their impetus and floundering at times. About this period there was a report in the newspapers that both Colin Webster and Jackie Blanchflower were waiting to speak to Busby about a transfer. Webster wanted a regular position in the first team which was understandable.

Blanchflower went to great lengths to distance himself from earlier reports that he would seek a move because his friend Mark Jones had displaced him.

Competition was fierce. Jackie had been playing in the first team and stepped out of the side in order to play for Ireland against Italy. "I did not say, as was reported, that I would seek a move," said Jackie. After a few days, he had a 'clear the air' meeting with Busby about his future. "All right, boss, I accept the position. And now I am going to try and win back my first-team place," he promised.

Ray Wood, the team's quiet, but consistent goalkeeper, came in for a great deal of criticism. Harry Gregg, from Doncaster, was an immediate replacement. The Northern Ireland goalkeeper was big, commanding and very confident, and a record signing for a 'keeper, costing £25,000.

Wolves, of course, had now got an eight-point lead over the Reds, at the halfway stage of the season. Matt Busby had given his team the chance to settle back into their winning ways, but after a few indifferent performances and having lost 1-0 to Chelsea at home on 14 December, the United maestro decided changes were necessary for the following week against Leicester when Gregg, Jones, Morgans, Charlton and Scanlon replaced Wood, Blanchflower, Berry, Whelan and Pegg.

This was the ruthless side of Busby. He was a very calm and patient manager, as loyal as can be to his players. But he had replacements for every position and all eager to show their ability in the first team. Leicester were cynically taken to pieces and hammered 4-0. Dennis Viollet getting a brace of goals, with one each for Charlton and Scanlon.

Albert Scanlon: "After the boss made the changes, we hit a good patch. We had so many great players that everyone had to be on top form otherwise you would lose your place in the side. The boss never dropped a player from United's first team. They were 'rested,' he told them!"

It was like previous seasons with the football flowing beautifully, and the team providing excitement and thrills galore. The team believed they could catch Wolves and overhaul them and take the Championship once again. Kenny Morgans, a former Welsh schoolboy international, was spotted by Jimmy Murphy while playing for Swansea Boys at Maine Road. He joined United in 1955, turning professional in April, 1956. He was a speedy winger, who was comfortable on either wing.

He developed a reputation for his accurate centres. This chirpy Welshman looked set for a lengthy run in the first team. He was only eighteen when he displaced Johnny Berry, while Scanlon, on the left wing, was fast, direct and possessed a cannonball shot in his left foot. He was the complete opposite to the man whom he had displaced, David Pegg, a beautifully balanced ball-playing forward. Bobby Charlton was a brilliant goalscoring inside-forward, with all the subtle skills of Billy Whelan whose place he had taken. Bobby had been on the fringe for quite some time, though still only a teenager. Like his partner, Scanlon, Charlton had tremendous shooting power, but with either foot. Bobby was a true Manchester United thoroughbred.

Paddy McGrath, was a long standing and close personal friend of Matt Busby and his family. An old St. Patrick's lad, he was an ex-boxer in the famous Collyhurst stable of Brown, King, and McAvoy and he owned the luxurious Cromford Club in Manchester's city centre, where all the sporting celebrities congregated as well as stars of radio, and television when in Manchester. Paddy was a regular at Old Trafford and knew all the players and their families intimately.

In fact, Roger Byrne held his wedding reception in the Cromford club. Many players came along with their spouses or girlfriends and would drop in after the game for a meal and a drink. They knew they could relax in peace. It was an excellent, well run establishment, strictly members only. Paddy was a "character" of the highest order.

Paddy McGrath: "Matt was talking to me one day not long before the crash and during our conversation he happened to mention that perhaps the team needed an "older head" in the team to slow the play down and calm the young players who were brilliant individuals. Ernie Taylor, no relation to Tommy, was going to be sold by the Blackpool manager, Joe Smith, to Leeds for £8,000, and Blackpool were going to buy Colin Webster from United for £12,000.

"Now I knew little Ernie very well from my days in Blackpool. He had often told me how much he admired Matt and the young team. He went as far as telling me: 'I would play in United's second team and help develop the kids.' I told Matt, who was very interested, and he 'phoned the Blackpool manager, who told him: 'Right, we'll do a straight swop.'

'Hold on' said Matt, 'You were selling Taylor to Leeds for £8,000, and we have already agreed a fee of £12,000 for Webster.' Joe Smith smiled, and both men agreed the deal. Matt was getting ready for the second leg of that fatal match against Red Star and he told the Blackpool boss: 'We'll leave it until I come back from Prague, then I'll contact you and sort everything out'. Of course, its now history what happened, but he would have been a wonderful asset to United's fantastic assembly of young talent."

Tommy played in the following six League matches in which United were unbeaten. But missed the 2-2 draw with Manchester City. He had notched sixteen First Division goals in nineteen games, besides helping to make many more for his team mates with his unselfish service and hard running. What a goalscoring record! What would modern day strikers give for a goals haul like that?

Kenny Morgans: "I had played in two winning games for the first team in five days in which we had scored seven goals, my confidence was high. I was feeling terrific. It was Christmas time and we were training at Old Trafford. I was floating crosses into the box for Tommy to practice his heading and then did some lapping and then into the gym. Tommy was without doubt the best trainer at the club. I couldn't keep up with him he was much to powerful for me. After training had ended, I was sat down having a breather when the boss, Matt Busby, came and sat down beside me.

"I thought he was going to praise me for my play in the two games. He looked at me and said: 'Kenny son. I'm leaving you out of the first team at Luton'. I was stunned. 'I am bringing Johnny (Berry) back I don't want you getting big-headed.'

The team only drew 2-2 and the following game I was back in the first team against Manchester City, and he never mentioned anything to me again. I wasn't getting big-headed of course; it was his way of telling me that I'd had a taste of first-team football action and it wasn't going to be easy. I couldn't argue with him could I?"

Tommy had also scored three goals in six European Cup matches. His last goal in this competition was against the Czech champions Dukla Prague, in front of over 60,000 delirious United fans. The Czechs were the much better side for the first hour at Old Trafford, but Busby's lads made it safe in a twelve-minute spell in the second half which saw them in their Championship winning form. After a mix-up in the Czech defence Colin Webster nipped in to score a glittering reward for his fast, do-or-die workrate. A couple of minutes later, with the Dukla defence deflated after giving away a silly goal, United scored again. Pegg made it 3-0 to wrap up a thrilling twelve minute scoring burst to win the tie, though they were beaten 1-0 in Prague a couple of weeks later.

Arriving back in Liverpool on the Friday night (they were diverted there because fog surrounded Ringway airport). The whole party were tired after the match in Prague. After a few hours sleep, the team were on their travels again, this time a three-hour coach journey to Birmingham where they faced City at St. Andrews. After an exciting opening few minutes, Viollet put the Reds in front but it was a short lived lead because Murphy equalised. Then the Midlands team took the lead through Astall.

This was a remarkable game and United answered their critics who claimed they were stale. Billy Whelan had a fierce shot turned away by Gil Merrick the Birmingham 'keeper. The ball went to Berry, who looked up, saw Tommy lurking in the penalty area, and before the defence could re-group centred high and Tommy pushed his aching limbs off the turf and soared skywards to nod the ball ever so gently past the 'keeper. Four goals had been scored in less than four minutes.

Kinsey scored again for Birmingham before Viollet earned the Manchester lads a well-deserved equaliser. They were unfortunate to not come away with both points.

Colin Webster: "I went for a few drinks with Tommy one night and we got chatting about our position with the club. He was smashing, listening to my moaning and groaning, but he couldn't stay serious for long. He would break out into a big grin and get me laughing over something or other. He had a fantastic nature, he really did. Many people thought he was just a big lovable Yorkshire lad who hardly took anything seriously, but he was smart, very smart indeed.

"Yes, Tom knew he was a good player and in his own quiet manner proved it. One night I told Tom that I was going to confront Matt Busby about a move. The big feller laughed at me. He didn't believe me. 'You just wait', I told him, and I arranged to meet the boss in his office. I had practised what I was going to say to him over and over again in my mind. I wanted regular first-team football so I went to see Matt Busby a few times concerning my position with the club. I was always involved with everything which was going on in connection with the first team, but like a few others I wanted regular first-team football.

"I don't know how he did it, but he had a knack of defusing the situation, and before you left his office, Matt would get out of his chair, put his arm around my shoulders and thank me for all I had done for him and the club.

"I would walk down those few stairs and think to myself: 'Hey, I never told him what I wanted to tell him.' He was a crafty man.

"This happened quite a few times with me. I'd be determined to tell him what I thought, I would rehearse my speech for a few days then when I walked up to his office . . . Bang! He completely wrong footed me. Later, bumping into Tom he winked at me and said: 'Did you tell him then?' knowing bloody well that I had been thrown out of my stride."

Sandwiched in between the fight for the First Division title was a trip to Workington Town, in the F.A. Cup, for a 3-1 victory, followed by a 2-0 win over Ipswich Town.

Bobby Charlton: "We had won our way to the fifth round of the F.A. Cup with wins over Workington and Ipswich Town. Two unfashionable sides, it's true, but they are often the hardest nuts to crack in this type of competition. Mind you, if you can't beat them, no matter how unfamiliar the hazards, you don't deserve to win the Cup."

The Red Devils had been drawn against another Iron Curtain country when facing Red Star of Yugoslavia in the quarter-finals of the by now popular and exciting European Cup. They had of, course, played the first leg at Old Trafford in January, winning by the slender margin of 2-1 with Charlton and little Eddie Colman getting the goals. Red Star had in their forward line a brilliant individualist inside-forward Secularac, who many Continental observers reckoned was another Puskas. On the Saturday before flying out to Yugoslavia for the second-leg they were playing against the once mighty Arsenal at Highbury.

This was a much awaited meeting between these two wonderfully attacking teams. All gates were locked well before the three o'clock kick-off. It was a game which is still regarded as one of the finest matches ever to grace a football stadium. A classic!

Albert Scanlon: "On the Friday afternoon before the Arsenal game we went down to London to our team hotel, the 'Lancaster Gate'. Myself and Eddie Colman went to the pictures in Marble Arch. 'Pal Joey' was showing and we were both big Frank Sinatra fans. It was a smashing feeling. Since I had got into the first team as a sort of regular the side had remained unbeaten. The confidence in each player was something hard to describe, but we believed we could beat anybody, and I mean anybody."

Bobby Charlton: "In the League we were poised just behind Wolves, the leaders, ready for a gallop down the rails in the last furlong. Our League match away to Arsenal was one I shall always remember for many reasons. When we ran on to the field at Highbury in our all-white Wembley strip we were wearing black armbands as a mark of respect for one of our directors, Mr. G.E. Whittaker, who had died in our team's London hotel that morning.

"It was our first visit to London that season, and Highbury was packed with 63,000 spectators, no doubt hoping to see the Gunners wipe out the shock of their recent Cup defeat at the hands of little Northampton. Present in the crowd, we learned, was a small group of Yugoslav observers, there to assess our form before the second leg of our European Cup quarter-final in Belgrade on the following Wednesday. We were resolved to give them something to think about."

These were the teams: Arsenal: Kelsey; S. Charlton, Evans; Ward, Fotheringham, Bowen; Groves, Tapscott, Herd, Bloomfield, Nutt. (David Herd, of course, would join United a few years later and prove a great goalscorer and loyal servant to United).

United: Gregg; Foulkes, Byrne; Colman, Jones, Edwards; Morgans, Charlton, Taylor, Viollet, Scanlon.

Once the game got underway, United were cruising, putting on the style for the London soccer fans. After ten minutes of fierce exchanges, Kenny Morgans weaved his way past two Arsenal defenders as if they didn't exist, side-stepping before rolling a pass along the ground for Duncan Edwards, who had come crashing through the middle. Timing his run to perfection, Duncan unleashed one of his "special" cannonball drives which sent the ball like a rocket through Jack Kelsey's hands and into the net.

Bobby Charlton: "Eighteen-year-old Kenny Morgans, my right-wing partner, had been skippering our youth side with tremendous success, and what a fabulous game our Welsh wizard had that day. Albert Scanlon, playing a great game on the left wing, made our second goal. Picking up a loose ball in his own half of the field, Albert set off on his own like a scalded cat with the rest of us, Arsenal defenders as well, chasing him for all we were worth.

"Only Tapscot and I managed to keep up, and when Albert, after his amazing hundred-yard run, reached the left corner flag, he swung a perfect ground pass across to me. My breath was coming in gasps and my socks were sagging round my ankles, but I managed to smack that ball into the net."

Scanlon was on the rampage and after another mazey dribble he sent a long, raking cross out to Morgans on the opposite wing. Kenny saw Tommy Taylor moving forward and stroked the ball into his path for the powerful centre-forward to shoot United's third goal. 3-0 up at half-time was a marvellous position for the "Babes."

They were obviously jubilant and Matt Busby was delighted. This was the type of soccer spectators dreamed of watching. What a turn around the second half brought.

With the huge crowd in hysterical mood, Arsenal equalised with goals from Herd and a minute or so later Bloomfield got the second before heading the equaliser past a bewildered Harry Gregg. Most teams, after conceding a 3-0 lead, would have gone to pieces, but United, driven on by Colman and the rampant powerhouse, Edwards attacked even more ferociously.

Albert Scanlon: "Big Dunk was shouting like mad for everyone to surge forward, but to be perfectly honest, though Arsenal had pegged three goals back, we were really confident that we would win. Why? With players like Edwards, who was playing like two men, Roger Byrne so commanding at the back, Big Mark Jones showing toughness and durability and we had the jewel in our crown . . . Tommy Taylor. We felt we would beat anybody."

Bobby Charlton: "Our brilliant young wingers kept the air round Arsenal's goalmouth electric. A goal had to come, and did when Scanlon darted round Stan Charlton and placed a perfect centre which Dennis Viollet nodded home.

Tommy celebrates a goal at Highbury.

"Then in the seventy-first minute, after Gregg had saved at Herd's feet, Kenny sent a long ball up to Tommy Taylor, who scored a goal which surprised him almost as much as it surprised us. Tommy ran along the goal-line and shot hard and low from a ridiculous angle, leaving Kelsey helpless. Jimmy Greaves of Chelsea is the only other player I know who might have scored such a goal."

The Gunners came back to make the final score 5-4 to United in a game that had the spectators in raptures for the whole ninety minutes. This was blissful soccer, with both teams attacking in brilliant fashion. United were back on top form now and everyone was in good spirits after this wonder performance in the capital.

Dennis Viollet: "What a wonderful game to play in. I got a rare headed goal from Albert Scanlon's cross. It was meant for Tom who liked the ball centred fast, direct and hard and high. Albert could certainly do that all right. Tommy scored twice and with his arms aloft and a big smile on his face he looked the picture of happiness as all the team were, of course, after such a game."

Albert Scanlon: "What a game. Me and Kenny Morgans tore holes in their defence. The boss wasn't upset that we had conceded four goals; he was delighted at the character and style we had shown in the Arsenal game. Mind you on that train journey home, everyone was elated."

When they arrived at London Road station, Albert went along with Tommy, David Pegg and a couple of the lads into the Plaza Ballroom. Everyone was drinking and dancing and Jimmy Savile was dee-jaying from the stage. It was soon action stations as a buxom young lady and her friend paraded before them, sniggering.

Tommy and David marched after the girls, passing a table occupied by Mark Jones, Eddie Colman, and Wilf McGuinness, who was holding hands with a young lady. Jimmy Savile took the microphone and tells the crowded ballroom that the lads who thrashed Arsenal were still on their feet. The crowded room erupted in applause and Jimmy called Eddie and Mark to the stage to give their version of the Frankie and Johnny song.

While the lads were doing something awful to the song, Tommy was smooching with a well endowed young lady in the body of the room. It was all good, clean fun, and their way of relaxing after a torrid game. Later, Tommy, David Pegg and Albert Scanlon made their way to the "Costa" night club. They were bubbling with excitement.

Sat in the club was Denis Law, who was still playing for Huddersfield. By this time, Tommy was courting strongly; in fact he was planning to be married in June or July of 1958. As Tommy and his team mates were enjoying their drink, he smiled for his future was bright indeed. He had so much to look forward too. If United got through against Red Star in a few days time, there was a second successive semi-final in the European Cup.

The team were still involved in the F.A. Cup, and they were scheduled to face

Tommy on board with Wilf McGuiness.

Wolves on their return from Belgrade. Many soccer sceptics considered this match against Wolves a virtual Championship decider. On the international scene after taking unmerciful criticism, he was now England's number one centre-forward, an automatic choice for his country and the prospect of leading England's attack in the 1958 World Cup finals in Sweden during the summer gave him a warm satisfied feeling.

Wilf McGuinness: "If you were injured or had a knock a sprain or anything, you had to report to Old Trafford on the Sunday morning for treatment. I desperately wanted to travel with the first team to Belgrade for the return with Red Star. I had been carrying an injury for awhile but on the Saturday I was injured again. I was told to stay behind for treatment. Of course I was disappointed, but it was perhaps lucky or fate or whatever that I wasn't destined to travel with the lads on the Monday."

Colin Webster: "I was told that I would be making the journey to Belgrade a few days before, but I went down with a real bad dose of the flu. I felt terrible. Obviously I couldn't go. I was feeling in low spirits because I wanted to go with them. We always had great fun, but it wasn't to be for me."

Jackie Blanchflower: "I was a regular first-teamer from the start of that season, but had dropped out and played for Northern Ireland and lost my place to Mark Jones. I hadn't played in the previous nine League matches, when the boss asked me to travel with the team. I could have stayed behind, but decided to join the party to Belgrade."

On a cold, miserable and depressing Monday morning, Tommy said farewell to Mrs. Swinchat, his landlady, and made his way to Old Trafford accompanied by Duncan Edwards and Kenny Morgans, and boarded the coach taking them to Ringway to commence the long, arduous trip to Belgrade, on their chartered flight. Poor old Mark Jones took some ribbing from the players for being late.

They were all in good humour after reading reports of the Arsenal game. There was some early fog at Ringway which delayed the take-off for almost an hour. It was a six-hour flight with a stop at Munich to re-fuel. Continuing on their journey, the Elizabethan aircraft ran into poor visibility going into Belgrade. In fact, United's 'plane was the only aircraft to land in Belgrade that day because of the dreadful conditions.

However, the Manchester party arrived in their destination around tea-time. The Hotel Metropole was sparse and minus the usual comforts of most other establishments, though there was a beautiful view from the rear of the hotel. The Danube wound it's way along the banks, but there were armed guards on every floor for some unknown reason. These Communist countries seemed to have soldiers everywhere. The team were situated on the fourth floor.

Though United officials took care to ensure the players only had English-style food. The players had been tipped off to take plenty of razors, chocolate bars, and toothpaste these items were better than having money. They were a better bargaining inducement.

Tommy and a few players went for a walk and were amazed and startled to find people actually walking about in shoes made from old car tyres; it was unbelievable and sad. There were long queues for the shops and almost everything else. Belgrade looked a dour dismal place with little or nothing of interest to the English party.

Their recent run of ten matches without defeat led to talk about the Wolves game a few days hence.

"We can pull them back to just two points if we beat them," said someone. Duncan Edwards replied in a forceful manner: "Let's get this Red Star beaten first and out of the way, then we can think about Wolves. I'll tell you this, if we play and attack like we did against Arsenal, Wolves will have to pull out all the stops to beat us."

Tommy and Jackie Blanchflower thought they had found a skating rink, but it was a lake which was frozen solid. The two chums went for a little whirl on this makeshift rink, laughing and larking about. It was fortunate for them that Busby or any other United official never caught them.

There was talk that the ground where United were due to face Red Star was frozen solid in places this surprised nobody because everything was cold and frozen up. But the team were assured that the game would be played. On the Tuesday the team, accompanied by the press, and also the crew from the aircraft trained on a pitch which now resembled a swamp.

Most of the snow on it was melting and the players were soon covered in mud, much to the delight of cabin staff Margaret Bellis and Rosemary Cheverton.

These two young ladies were delighted as the team splashed and sploshed their way through a light training session. "Look at that Tommy Taylor. He moves like a thoroughbred. He's a real rum bugger," remarked steward Tommy Cable, a United fanatic. "Look at the way he moves with that high-stepping graceful running. He's brilliant."

There was a doubt about Roger Byrne, and Geoff Bent was ready to step in and take his place. But Byrne gave himself a thorough fitness test and declared himself fit. Later, everyone was washed and spruced up, they all went to the cinema where the first couple of rows were put at their disposal. People who had obviously paid to watch the film were quickly ushered to other places.

How on earth they could understand the film was anyone's guess, because it was all in English. Tommy and the rest of the team could not wait to get the game played and head home for some old-fashioned home comforts.

The hotel lounge was a hive of activity with autograph-hunters everywhere. As the team boarded the coach which was to take them to the stadium, warm sunshine greeted them. The pitch had been frozen but was melting, which suited the United lads. All along the route to the ground there were thousands walking joyfully, singing and chanting "Red Devils," or "Busby Babes." This match had certainly caught their imagination. It brought home to the United lads they were acting as ambassadors for England.

There was an estimated crowd of 52,000 inside the ground, with thousands more sneaking in. The first few rows of seats were occupied by soldiers.

It was a hard fought battle which ended in a 3-3 draw. Dennis Viollet put his team into the lead within ninety seconds. Tommy picked up the ball in his own half, set off on a run taking the Red Star defenders wide, but keeping possession as he was challenged.

Viollet was moving alongside him. Everyone expected Tommy to shoot, but increasing his pace he left the defence spreadeagled and passed the ball to Dennis to do the necessary.

Bobby Charlton scored a brace of goals, one a rocket of a shot which whistled into the Red Star net. Tommy, though not on the scoresheet, fought a valiant and sterling battle with the tough Yugoslav defenders. There were many niggly fouls, free-kicks and disputed decisions but above everything else, excitement!

Kenny Morgans was kicked deliberately on the knee, and had his right thigh ripped open by a Red Star defender. The Red Star side fought back splendidly and through the referee's generosity equalised.

At the final whistle trainer Bert Whalley and coach Tom Curry quickly got the United lads back into their dressing room where they were joined by the reserves, press and the aircrew who shared in their delight. Eddie Colman and Tommy, with towels round their waists, did a Latin-American rumba with Eric Thompson clicking his fingers castanet-style in accompaniment. Even pilots Thain and Rayment joined in the merriment.

"Bring those stewardesses in here," shouted a laughing Tommy. Matt Busby gave him a cold stare. "The ladies will wait outside," said Busby winking at Captain Rayment, who smiled and shouted over to Tommy: "I imagine they're a bit shy, Tommy." It was all good natured fun. Tom Currie and Bert Whalley were busy collecting the player's kit which was littered all over the dressing room floor. The charismatic Jimmy Murphy, would have been delirious in this atmosphere, but as the Welsh team manager, he was with the Welsh team in Cardiff for their qualifying World Cup game against Israel.

"Well, that's another one out of the way. We are in the semi-finals again," said an elated Busby. The Red Devils had triumphed 5-4 in this two-legged tie. The whole United party were relieved to come through this ordeal. Back in the hotel everyone was getting ready for the official post-match banquet, which was being held in the British Embassy that night. Each player received a beautiful tea set

Passing time in the departure lounge, Ringway Airport.

and a bottle of gin. With the tension of that afternoon's match over the players were in a happy and relaxed frame of mind. As the speeches were drawing to a close, and it was the port-and-cigars stage, Matt Busby stood up and gave a speech.

The Belgrade chairman rose, shook Busby's hand warmly. At the players table, Mark Jones, Tommy, and David Pegg broke out loudly with a rendering of their song "Ilkla Moor Bah Tat'" with the rest of the players joining in the chorus. Roger Byrne was busy scribbling a note "Boss, we've been invited for a few drinks at the American Embassy can we leave now, Roger." The singers followed the progress of the note as it moved from hand to hand to the top of the table.

Matt glanced at it, half-smiled, looked straight at Roger and nodded a 'yes.' Immediately the singing picked up added gusto and at the conclusion of the verse, the players clenched their arms in a farewell salute, and withdrew. The manager wanted his lads to enjoy themselves. "Football is a funny game, isn't it?" Roger Byrne remarked to journalist, Frank Taylor. "I thought we were going to ease our way through after taking a three goal lead, but you can't give these teams an inch."

The match against Red Star would be sadly the last time that this truly wonder team, a side full of artistry, would ever be seen again in it's full glory and majesty. For decades to come, every football follower, critic, or member of the media corps, would be pondering just how great this young team could have become. The side had already gone a long way over the previous three years. There is little doubt they would have become the greatest club side ever assembled in Europe. It is possible they were already one of the greatest teams!

Tommy and some of the reporters visited a night club named "The Crystal" where they were entertained by dancers and a cabaret. Compared to the night spots in Manchester, it was modest but friendly. Feeling tired after a physically hard game a few hours earlier, Tommy decided he was going back to the hotel to catch up on his sleep. The night was quite mild compared to when they first arrived in Belgrade. Walking back he saw teammates, Viollet, Charlton, with Frank Swift, the former Manchester City and England goalkeeper, now a journalist. Tommy seeing Bobby didn't have a coat on, lent him his while he proceeded to bed.

Early next morning, Tommy and Eddie Colman were on the hotel landing, switching everybody's shoes which had been left outside the rooms to be cleaned. Eddie shouted: "No, not those. That's the boss's room," just as Tommy was about to switch Matt Busby's shoes.

Later that Thursday morning the United party had breakfast, said their farewells to hotel staff and boarded the coach which took them to Zenum airport for the return flight to Manchester. The 'plane, the British European twin-engine Elizabethan, RMA 'Lord Burleigh,' G-ALZU AS 57.

While the aircraft was being refuelled in Munich the party were in the lounge having coffee and sandwiches. The call came to board the plane. There was a great deal of snow all over the airport. As the aircraft made ready for take-off the engines died down and the plane taxied back to the runway to get ready for a second, attempted take-off.

As the plane moved forward something was obviously wrong for the same thing happened. Everyone was asked to go back into the lounge. After a few minutes, the message came over the loudspeakers for everyone to make their way back to the aircraft.

Albert Scanlon: "I was walking up the steps behind Frank Taylor. Frank turned and said: 'Sod this! If you didn't take off first time in the R.A.F., the flight was scrapped.' I didn't reply, because I just did what I was told. I sat down with Bill Foulkes and started playing cards. Bobby Charlton and Dennis Viollet came to the front of the plane and swapped places with Tommy Taylor and David Pegg who were now in the back because they thought it would be safer. Eddie Colman followed them. As we started the third take-off I looked around and noticed Tommy wasn't in his seat.

"Then as I turned back towards the front a steward came rushing out and quickly strapped himself into his seat. That wasn't reassuring I can tell you. Someone told me later that both Tommy and David were in the toilets at the back of the plane.

"I remember going down the runway and then suddenly everything just went blank. You know the rest."

The tail end of the aircraft came away and burst into flames. Eight players died: Roger Byrne, Geoff Bent, Eddie Colman, Mark Jones, David Pegg, Billy Whelan, and England's greatest centre-forward, "The Smiling Executioner" Tommy Taylor. Three members of the club staff, Bert Whalley, secretary Walter Crickmer, and old 'Tosher' Tom Curry. Duncan Edwards died a short while later.

Eight members of the press team perished: Alf Clarke, Don Davies, George Follows, Tom Jackson, Archie Ledbrooke, Henry Rose, Eric Thompson and Frank Swift. There were forty-four people on board the aircraft.

It was a terrible tragedy felt world wide. These world-class players were taken away in the prime of their lives when they had so much more to offer football and life itself.

Tommy's life and career was tragically short because of the Munich disaster. He loved life to the full and was enjoying the fruits of his hard work and dedication to his chosen profession. From starting with Barnsley's first team, his career lasted barely a decade. But what an impact he made in those few short years, he set the football world alight with his glorious goal scoring exploits.

He played alongside some of soccer's greatest legends, and he was on equal terms with them all, because he himself was an all-time great. Just before his death Tommy had the world at his feet. He has never been forgotten in Barnsley and Manchester. We have not seen his equivalent since.

Colin Webster: "When the coffins were brought home, I attended eight funerals in eleven days. It affected me deeply. It could so easily have been me in one of those coffins. It did my head in completely. I became more irritable and was sent off the field a few times and it was mainly down to the stress and strain of what happened at Munich. I visited Tommy's parents and obviously they were distraught and heartbroken. Speaking to his parents and his brothers and sisters was a very emotional experience for me personally."

Tommy was buried at the small cemetery at Monk Breton Parish Church, on 13 February, 1958. As the cortege made its way along the streets and roads from the family home in St. Helens Avenue, Barnsley, thousands of people wearing red rosettes, the colour of both Barnsley and United, but with a black ribbon attached, four deep wept openly as they packed the route. As the funeral cortege passed his old school, there stood in silence paying their respects, were eleven youngsters all dressed in red football kits.

At the Barnsley Town Hall, and at Oakwell and Old Trafford, flags were at half mast. Outside the church the Barnsley players formed a guard of honour as the coffin was carried by close friends of Tommy's from Smithies. Harry England was one of the bearers. After a short and simple service by the Reverend W.A. Jubb, Tommy was laid to rest as the sound of the "Last Post" was conducted by a lone bugler.

Joe Richards and Walter Winterbottom were at the graveside along with United players and officials, Louis Edwards, Mr. W. Petherbridge, Les Olive, Joe Armstrong, Sandy Busby, Gordon Clayton and Don Gibson, plus hundreds more.

The Greatest Partnership in Football

The story of Tommy Taylor would not be complete without introducing the two men who made the story possible. The first is Matt Busby, the greatest manager in soccerdom. Busby became manager of Manchester United on 22 October, 1945. His first signing was his most inspired as Busby himself always claimed . . . it was Jimmy Murphy.

These two helped mould great teams which football followers world wide came to admire. Busby was a quiet man who thought before he spoke. There were certainly more tougher, more abrasive, more aggressive and more sergeant-majorish, but none with his wisdom and passion for the great things in football. He was a dreamer.

His philosophy was: if you don't get it right to-day, don't worry; there's always tomorrow. Busby dreamed of producing his own world-class footballers, teams of home-reared youngsters. He had gifts other managers lacked . . . imagination, patience and foresight.

Jimmy Murphy was the inspirer of greatness. This fellow was known as the the "Starmaker." He was not motivated by money; in fact he was offered jobs with other clubs, Arsenal among the many, and a host of Continental clubs. But Jimmy also dreamed of coaching and producing fascinating players of the calibre of Duncan Edwards, Bobby Charlton, George Best, Denis Law, and Tommy Taylor.

He moulded these men into brilliant, world-beaters. Busby and Murphy were visionerires. What they achieved is in the record books and the players that they produced bear testimony to their coaching and foresight. They created the legend that is now a dynasty . . . Manchester United. Tommy Taylor had the greatest respect for both of them along with the other stalwarts of the club. Their achievements will never be forgotten.

In Conclusion

Well, that is the Tommy Taylor story concluded. What a sad ending for such a wonderful player and his colleagues and also the others who perished on that snow covered runway at Munich. Some memories never fade, years crowded with nostalgic memories of those Busby Babes feats of unadultred brilliant, breathtaking skills on the soccer fields of England and Europe. Memories that would fill volumes if set down on paper, but don't let us feel despondent and sad. Let us instead remember the warmth and happiness Tommy Taylor and his colleagues gave us.

Tommy's goals, in particular, can never leave the memory. When I decided to undertake the writing of this book, my sole object was to highlight Tommy Taylor, my idol, who, in my humble opinion, was the best centre-forward ever. Then I also wanted to give full exposure to the whole Manchester United team, not just the players, but the stalwarts of this magnificent club, men such as Jimmy Murphy, Tom Curry, Bert Whalley,

Tosher Powell, Bill Inglis, scout Joe Armstrong, Arthur Powell, Joe Travis, Bert Fishburn Ted Dalton, Johnny Aston and Jack Crompton. These men earned very little in moneytry terms from United's success. These loyal servants built the rock-solid foundations for the huge turnover in money which the club is still enjoying to this very day.

After spending endless hours talking to Henry Cockburn, John Aston Snr, Jackie Blanchflower, Ian Greaves, Albert Scanlon, Colin Webster, Alex Dawson, Kenny Morgans, Wilf McGuinness and other former United players, the one thing which shines through the darkest patches, which were obviously so painful and which did they not relish speaking about, was their overriding love for Manchester United . . . their club!

These were very, very proud men who are loyal, honest and devoted to the well being of the club.

"Magnifico"

Alfredo Di Stefano

Alfredo Di Stefano, an Argentinian, was the first signing of Santiago Bernabeu, The President of Real Madrid, in the 1950s. His fee? £20,000!

Di Stefano's contribution to the Real Madrid is etched into the record books. Who could ever forget that wonderful 1960 European Cup final against Eintracht Frankfurt, in front of 135,000 people in Glasgow's Hampden Park. Real reached their peak that night; their performance has never been surpassed.

Di Stefano was a brilliant player, a soccer genius, he made the game look easy with his flowing style of play covering every blade of grass. He played 510 games for Real Madrid and scored 428 goals, forty-nine of which came in European Cup ties.

We thought it would be nice to ask the great man for his view on Tommy Taylor. John Donohue who helped with a great deal of research for this book, wrote to Real Madrid for Di Stefano's address. Officials put him in touch with the "great" Alfredo.

"Could you please give us your opinion of Tommy Taylor, for a book to be published about his career," John wrote.

Not expecting to receive a reply, he forgot all about his request to the Argentinian who now calls Spain his home. When through the post from sunny Spain came a very poignant reply.

"In answer to your question about what I think of Tommy Taylor as a centre-forward. There is only one word necessary to describe my opinion of the great Manchester United player, Tommy Taylor — he was simply: Magnifico"

It was signed by the the man Sir Matt Busby described as the greatest footballer he had ever seen. What a tribute.

"Among the very best"

Sandy Busby

Matt Busby's son Sandy was a fine footballer in his own right. He played in the F.A. Amateur Cup for the famous Surrey team, Kingstonian, and had a few games for Bury before joining Blackburn Rovers for some years. Sandy was a close friend of all the United players during the fifties.

"Tommy Taylor was one of my father's truly great signings. I accompanied Dad to Oakwell, to watch Tommy play for Barnsley. My Dad was excited by Taylor's style of play. When it became certain that Tommy was going to join United, I know that my father, as astute as usual and being a canny Scot, did not want to pay Barnsley the £30,000 transfer fee which the Yorkshire club were demanding for the young Taylor in 1953.

"Dad didn't wish to burden Tommy by having such a huge fee hanging around his neck. This was because when Dad met Tommy and his family, they seemed concerned over the size of the fee which was the second highest of those days. Tommy seemed nervous that he might be saddled with this huge burden.

"In the beginning Dad worried that this situation might effect Tommy's form. Yet his fears were unfounded and later he always said: 'I had no need to have worried on that score, because Tommy took it all in his stride. The fee never did upset him in any shape or form. The lad was the perfect professional.'

"Over the proceeding years, I well remember my father having several discussions with various newspaper journalists and soccer officials regarding the merit of Tommy Taylor. He was forever singing the praises of his centre-forward. I recall listening intently as my dad explained Tommy's many great attributes to the Manchester United team of the never-to-be-forgotten Busby Babes teams of the 1950s.

"Dad praised Tommy's unselfish running for his team mates, and his

wonderful awareness plus his goal scoring. 'As a player Tommy was among the very best centre-forwards. And as a person, he was first-class,' he often commented.

"And what a wonderful club man, he stuck to the rules regarding being in his digs before 10pm two nights before a game. He loved his pint and a night out with his side kicks, Jackie Blanchflower and David Pegg, but I have seen and tried to stay the pace on a Sunday morning when he would run at three-quarter pace twenty-two to twenty-four laps of the ground to get rid of the liquid from the night before.

"I remember watching Tommy in action and like thousands more being thrilled as he would rise about four feet of the ground and crash in one of those unstoppable power-house headers into the back of the opposition net. When recalling the many goals Tommy scored for United, a big smile would cross my father's face.

"He was the perfect centre-forward mentally and physically. Brian Douglas, a pal of mine from Blackburn Rovers, wrote an article stating that if Tommy, Roger Byrne and Duncan Edwards had not perished at Munich, England would have won the world Cup in 1958.

"All the players from that era were truly brilliant, fascinating characters and a credit to their families and their profession. Dad loved the big fellow dearly, as he did all the players under his wing. I think Tommy's smiling devil-may-care attitude to life and his immense bravery left a big impression on him. How I miss that baby-face smile with that lovely Yorkshire accent.

"On behalf of the Busby family, we fully endorse this tribute to a man who will always be a legend as long as there is talk about the great teams of Manchester United. I know that if my father was alive today he would be thrilled that this book about the life of one of the greatest ever centre-forwards has been written, and that the proceeds were going to help the youngsters of the Collyhurst and Moston Lads' Club.

"Because it is a fact that though his goal scoring record was phenomenal, Tommy Taylor never really got the credit he deserved. Tommy Lawton was one of my father's favourite centre-forwards, and I know he rated Tommy Taylor in the same bracket as Lawton. Praise indeed! This book will go a long way giving Tommy the recognition he deserves."

"My number-one choice at centre-forward"

Ronnie Cope

Ronnie was an England Schoolboy international. He joined Manchester United as a sixteen-year-old from Crewe Schools football in 1950, turning professional on his seventeenth birthday in 1951. He played ten years for United and registered ninety-two League games in United's colours, before moving on to Luton Town.

"When Tommy was signed by United, none of the other players knew what to expect from him. When I first met him he was very quiet and seemed rather shy. I could not understand his Yorkshire accent. The other players jokingly said that they would ask Mr. Busby for an interpreter so we could fathom out what he was saying. Tommy took it all in good spirits. I soon picked up his meanings and manner of speaking.

"When he first arrived from Barnsley, he used to just mix socially with the older players. But when he settled into the pattern of things at Old Trafford, and he got to know the younger pro's he was great. He loved to play jokes on us, and always joined in with the younger players games of head tennis and our five-a-side matches.

"I can tell you though, he was a very affable, pleasant man, he was as hard as nails. He never held back in those games. Though I never saw him lose his temper with us kids or his team mates in the first team. I don't know if he ever snapped with opponents. What we all liked about him though, was although he wasn't much older than many of us, he would make us feel ten-feet tall by telling us individually what fantastic players he thought we were.

"For example, I was a centre-half so he would say: 'Whew, Ronnie, you're some player. I've played against Billy Wright, Harry Johnston or whoever was a well-known centre-half of that period, and you gave me a harder time.'

Many years later and with the benefit of hindsight I realised he was just saying this to boost my morale and make me feel great, and it did make me feel confident.

"But he would also encourage the full-backs and goalkeepers, and he would tell the forwards: 'I'll have to watch myself,or you will be taking my place.' You don't know the wonderful feeling a kid gets when the likes of Tommy Taylor says things like that to you . . . Magic!

"I sincerely can't think of one player who was in any way jealous of Tommy. He was an extremely well-liked person by players and staff and fans. He would go out of his way to be of any help to anyone. What impressed me most about him was his honesty and sincerity.

"And what a hard trainer, he would be the last player to leave the training pitch, practising his shooting at goal, and his heading technique, he would spend hours doing this when most other players had long since gone their way.

"In my humble opinion I don't think the £29,999 fee which United paid for Tommy ever bothered him in the slightest. He was an ebullient character and he had confidence in his own ability to produce goals. I would say without any hesitation that he was arguably one, if not, the best centre-forwards England and Manchester United have ever had. And the most underrated.

I was recently asked in an issue of United's programme to name my all-time best Manchester United XI, and the name of Tommy Taylor was my number-one choice at centre-forward."

"A world-class centre-forward"

Jack Crompton

Jack joined Manchester United from the famous local side called Goslings. He was United's regular goalkeeper between 1945 and 1950, lost his place in the team to Reg Allen, but won it back two years later, playing his final game in the 1955–56 season. Jack proved a wonderful servant for United, as a player, and coach until 1981.

"At seventy-four years of age my memory is not what it was, but of one thing I am certain of and that is Tommy Taylor was a world-class centre-forward. I well remember Matt, or Sir Matt, paying the near £30,000 for Tommy. Let me tell you I believe the size of the fee worried Matt much more than it ever bothered Tommy. A Scot spending all that money, when previously he had produced so much home produce. Seriously, by this I refer to those wonderful, fantastic young players like Roger Byrne, Geoff Bent, Eddie Colman, big Duncan, Mark Jones, Bobby Charlton and the rest.

"I was in the team when Tommy made his debut. Some people say that when a new player joins a club for a transfer fee, the rest of the team are a little bit envious or resentful toward the new lad. Well, I can tell you that was not the case with our team at United. In fact, we all went out of our way to welcome him. Mind you, Tommy was such a pleasant working class lad like the rest of us, that you couldn't fail to like him. The rest of the players like myself, saw him as a potentially great player who could help us win some bonus. There was no edge about him despite the fortune (as it was in those days) which had been paid for his services. It did not alter Tom at all.

"What a diligent trainer, he worked hard, and was a very fit lad and so unselfish in his play. He also had a very deceptive style of running, but could run for hours, yes, a great runner. He loved heading the ball. I would spend many an extra hour or so with him while he practiced what he was outstanding at doing . . . heading. There is a little piece of advice to all aspiring

young players, practice and practice some more, like Tommy Taylor used to do. Even after he became an England international, Tommy worked at perfecting his skills, be it shooting or heading or whatever.

"Like most human beings he lost his temper occasionally if provoked, didn't we all. But on the whole he was absolutely superb; in fact, I don't think that he was ever cautioned or sent off in a game. He created space for other players to ultilise to their advantage because of his unselfish movement. A very unselfish player. I know Dennis Viollet loved playing along side Tom, because he created so much space for Dennis.

"I am sure that as good as he was, there was even better to come had the good Lord spared him. In his early days I think critics could possibly upset him, but the older players helped him to put criticism in its true perspective. A great, great player and a first-class human being was Tommy Taylor, the lad who practiced to make himself perfect!

"The Greatest"

Tommy Docherty

Tommy Docherty, the former Manchester United manager, was a formidable player with Preston North End and Arsenal and a Scottish international wing-half.

"Do I remember Tommy Taylor? How could I ever forget him? I was in the Preston team when he made his debut for Manchester United at Old Trafford in front of their biggest crowd of that particular season. He was the greatest centre-forward ever!

"I had never heard of him until that day in March, 1953, when the Preston team played United. But I certainly could never forget him after that match, and the other occasions when he played against us over the short period of time he played.

"Talking about that first game Tommy played for United, we had a very good centre half at Preston, after about twenty minutes of play a ball came across into the box and our fellow and another defender went up for it, then in a flash, this big, curly-haired United player was up head and shoulders above them, and whoosh, the ball was nestling in the back of our net.

"That was Tommy Taylor's introduction to the First Division, and also to the United followers. What an entrance. The fans loved him. And Preston had a damn good side in those days, a great First Division outfit. Tommy seemed to make a habit of playing exceptionally well against us. I remember he always used to score goals when facing Preston, and our defence was pretty solid, and good in the air. But Tommy seemed to jump a foot higher than us.

"The lads at Deepdale had great admiration for his ability. I watched his progress with admiration. He was the type of player any manager would want in his team. He proved his worth over the five years or so when he was in that brilliant United, 'Busby Babes' team.

"How much did Sir Matt Busby pay Barnsley for him? £29,999 he was the biggest bargain of all time. With the millions of pounds being paid by present

day managers, what would Tommy Taylor be priced at? Priceless I should imagine.

"I might not have cherished playing against him. But I would have deemed it a privilege to have played in the same team as Tommy. And as a manager, It would have been a pleasure, and I would have been honoured and very fortunate to have had him in any of the teams I later managed.

They don't come round that often — the likes of a Tommy Taylor. He was a magnificent player and wonderful, warm, human being. He was a chirpy, ever smiling lad, a true sportsman in every sense. It was a tragedy what happened to Tommy and his team mates at Munich."

"Outstanding . . . a clinical finisher"

Tom Finney

In twenty-one years in football Finney played 432 League matches and forty cup-ties for Preston, scored 187 goals in the League and twenty-three in the Cup and was capped for England seventy-six times, scoring thirty goals. He was also twice voted Footballer of the Year. Those who saw him play will always remember not just his brilliance, but his impeccable behaviour on the field.

"I remember Tommy joining Manchester United from Barnsley for a near record fee of £30,000, which in those days was a lot of money, but what a bargain he was.

"I played against him on a number of occasions and I recall one particular game at Old Trafford when United beat us, if I remember correctly, 5-1, and Tommy scored three goals and had a brilliant game against a very good centre half we had at that time at Preston, called Joe Marston. Yes, indeed, Tommy Taylor was outstanding and what a clinical finisher. He had everything and was so young and strong.

"I know the United lads harboured no petty jealousy after Tommy's signing for such a big fee, in fact I know that they were glad he was playing for them and not their opponents. When players like Tommy come along in your team they take a great deal of pressure of everybody, and he was such a lovely willing player. He gave the side a boost, as the Champions they were struggling a little, but still had wonderful players such as Johnny Carey, Allenby Chilton, Henry Cockburn, Johnny Aston and Jack Crompton, beside Stan Pearson and Jack Rowley.

"Tommy was exceptionally fast for his size and excellent in the air, good ball control and a good shot, and from experience with him with the England squad a very good trainer indeed, It was obvious he had outstanding ability as a centre-forward and was a prolific goal scorer. He was eager to learn from us older and more experienced players, a very likeable person, pleasant and full of

fun, he really enjoyed his football and wasn't easily provoked, although having said that, he could certainly take good care of himself.

"Most players are very nervous before a game but once they get out on the pitch they never worried. Tommy, never seemed to suffer in this respect and in the games I played with him for England I never noticed any superstitions. He was on the South American tour in 1953 and he was with the England party for the 1954 World Cup in Switzerland and we enjoyed each other's company. He had a tremendous future to look forward to in the England side and there's no doubt he would have gone on to earn many more international caps.

"Tommy and the many other United players who perished in the air crash were a great loss to the game. They were in the prime of their careers and no one knows how great they may have been.

"I remember what a wonderful game he had for England against Brazil at Wembley when England won 4-2, I think you can't play well against any better world-class side than the Brazilians. I am certain that Tommy would have progressed to become one of the all-time greats of British football.

"When I retired my wages were £20 a week in the season, plus bonuses of £2 for a win and £1 for a draw. For international games I was paid £50. Tommy Taylor and his team mates were on the same. What would he be worth today? . . . Millions, I suspect!"

"A sartorial elegance"

Freddie Goodwin

Freddie made his United first-team debut in the 1954–55 season. Edwards and Colman were holding down the two wing-half positions. He played 106 games and scored eight goals. A tall, elegant player who could have commanded a first-team place with any other club. Was one of the heroes after Munich. He remembers his period with United with affection.

"Tommy Taylor had a sartorial elegance about his play. He was a true thoroughbred. When training I used to watch open-mouthed at the incredible heights to which he could soar and then nod the ball into the net with ease. He did of course achieve these feats in competitive matches. He will always be remembered for his goal scoring feats, though there was so much more to his game than merely scoring. However, he must be among United's all-time top scorers.

"A centre-forward in those days was a dashing, shoulder-charging, fearless spearhead who usually stayed in the middle. Tommy could do all that of course, but he advocated a roving commission, drifting out to the wings, in order to draw the centre half and so make openings for the other forwards. Tommy could send accurate long passes to either winger. And as a goal-poacher he was second to none.

"Tommy was a cog in a great team, but a very important cog. He and Dennis Viollet were a splendid pairing. Viollet, not heavily built, but very wiry, used to anticipate where Tommy would nod the ball and be on to it like a streak of lightning.

"And who can forget Tommy's international record? What was it? Only on the losing side for England on two occasions? It is quite possible that England could have won the World Cup in 1958 had Tommy, Roger and Duncan not perished at Munich. Tommy was his country's first choice centre-forward. A true Barnsley legend!

"As a person he was first-class. Some of the memories never fade, years crowded with memories of that wonderful club and those marvellous players. Arguments and discussion are the lifeblood of soccer. Football folk have a reputation for varying opinions, but for me, Tommy Taylor was the best centre-forward, and that Busby Babes team was the greatest side ever. I am proud and honoured to have been a part of it."

"A great player and a gentleman"

David Gaskell

David Gaskell played in United's first team when barely sixteen, he replaced the injured Ray Wood in the 1956 Charity Shield game at Maine Road. Played 118 first-team games for United. A flamboyant goalkeeper who was also very athletic, David (although suffering with ill health) recalls his time at Old Trafford:

"I was only a youngster of course when Tommy was playing with United. But like the others I have to say what a smashing fellow he was. Always ready with encouragement, and also ready for some pranks. He pulled my leg something rotten. But all in good fun. You couldn't help but notice the way he trained. He never shirked anything. He did his running and practicing every day.

"Sometimes after training had finished Tommy would ask me to go into goal while he practised shooting or heading. My hands used to be stinging from the effects of his ferocious two-footed shooting, and my head dizzy from the speed, power, and accuracy of those bullet-like headers. Afterwards I would go home and proudly tell my friends that I had been helping Tommy.

"When I wasn't playing for one of United's junior teams I would be at Old Trafford watching the first team in action. What a brilliant team, Roger Byrne, Duncan Edwards, Eddie Colman, Billy Whelan, Dennis Viollet, Johnny Berry and David Pegg and those other fantastic players. They made football look easy, which of course it wasn't. But Tommy was a special kind of player.

The crowd could associate with him more readily, perhaps it was his bubbling personality, or the way he celebrated a goal. Whatever it was the United supporters idolised him.

"I had the thrill and pleasure of actually playing in the Busby Babes team. I think I was only fifteen years old, not long out of school, Matt Busby told me to get on the coach taking the team to Maine Road to play City who were the F.A. Cup winners. 'Don't forget to pack your boots,' he said, in that quiet tone

of his. Lo and behold, Ray Wood got injured and I went out for the second half.

"The lads were terrific with me, absolutely marvellous; I was walking on air for weeks afterwards. Roger Byrne gave me my instructions, but all the players helped me. Tommy of course often pulled my leg about this game, but it will live in the memory for ever.

I'm glad this book has been written about Tommy Taylor because he deserves it: a great player and a gentleman. I hope it is a bestseller."

"It's hard to be flash when you ride a bike"

Ian Greaves

Ian, a solidly built six-foot, full-back gave United splendid service after joining them as a professional from the Cheshire League club Buxton in 1952. He made the first of his sixty-three appearances for United in October 1954, away against Wolves, and left in 1960 to join Lincoln City.

He won a League Championship medal with the Reds in 1956 and was a stalwart after Munich when he played in the F.A. Cup Final against Bolton. A brilliant manager in his own right he has pleasant memories of his friendship with Tommy Taylor.

"Talking about Tommy Taylor brings back many happy memories for me personally. Can it really be nearly forty years? I had joined United a few months before Matt Busby bought big Tommy. I had just finished my National Service. In relative terms Sir Matt paid the equivalent of five million pounds for Tom. Hard to believe I know but on today's prices that would have been the figure. And I can vouch that the smiling lad from Barnsley would have been worth every penny.

"As a lad, Tom was just an ordinary Yorkshireman who enjoyed nothing better that a pint at his local. He was easy to get along with and had no airs and graces — we always said how could he, coming from Barnsley!

"He had a great build and it was rumoured that he had done some boxing, but no-one ever tried to find out, by testing him. He was a superb athlete and did a lot of running that was not on the training schedule. He also stayed behind a lot after training had finished to improve his heading. Considering he was one of the best headers of the ball I have ever seen, I used to wonder why. But that was dedication for you. He was never satisfied to be good, he strived to become the best.

"When we broke up at the end of the season after the tours and whatever had finished. The big lads were instructed to put on weight during the summer break. I know it must sound stupid but that's what we were told. Then when we reported back to Old Trafford for pre-season training myself and Tommy would be put together on the 'heavy gang' and train in a group on our own. I can close my eyes and see Tommy now with a towel around his neck sweating like one of the boxers from the Collyhurst and Moston Lads Club. It used to take us a full month to get the stone off that we had been told to put on! Tommy, Mark Jones and yours truly were founder members of that group.

"I can remember Tom coming to the ground on a bike, along with Duncan Edwards. It's hard to be flash when you ride a bike!

"128 goals in 189 appearances is truly remarkable even for a poacher but Tom was far more than that. He was an all rounder, who worked as hard off the ball as he did on it. His ability in every department of the game was outstanding and his build could frighten most central defenders. He was aggressive but not in any way beyond the rules.

"The Old Trafford crowd loved him like a son. He was not only very talented but one hell of a trier, and everybody loves an honest trier.

"6 February never goes by without memories for me. Only by the luck of the Devil did I miss the crash, an escape for which I have always been grateful. It was not just a lot of star players who died as the result of that terrible crash, but my personal friends.

"To sum up, Tommy Taylor was the best striker I ever saw, never mind having the good fortune to play with. He was normally a very happy-go-lucky lad with very simple values. As a man, he was modest, honest and a good Yorkshireman with no fancy ideas. The last thing Tommy would have liked would to have been called a 'Legend'; he was far too modest for that. But in fact he is a legend and the greatest striker of all time. To me, he was just a very good friend."

"Sheer class"

Denis Law

Denis made his League debut in 1956 aged sixteen. At eighteen he became the youngest player this century to be capped by Scotland. He was one of the most exciting, flamboyant and controversial players of his generation. In a career spanning eighteen years he played in more than 600 first-class matches, and scored over 300 goals.

"I was only a kid when the Busby Babes were at their peak, and playing a brand of football which is still talked about today. Of course I read everything about their exploits at home and in Europe. They were a brilliant team.

"I did play for Huddersfield, against United's Youth team. My old school chum, Alex Dawson, was playing for them at the time, and I could tell that they were a wonderful club for producing young players. A few years later I spent the best years of my career there, and some of my happiest moments were the years I spent with the club.

"Talking specifically about Tommy Taylor, I must be honest and say that I did not see him in action a great deal. I knew that he was a terrific centre-forward and England's leader. His record as a goalscorer speaks for itself. And from what I heard from much older and experienced players in Huddersfield he was very highly respected.

"One match I do remember was in 1957. I saw United play Aston Villa in the F.A. Cup at Wembley. Though United were beaten through a controversial charge by Peter McParland on Ray Wood. What sticks out in my memory was the header which Taylor scored for United.

"People were kind enough to say that I could get up high for headers, but that header of Tommy's would take some beating. The way he soared above everybody and directed his header into the net was sheer class. I can never forget it. If my memory is right, Duncan Edwards took a corner, the ball seemed to hang in the air for an eternity. But up rose Tommy, he knew what to do."

"A brilliant player"

Jimmy Greaves

Jimmy was arguably the greatest ever goalscorer in this country. For example; 200 League goals before the age of twenty-four; 114 goals as a Chelsea apprentice; 357 goals in 516 First Division matches; 491 goals in all first-class matches.

"Not long after I managed to force my way into Chelsea's first team, Walter Winterbottom selected me for an England squad. I was only a teenager, and I roomed with Big Tommy. This was, I think, if memory serves me right, in 1957. I might not be able to remember the exact date but what I vividly remember clearly was his easy going attitude. What a terrific fellow he was, we got along really well. Listening to us talk, the other players said they needed an interpreter to understand what we were saying, me with my Cockney accent and Tommy with his broad Yorkshire tone.

"Though I wasn't selected for this particular game and never managed to partner Tommy, I had nothing but admiration for his play. Obviously his strong point was the masterful way he could rise above defenders for those amazing headers. His timing was so good that he seemed to get into the air and wait there until the ball came across.

"However high the centre, he seemed to get above the ball and put it low into the goal where it gave the goalkeeper most trouble.

Considering the fact that he was a big fellow, Tommy was a light mover; he was six foot or more, and weighed about thirteen stone. He had perfect balance, that for me was his secret. He was not merely a goalscorer. His head flicks made many openings for his inside men, and he held the line together. Yes, a truly great centre-forward.

"This fellow would have stood out in any era, great players always would, and he was a brilliant player with bags of old-fashioned guts."

"My dad loved Tommy"

Nick Murphy

Nick Murphy is the youngest son of the great Jimmy Murphy who was Assistant Manager at United for more than twenty-five years. Nick has played for United's junior teams and the reserves with Brian Kidd; he also played for Reading. He was on United's books for over six years. Like Jimmy, Nick is the proud father of six children.

"Speaking on behalf of my mother and family, we consider it a great honour and a privilege to be asked to write our tribute to Tommy Taylor. My father, the late Jimmy Murphy, thought Tommy was the greatest ever centre-forward in English football. Taylor was christened by one sports writer "The Smiling Executioner" and when at Barnsley was one of the most sought-after players of all time.

"My Dad had great affection for the big feller, as he did for every player on United's staff. 'If Tommy has one fault it is simply that he does not realise how good he is,' said my Dad, many times to various people who enquired about Taylor. 'He was a superb mover, a man possessed of grace and athleticism not normally found in a tall man. He could crack a ball with power with either foot and when it came to heading he was absolutely magnificent and could be ranked alongside the greats in any era.'

"On many occasions Tommy would walk round to our house in Whalley Range. I was only a young boy, but vividly remember him and my Dad in deep discussion about his play. If he had any kind of a problem he would ask my father for help and advice. That was one of the things my Dad liked about him, he asked and listened intently to the advice passed on to him.

"He would spread himself out on the floor, my mother would make a pot of tea and toast and he would be as happy as anything. It was marvellous to watch Dad explaining and demonstrating moves or techniques which Tommy wanted help on. They had a strong bond of friendship. If the newspapers

criticised Tommy, it hurt my father deeply. He spoke many, many times of Tommy's strong points and unselfishness in regards of the team.

"If my father was alive he would be proud to be associated with this book, a tribute to a truly great, great centre-forward. And knowing that all the proceeds are going directly to the Collyhurst and Moston Boys Club, would have made him doubly happy because he had a warm regards for the area and the people living there. The Murphy family wish this venture every success.

"Some of the goals he scored were breathtaking"

Nobby Stiles

Nobby became a legend with Manchester United and England. Born in Collyhurst, he joined United as a ground-staff boy in 1957. He played 392 games and scored nineteen goals for the club before moving on to Middlesbrough. Who could ever forget his exploits for England in the 1966 World Cup? Nobby has fond memories of the brief time he knew Tommy Taylor.

"As a youngster, my idol was Allenby Chilton. Then in the Busby Babes team I admired Duncan Edwards and Eddie Colman, perhaps it was because they were wing-halves or inside-forwards like myself. When I joined United's ground-staff, one of my tasks was to clean about sixty pairs of boots and shin pads for the senior players. I paid special attention to the boots of Colman, Edwards and Taylor, always giving them an extra polish.

"Tommy was a down-to-earth person, very polite and understanding with us younger kids. I remember how he would encourage all the youngsters. Though he was busy, he always had time to spare for a chat. Yes, Tommy had a warm smiling personality, and a wonderful disposition. He was a wonderful ambassador for United and football.

'He played his football with a smile. As a player he was a sharpshooter, tall and graceful, full of enthusiasm. I thought Stan Pearson was the most elegant header of a ball I had ever seen, but I must admit that Tommy could get higher and he looked so graceful going up for the ball and carved out many a goal from out of the clouds, always keeping his eye on the ball. Goals are a powerful commodity, and players like Tommy, with a gift for scoring goals on a regular basis are rare indeed, but goals were his business, he was a master at taking the half-chance.

"Some of the goals he scored were breathtaking in their execution. He was a

clinical finisher and I admired the way he would race through the middle from through passes from Viollet or Whelan. Tommy achieved his ambition of playing for England and from what I'm told, he was always proud to wear the white shirt of England.

"Another good point about Tommy's play was his awareness. And he was great at moving out to the wings and running off the ball for his colleagues. He was playing the kind of centre-forward role with which Geoff Hurst gained fame and adulation when playing a similar style for England a few years later. Jimmy Murphy always said: 'Tommy is a good listener.' How right he was. I remember watching him training and running like mad, then practicing and continue practicing until he was satisfied he had mastered what he had been trying.

"After Munich, like everbody else at the club, I was devastated. I cried for weeks. One day, not long after the disaster, I remember asking Jimmy Murphy if I could keep Tommy's size seven-and-a-half boots, and he told me I could. I treasured those boots for over thirty years until I donated them to the United Museum. Those boots reminded me of a truly great, great centre-forward. Tommy Taylor was world class in every respect!

"I am delighted that this book has been published, because it pays tribute to a fabulous centre-forward who was at times a very under-rated player, and who never received the recognition his ability merited. I wish the book success and I am delighted to be able to help in this way. Brian Hughes is an old school friend and neighbour, and as a schoolboy I enjoyed the facilities of the Collyhurst Lads' Club, as well as attending Hugh Oldham Lads' Club. I know the Collyhurst club well, and it has produced many great sportsmen through the years."

Tommy sporting the 1957 Cup Final kit.

Tommy Taylor's Complete Record

1944–46:	Barnsley Boys and Raley Secondary Modern School
1948:	Smithies United

Barnsley Football Club

February, 1948:	Signed amateur forms
July, 1949:	Signed as professional
May, 1950:	First-team debut v St. Mirren (Paisley Charity Cup)
October, 1950:	Football League debut v Grimsby Town (Second Division)
January, 1953:	F.A. Cup debut v Brighton and Hove Albion (Third Round)
February, 1953:	Last game for Barnsley v Lincoln City (Second Division)

Season	**Appearances**	**Goals**	**Division**
1950–51:	12	7	Second
1951–52:	4	0	Second
1952-53:	28	19	Second
F.A. Cup:	2	2	n/a
Total:	**46**	**28**	

Manchester United Football Club

March, 1953:	Signed for Manchester United
March, 1953:	First Division debut v Preston North End
January, 1954:	First F.A. Cup game v Burnley (Third Round)
September, 1956:	European Cup debut v Anderletch (First Round)

Season	**Appearances**	**Goals**	**Division**
1952–53:	11	7	First
1953–54:	35	22	First
1954–55:	30	20	First
1955–56:	3	25	First
1956–57:	32	22	First
1957–58:	25	16	First
F.A. Cup:	9	5	n/a
European Cup:	14	11	n/a
Total:	**189**	**128**	

England Appearances

Full Internationals

Year	*Opponents (goals)*
1953:	Argentina, Chile (1), Uruguay (1).
1954:	Belgium, Switzerland.
1956:	Scotland, Brazil (2), Sweden, Finland, West Germany, Northern Ireland. Yugoslavia*(2), Denmark (3).
1957:	Republic of Ireland (3), Denmark (2), Republic of Ireland, Wales, Northern Ireland, France (2).
Total:	**19 games (16 goals)**

"B" Internationals

Year	*Opponents (goals)*
1956:	Scotland (1), Switzeland (3).
Total:	**2 games (4 goals)**

Career Total: **253 appearances (176 goals)**

Tommy also represented The British Army, The Football Association and The Football League.

*as a substitute

"A truly magnificent centre-forward"

Sir Bobby Charlton

A legend with Manchester United and England, Bobby hardly needs an introduction. A Busby Babe. He won League Championship medals, playing over 700 games for United's first team, scoring 247 goals. European Cup honours and was an F.A. Cup winner, beside playing over 100 games for England. He is a Manchester United director.

"I was playing for East Northumberland schoolboys at Maine Road on the Saturday morning that Tommy was due to make his Manchester United debut. After our game we had lunch at an hotel near Old Trafford. On the way back home our coach slowly passed the top of Warwick Road, there were thousands of fans making their way to the ground. Even sat in the coach I could feel the buzz of excitement and anticipation in the faces of supporters as they seemed to be discussing Tommy Taylor while making their way into the ground.

"I had of course been reading the newspapers about his £29,999 transfer to United and read that several other clubs had been chasing Tommy. But I had never seen him play. In the summer of 1953, I signed for United as a schoolboy, and saw Tommy on a personal level. We were of course from similar backgrounds. I lived in the same digs with him for a while and a short time later I became quite friendly and close to him, along with David Pegg. We had some wonderful fun.

"On a Sunday morning myself, Tommy and David and sometimes Eddie Colman would go along to Longford Park and watch the amateur matches, we all socialised together a lot. If I was playing in the reserves, and they were with the First team, we would agree to meet up later that night. We were all in the same boat, away from home and our families and living in a big city we tended to stick together.

"My first impressions of Tommy as a player was that he had a big heart, brave as a lion. He was very fast, immensely strong, and he was absolutely

sensational in the air, this was one of his greatest assets, and remember, this was when the ball was one of the heavy leather types with laces. He was a powerful header of the ball and so accurate. It wasn't everybody who liked putting their head there when the ball was crossed into the box, but Tommy would defy gravity and was so spring-healed he would rise up so majestically to meet it, absolutely brilliant!

"When I played in the First team alongside him, I found him very helpful and encouraging. When the ball was in the air, I would dart away anticipating where he would direct the ball with his neat head flicks, we got many a goal by this method. He suffered a great deal with injuries, having a troublesome knee, which sometimes restricted his appearances in the First team. His control for a big man was quite good, he trained hard and with plenty of enthusiasm. Tommy was aggressive but only in a competitive sense, I cannot remember him having ever been cautioned or sent off.

"He was a big tough lad and came from good Yorkshire mining stock, and all those type of fellows were tough, very loyal, and very committed.

"I've heard about players from other teams who worried about facing certain teams or opponents, but this never happened with Tommy, no, it never bothered him in the slightest who we were playing against or what defender was marking him, never. He was super confident, really. Yes, Tommy was always a handful for any defenders, but I vividly remember his duel with the Bilbao centre-half, Jesus Garay. I was not in the team that particular night but I watched it. Whew, fascinating. Tommy was like a man inspired. I couldn't put my finger on it and say what I thought was his greatest game for United because he had so many momentous games, but the Bilbao match must have been close to his best.

"His best game for England was undoubtedly when he scored two goals against Brazil. He was young, and the best around at that time and he had everything before him in the England set-up. Tommy was very proud when he played for England, it was like a new career for him. England could have done well in the 1958 World Cup with Tommy, Duncan Edwards and Roger Byrne in the team. I'm not saying we could have won the trophy, but we would have had a better chance with those three great players in the team.

"Comparing Tommy with centre-forwards who I played with for England such as, Nat Lofthouse, Gerry Hitchens, Bobby Smith, and Geoff Hurst, is impossible because the players mentioned fulfilled their ambitions and had full careers, but Tommy was cut off in his prime. He had achieved a tremendous amount and I personally feel that he would have got better and better. I really do believe that, because he was forever trying to improve his technique and other aspects of his play.

"Any youngsters taking up soccer today could do no worse than follow Tommy Taylor's example. He trained hard, practised and practised until he perfected his skills. And he lived a good clean healthy life. He achieved greatness mainly because he was always ready to listen to good advice from Sir Matt and Jimmy Murphy plus all the other coaches at the club.

"I wish this book every success and I am sure that anyone reading it will be inspired by Tommy's rise to soccer stardom. He overcame many set-backs and played a role in Manchester United's history. I can never forget him. A truly magnificent centre-forward and a dear friend."

"My Best Man"

Jackie Blanchflower

Jackie Blanchflower was one of the original Busby Babes. A thoroughbred footballer. He played 116 first-team games scoring twenty-seven goals. He played on twelve occasions for Northern Ireland when his career was curtailed by the Munich Air Disaster. He never played again because of the injuries he sustained in the crash.

"Tommy Taylor any myself were the best of pals from the moment he joined Manchester United in March, 1953. I have explained in the pages of this book how close we were, in fact, Tommy was my best man when I got married to my wife Jean. But to describe Tommy the centre-forward into a few brief words is virtually impossible because he had so many attributes. My mind drifts back to a pre-season game during the fifties which United played against a German team named Lower Saxony, in the giant stadium in Hanover. We should have scored twelve but we were stroking the ball around playing exhibition soccer. The Germans scored first after sixteen minutes, it jolted us into action and we retaliated two minutes later. I can visualise the goal even now. Johnny Berry took a corner and though tightly marked, Tommy made what was described by one journalist as a helicopter take off and glided the ball into the net. The crowd of 25,000 were absolutely stunned by his ballet-like leaping manoeuvre.

"Dennis Violet scored a goal and Tommy repeated his high flying act by getting up to an incredible height and blasted the ball into the German goal. Everyone knows how brilliant he was in the air but he was very versatile as well, for his first goal he had scored from a right wing corner, for the second goal, he accepted David Pegg's high centre from the left flank. We got used to watching him soar to amazing heights for headers but the German defence didn't know whether to laugh or cry at his exploits, instead they sighed in wonder at his towering headwork. Yes, Tommy was a brilliant centre-forward.

"I remember reading a soccer magazine in the fifties and the writer was

discussing Tommy's merits as England's first choice leader of the attack. "I was talking the other day about centre-forwards and, inevitably, the name of Tommy Taylor came up. Why? There are one or two more mentionable centre-forwards than the Manchester United boy," wrote the journalist. "There is Trevor Ford and Arsenal's Vic Groves and Bobby Johnstone who is actually an inside-forward. Centre-forward is the most glamorous position. Every time I Have a conversation about the position, Taylor's name creeps into the conversation, too. The reason is not far to seek. I have spoken before of the natural ball-player who typifies British football as opposed to the manufactured ball-player who typifies the game outside this tight little isle.

"Taylor is one of them. He is fast off the mark. He knows how to take up position and he knows how to place the ball to a colleague and race into open space for the return. He hits it naturally, with a freedom of body-action that none of the Continentals can match, and his rhythm on or off the ball is immaculate. I have seen him two or three times in the last twelve months and I have watched a lot of his opponents for the England centre-forward post.

"I have no hesitation in naming him as the most polished of the lot. The writer mentioned Tommy's effortless grace and his shooting ability with either foot which was so accurate. 'Tommy's shooting seems to come from a gun,' commented the writer. He also indicated what a quicksilver thinker Tommy was in tight situations. He ended his piece by stating. 'I am glad to include Tommy Taylor in the fine company of the great centre-forwards who have worn the white shirt of England.'

"That was praise. What memories this evokes!

"I sincerely hope that this book proves a success both as a tribute to my pal Tommy, a truly great, great centre-forward and his remarkable scoring exploits, and secondly, in order that the book helps the Collyhurst and Moston Lads Club. I know personally how hard Brian Hughes has worked in putting together this book and know also how pleased Tommy would have been to help the youngsters.

'Tommy was a legend"

Dickie Bird

Ask any sports fan to name as many cricket umpires as they can and, no matter how many they come up with, one thing is a near certainty — the list will include Dickie Bird. As such he requires no introduction, but few of those people will also know that he was a close school pal of Tommy Taylor.

"Tommy was my friend — we were brought up together in Barnsley in a little place called Smithies, we went to the same school, Burton Road Primary, and then Raley Secondary Modern School. We both played for the school team, he played centre-forward, and I played inside-right to him. At school, Tommy's nickname was 'Tucker' Taylor. I think he got this label because he tucked the goals away.

"Both our fathers were close friends with each other, having worked at the same coal face down the mine. At weekends, they would enjoy a pint of beer together, and then they would start their conversations on who was the best player, Tommy or me. Both our fathers said that Tommy and myself would not go down the coal mine for a living, and it gave them a tremendous amount of satisfaction when Tommy signed on for Barnsley F.C. and I signed on for Yorkshire Cricket Club. Tommy went into football and I went into cricket. That's how it all started for us both.

"We used to practise for hours together the two of us. Tommy, from a standing start could jump over a garden gate. Later, people told me that he could jump on top of a snooker table from a standing position, this is some feat. He always wanted me to cross the ball for him at head height so that he could rise and head the ball. He had this remarkable gift as a young kid, he could ride and hang in the air. I am convinced to this day that this gift made him into the best header of a football that I ever saw.

"I've seen four defenders marking him in the box, waiting for a ball coming in high, and though being pulled and tugged he has left the markers flat-footed

as he suddenly took off into the air. It was as if he was on a cushion of air or something. Majestic. On top of that he had pace, he had two very good feet, and he was tremendous at getting himself into the right positions. And his bravery knew no bounds. Really, he had everything! Which is why, if the newspaper reports were accurate, Real Madrid were prepared to pay United £70,000 for his transfer and the Italian clubs were also bidding £55,000 or £65,000 for his services.

"Tommy was in digs next to the Lancashire County Cricket Club at Old Trafford. He loved watching cricket and you would always find him at Old Trafford. He loved it when Yorkshire were playing Lancashire there and he always came into the dressing room to see me. Though he was idolised in Manchester, there was not the slightest sign of any "big-headedness" about my old school chum. If anything, he was rather shy. He was proud of his roots, a typical warm-hearted Yorkshire lad.

"Tommy, I know you will be in heaven mate, because you were a good and honest man. You gave millions and millions of people a lot of pleasure. You were the greatest centre-forward that I ever saw, and I have seen them all from Tommy Lawton to Alan Shearer. Your achievements are all there in the record books. What would you have achieved if you had not lost your life so tragically in the Munich Air Disaster of 1958?

"I always talk about you whenever football is mentioned, no matter what company I happen to be with. It only seems like yesterday when we were both kids practising football and cricket on broken glass, in fields, and any old rough ground. I think it gave us both the will and determination to succeed in our chosen professions. They were poor, but happy days all those years ago.

"I do hope that sports lovers will support and buy this book because it is for a tremendous cause, and it also gives everyone the chance to remember the great Tommy Taylor. It has given me a tremendous amount of pleasure to write these recollections of the greatest centre-forward to ever wear the England shirt. Tommy was a legend and I'm proud and honoured that he was my friend.

Afterword

Arthur Bower

A few weeks ago, myself, Dickie Bird, the famous test umpire, Michael Parkinson, who is now a television celebrity, and a few more Barnsley people were having a meal and talking about the sporting heroes from our home town. We discussed cricket but when our conversation got around to football, Mike and Dickie both said in unison . . . Tommy! I knew instantly who they meant, there was only one Tommy, and that was . . . Tommy Taylor! I can never forget this player, he is a Barnsley legend!

He only played forty-six games for his beloved Barnsley, scoring twenty-eight goals, but let me tell you those goals were all memorable goals and will never be forgotten by those of us who were fortunate to have witnessed them.

Tommy was absolutely fantastic for Barnsley. Many folk say that he wouldn't have become such a great centre-forward if he hadn't joined Manchester United, but I disagree with that theory. I firmly believe that he would still have become a world class forward even if he had stayed with the Oakwell club. He loved it playing for his home town club, he was very proud of that distinction. The memories of him come flooding back at the mere mention of his name.

I first saw Tommy play during the season 1944–45 when he played both full-back and centre-forward for the Barnsley Boys Town team. My recollections of these games and the players are somewhat blurred with the passing of time, although I do recollect him scoring a goal when playing centre-forward against Leicester Boys in a 2-2 draw on New Year's Day, 1945.

I didn't see much of him during the following years although I was aware that he had signed on amateur forms for one of the Barnsley and District local teams — Smithies United — and that at the start of the 1949–50 season he had signed professional forms with Barnsley Football Club. It was the 1950–51 season when Tommy paraded his skills for the first time as a First team player.

He had been called up for his National Service in May 1950 and although the Army had priority over players when it came to matches, they were nevertheless quite generous in allowing serving professional footballers time off whenever possible if required by their respective clubs. It was such an occasion on 7 October, 1950, when Tommy made his League debut in a Barnsley 3-1 home victory over Grimsby Town, and although not scoring, he certainly impressed all my friends and myself by his play, especially his head work, but more of that later.

It was, however, his next home game that put the name of Tommy Taylor on all Barnsley supporters lips as he scored a superb hat-trick in a 7-0 win over Queens Park Rangers. Alas, 'Father Time' has once again wiped out most of the memories of that game, but I do remember clearly one of his goals when he ran on to a pass, in that beautifully balanced long stride of his, and hit the ball firmly into the corner of the net.

I also remember quite clearly my father (he stood with my grand-father behind the goal at Bramhall Lane in 1912 when Barnsley won the F.A. Cup) saying after the game saying that "it looks like we've unearthed another good 'un but I expect we'll have to sell him, like we always do". Such is the fate of clubs like ours who have to sell to survive. Tommy made a total of twelve appearances that season scoring seven goals and whetting our appetites of greater things to come.

A horrendous injury while playing in an Army game nearly finished Tommy's career virtually before it began during the 1951–52 season, and limited him to only four League appearances with Barnsley. Discharged from the Army in June 1952 he worked hard on his rehabilitation and by the start of the 1952–53 season was fit and raring to go in what proved a brilliant personal season for Tommy although sad to say saw Barnsley F.C. relegated to the Third Division. I didn't see Tommy play many games that season as I had been called up in July, 1952, for my two years National Service at Reading, but I tried to arrange my monthly forty-eight hour pass, whenever possible when Barnsley were playing at home.

On such occasion (17 January, 1953) I remember seeing Barnsley lose at home by four goals to two, but what made this game unique was that both goals were scored by Tommy, both from the penalty spot. This was the first and only time I ever saw Tommy score two penalties in any kind of game.

Alas, from the point of view of Barnsley supporters, the inevitable happened for a player of his potential, he was transferred on 4 March 1953 to Manchester United. There has been a close bond of friendship between Barnsley and Manchester ever since and that is down to Tommy. Tommy's loyalty to Barnsley was highlighted by Sir Matt Busby, on the day Tommy made his home debut at Old Trafford when the great United Manager wrote: "As you will have read, I have been pretty busy recently with the bid for the transfer of Tommy Taylor, the Barnsley forward. I write before knowing whether Taylor is coming to Old Trafford, but, arising out of my visit to the Yorkshire town, I can say it gave me a new slant on a player's loyalty to his club.

"Everybody knows that a player has the last word in a transfer bid. Here we had a twenty-year-old boy who came up the hard way with his club, Barnsley. Despite the fact that many clubs apart from United, were interested in him, he expressed the wish, early on, to remain with Barnsley with whom he had always been very happy. But Barnsley need the money and whether they have transferred him will be known by this time. I should like to add that for the last seven months United have been watching Taylor — before any of the other clubs credited with an interest in him, were on the scene. And I would like to add that Taylor's club spirit is something to be admired. I shall always remember that and I am sure, wherever he goes, he will always be just as keen to display that characteristic spirit which is so essential to success". Those comments of Sir Matt's say it all, Tommy loved his home town club and the Yorkshire folk.

After my completion of National Service most of my Saturdays over the ensuing years were spent playing local amateur football, but once again the link with Tommy was kept as a team I played for ran a 'bus' to most of the Manchester United European Cup games which were played mid-week.

I certainly saw some wonderful performances from the "Busby Babes" against the likes of Anderlecht, Dukla (Prague), Real Madrid, just to mention a few of the teams, and all of us from Barnsley were thrilled to witness some glowing performances from Tommy. What a wonderful attractive team United were, with Eddie Colman, Dennis Violet, Roger Byrne and not forgetting that other Yorkshire lad, Mark Jones, a brilliant sturdy centre-half. But they were all great players. I little thought that night on 14 January 1958, when our bus journeyed over the Pennines to see United play Red Star of Belgrade in the European Cup that it would be the last time I would ever see Tommy perform on the field of play.

Sad to say, I also saw him play in his last International match for England when on 27 November, 1957, a colleague and I journeyed down on the train to see England beat France by four goals to nil. Tommy had a wonderful game, scoring two goals, and leading the line with is usual zest and enthusiasm.

It was very poignant that also playing in the England team that day were Roger Byrne and the great Duncan Edwards, who along with Tommy would have formed the nucleus of the England side for years to come. What a player Edwards was, I've never seen one better!

Players today are earning thousands of pounds a week, good luck to them I say. But the mind boggles at what the like of Tommy and the rest of that fantastic "Busby Babes" team would be getting in wages if they were playing now. They were priceless. Yet, they, and every other player for that matter, were only earning fifteen pounds a week because of the maximum wage structure of that period. So it cannot be said that players in those times were performing for the financial rewards.

The tributes paid to Tommy whenever his name is mentioned over the years by some of the greats of the game we have all heard or read about. Beautifully balanced, brilliant in the air, two good feet, quick, a great finisher, totally unselfish and a great lad to boot, is the ideal epitaph. Whenever I think of Tommy, of all those qualities mentioned, the one that I forever will remember was his magnificent heading, and I can't think of anything better to conclude with than the tribute paid to him by the late Billy Wright C.B.E. who described him as a "young Tommy Lawton" — praise indeed.

Rest in peace, Tommy.

Arthur Bower
(The Official Barnsley F.C. Historian)